Translating the Untranslatable

CSLI Studies in Computational Linguistics

This series covers all areas of computational linguistics and language technology, with a special emphasis on work which has direct relevance to practical applications, makes formal advances, and incorporates insights into natural language processing from other fields, especially linguistics and psychology. Books in this series describe groundbreaking research or provide an accessible and up-to-date overview of an area for nonspecialists. Also included are works documenting freely available resources for language processing, such as software, grammars, dictionaries, and corpora.

Series edited by Ann Copestake

CSLI Studies in
Computational Linguistics

Translating the Untranslatable

A Solution to the Problem of Generating English Determiners

Francis Bond

 CSLI
PUBLICATIONS

Center for the Study of
Language and Information
Stanford, California

Center for the Study of Language and Information
Leland Stanford Junior University
Printed in the United States
Copyright © 2005
CSLI Publications
09 08 07 06 05   5 4 3 2 1

Library of Congress Cataloging-in-Publication Data

Bond, Francis, 1967–
Translating the untranslatable : a solution to the problem of generating
English determiners and numbers in machine translation from Japanese /
Francis Bond.
p.   cm. – (CSLI Studies in computational linguistics)
Includes bibliographical references and index.

ISBN 1-57586-460-6 (pbk. : alk. paper)
ISBN 1-57586-459-2 (hardback : alk. paper)

1. Machine translating. 2. Japanese language–Translating into English.
3. English language–Determiners. 4. English language–Number.
I. Title. II. Series: Studies in computational linguistics (Stanford, Calif.).
P309.B66   2004
418′.02′0285–dc22   2004010605

CSLI was founded early in 1983 by researchers from Stanford University, SRI
International, and Xerox PARC to further research and development of integrated
theories of language, information, and computation. CSLI headquarters and CSLI
Publications are located on the campus of Stanford University.

CSLI Publications reports new developments in the study of language,
information, and computation. In addition to lecture notes, our publications
include monographs, working papers, revised dissertations, and conference
proceedings. Our aim is to make new results, ideas, and approaches available as
quickly as possible. Please visit our web site at
http://cslipublications.stanford.edu/
for comments on this and other titles, as well as for changes and corrections by the
author and publisher.

Translation, you know, is not a matter of substituting words in one language for words in another language. Translation is a matter of saying in one language, for a particular situation, what a native speaker of the other language would say in the *same* situation. The more unlikely that situation is in one of the languages, the harder it is to find a corresponding utterance in the other.

Suzette Haden Elgin
Earthsong: Native Tongue II (1994: 9)

Languages differ essentially in what they *must* convey and not in what they *may* convey.

Roman Jakobson
On Linguistic Aspects of Translation (1966: 236)

Preface

This book is based on work I carried out on improving the quality of machine translation while at Nippon Telegraph and Telephone Corporation. The central part of it was developed into my PhD, but much of it is new, especially the work on lexical acquisition.

The book deals with the application of insights from linguistic theory into practical natural language processing. The main phenomena I consider, reference, countability and definiteness, are central to the semantic analysis of natural language. They are also of immense practical interest in machine translation, where the different ways these phenomena are expressed linguistically are the cause of significant mismatches. I show in this book how semantically motivated processing can deal with the link between meaning and expression.

I have been working on these problems for over ten years and received an enormous amount of help along the way. I would particularly like to thank Kentaro Ogura, who introduced me to the world of natural language processing at NTT, and the advisors for my PhD, Rodney Huddleston, Tsuneko Nakazawa and Roly Sussex. I would also like to thank all of the current and past members of the NTT Machine Translation Research Group, especially Satoru Ikehara, Satoshi Shirai, Akio Yokoo, Hiromi Nakiwa, Hajime Uchino, Matsuo Yoshihiro, Yoshifumi Ooyama, Osamu Furuse, Yasuhiro Akiba, Setsuo Yamada, Yamato Takahashi, Masahiko Haruno, Takefumi Yamazaki, Takaaki Tanaka and Sanae Fujita.

This book would not have come into being without the support of CSLI publications especially Ann Copestake, Dikran Karagueuzian and Christine Sosa.

I learned much from the programmers, analysts and assistants with our group at NTT: Satsuki Abe, Kazuya Fukamachi, Yoshitake Ichii, Minako Kamezaki, Junko Kimura, Sonomi Kobune, Hiroko Inoue,

Takako Matsumoto, Satoshi Mizuno, Nao Muramoto, Toshiaki Nebashi, Makiko Nishigaki, Shinsuke Okuyama, Yoshie Omi, and Izumi Watanabe. I would like to thank them for their patience with my incomprehensible Japanese and insatiable appetite for linguistic judgments.

It is not possible to enumerate everybody who supported me, but in particular, I wish to thank the following people, many of whom sent me copies of papers and data, as well as useful comments and discussion: Naoya Arakawa, Shipra Dingare, Laurel Fais, John Fry, Mark Gawron, Julia Heine, Ben Hutchinson, Tsuneaki Kato, Gen'ichiro Kikui, Kevin Knight, Takeo Kurafuji, Daniela Kurz, Emi Izumi, Chris Manning, Mayumi Masako, Masaaki Murata, Shigeko Nariyama, Christoph Neumann, Elena Not, Emmanuel Planas, Ivan Sag, Melanie Siegel, Leonoor van der Beek, Caitlin Vatikiotis-Bateson, and Lynn Wales.

I owe a special debt to those people who took the time out of their already busy lives to read and comment on my book (and dissertation) as it was taking shape. Their interest kept me going: Timothy Baldwin, Colin Bannard, Dan Flickinger, Kristiina Jokinnen, Yukie Kuribayashi, Guido Minnen, Stephan Oepen, Dylan Robertson, and Graham Wilcox.

My parents, Graham and Monique, and my sisters Denise and Helena, gave not only moral support, but also corrected my spelling, grammar and argumentation! My deepest thanks go to Kyonghee who kept my spirit up during the long slog. Her discussion and insight have helped me to see more clearly, and her love and support have been pivotal for the successful completion of this long journey.

Keihanna, Japan, November 2004

This book was written with EMACS, typeset with LaTeX and printed with Ghostscript. I would like to thank all the people who developed this and much other free software, without which it would have been much harder to carry out this research.

Contents

List of Figures

List of Tables

Notational Conventions and Symbols

- *Italic font* is used for citing sentences, words and other forms. Japanese forms are given in the Hepburn transliteration (Lunde, 1999, 30–35); long vowels are shown with a macron.
  e.g. *oo* and *ou* become *ō*.
- "Glosses" are given immediately after the words or phrase, quoted with double quotes.
- 'lit:' is used to mark literal glosses or translations
  e.g., *watashi-no kono hon* "I-ADN this book (lit: my this book)"
- **`Bold typewriter font`** is used for semantic classes or features.
- SMALL CAPS are used for names of types and grammatical glosses.
- **Bold font** is used to introduce technical terms.
- <u>Underlining</u> is used to highlight areas of interest in examples.
- <u>Wavy Underlining</u> is used to mark the target for agreement or floating quantifiers.
- * (asterisk) indicates that the following example is ungrammatical.
- # (hash) indicates that the following example is pragmatically odd — it cannot have the desired interpretation, although it is grammatical under some other interpretation.
- ? indicates that the following example is of questionable grammaticality (?* indicates questionable ungrammaticality).
- ⊢ is used to show the relation of entailment: S ⊢ W means S entails W.

The following abbreviations are used for Japanese adpositions and other markers:

Abbr.	Name	Ex.	Abbr.	Name	Ex.
NOM	nominative	*-ga*	Q	interrogative	*-ka*
ACC	accusative	*-o*	COL	collectivizing suffix	*-tachi*
DAT	dative	*-ni*	HON	honorific suffix	*-san*
ADN	adnominal	*-no*			
TOP	topic	*-wa*			
FOC	focus	*-mo*			
QUO	quotative	*-to*			

The following abbreviations are used for syntactic classes, functions and other categories:

Adj	adjective
AdjP	adjective phrase
Adv	adverb
AdvP	adverb phrase
CL	classifier
Detr	determiner
Detve	determinative
Demve	demonstrative
N	noun
NP	noun phrase
Obj	object
Obl	oblique
PP	prepositional phrase
pl	plural
POS	part of speech
Poss	possessive
PossP	possessive phrase
PossPro	possessive pronoun
Prep	preposition
sg	singular
Subj	subject
V	verb
VP	verb phrase
ϕ	a position where a determiner could be used, but is not.
Φ	a zero pronoun or other elided constituent.

1

Introduction

In this book, I present a solution to the problem of generating determiners (*a/an, the, my, your,* etc.) and determining number and countability. This is one of the hardest problems for accurate automatic translation because it is necessary to generate words and inflections that are obligatory in the target language, but not in the source language. The solution is specific to the problem of generating articles and determining number and countability, but the method is generally applicable, not only to machine translation, but to the wider field of natural language processing. In particular, I present the solution in enough detail to show the amount of information that is needed to solve similar problems. Further, I show some methods of acquiring this detailed information.

In Japanese, nothing directly corresponds to the English articles *a* and *the*. With a few exceptions, no distinction is made between singular and plural. This means that when Japanese is translated into English the choice of articles and number falls upon the translator. Consider the possible translations shown in (1). Depending on the context any of the ten translations shown are possible and there could be more. There are at least six different choices of determiner: *a, some, the, my, our* or none, and two different choices of number: singular or plural:

(1) 私 は   犬 を   見た
    Watashi-wa inu-o   mita
    I-TOP   dog-ACC saw

    I saw <u>a</u> dog

    I saw <u>the</u> dog

    I saw ϕ dog

    I saw <u>some</u> dogs

    I saw ϕ dogs

I saw the dogs

I saw my dog(s)

I saw our dog(s)

Not all the translations, however, are equally probable. In most cases the context provides information that makes only one of them the appropriate choice. Translation of number and determiners has long been recognized as a problem for human translators. The biblical translator Nida (1964, 198), in discussing contrasts between languages, points out that number presents problems not only because it is obligatory in some languages and optional in others, but also because of: "(1) its arbitrary values, (2) the exacting nature of some distinctions and (3) the necessity of different treatments within specific contexts". Translators, and more generally Japanese native speakers using English, often use articles and number incorrectly (Sakahara, 1996, 54) and problems with articles were found to be the most common type of errors made by Japanese learners of English at all levels of competence (Izumi et al., 2003).

An automatic solution to the problem of generating determiners and determining number is of interest for two reasons. First, it is an important practical problem for all translation systems that translate between a source language without obligatory determiners and/or number distinctions, to a target language that does need determiners and/or make number distinctions. Some examples[1] are Japanese-to-English (Nagao, 1989, Ehara and Tanaka, 1993), Russian-to-English (Ganeshsundaram, 1980), Polish/Russian-to-English/Swedish (Gawrońska, 1993) and Japanese-to-German (Siegel, 1996a, Heine, 1998). Second, the proposed solution provides tractable methods with wide-coverage for handling countability, number, reference, genericness and definiteness in natural language processing systems.

The problems of generating determiners and determining number in Japanese-to-English machine translation are both examples of a more general problem: specialization of under-specified input. In both cases, the problem is to make the correct choice from a small closed set, where the input may provide insufficient information to make this choice. The solution to this problem is useful not only for machine translation, but also for generation in other areas such as report generation or speech prosthesis (Copestake, 1997).

There are many areas in natural language processing where special-

---

[1] Japanese has neither articles nor number, Russian and Polish have number but no articles, and English, Swedish and German have both articles and number.

ization of under-specified input is necessary. Examples of choosing one from a set of closed class words (often including no word) include: choice of English locative or temporal prepositions in machine translation, where typically there is a choice between *in, on, at* or none (Trujillo, 1995); choice of numeral classifier when generating a numeral-classifier language such as Japanese or Thai, where numerals must be followed by a classifier (like English *piece* or *pair*) (Sornlertlamvanich et al., 1994, Bond and Paik, 2000); choice of subordinators (like *that, whether, which* or none); choice of determiners depending on the countability of their head (like *much* or *many*); and choice of appropriate pronoun (like *tu* or *vous* in French). These are all problems of tactical generation: the how-to-say part of natural language generation.

Considering the problems of determiners and number within the context of natural language processing, it is important that the analyses are detailed enough to provide useful results, but not so detailed as to be impossible to implement. Raskin and Nirenburg (1998) set out the following properties that an analysis must have for it to be useful within a natural language processing system:

- Wide coverage (can handle a variety of input)
- Tractable (can be implemented in a working system)
- Robust (can handle unknown or ill-formed input)
- Better than a baseline [e.g. all NPs are singular, definite]
- Portable to new domains and language pairs

Further, a machine translation system should ideally exhibit **target-source independence**: the output of the analysis is the same as the input to the generator for all languages (Gawron, 1999). In practice, this is impossible due to **mismatches** between languages. A perfect semantic analysis of Japanese will still not give all of the information needed to generate English.

The solution proposed here to the problem of generating determiners and determining number in Japanese-to-English machine translation has been implemented and tested in the wide-coverage Japanese-to-English machine translation system **ALT-J/E**: the **A**utomatic **L**anguage **T**ranslator — **J**apanese to **E**nglish (Ikehara et al., 1991). Because it was implemented in a working system, it benefitted from continuous large-scale testing on a variety of texts, which revealed many shortcomings along the way. The method splits the problem into two parts: (1) analyzing the meaning of the Japanese input and (2) generating the English from this semantic representation. Approaches that look only at one language, either the source or target, miss out on essential information. The method not only generates articles, it also appropriately generates possessive pronouns, a problem that is ignored by many current approaches.

The processing is deep, considering both the referential use of noun phrases and the boundedness of their referents. Such approaches are now feasible because of the existence of large-scale deep processing systems (Ikehara et al., 1993, Mahesh et al., 1997, Uszkoreit, 2002). The solution does not, however, rely on full context processing and resolution of all anaphora, as such processing is not yet reliable. Ultimately, the problem of determining number is unsolvable without world knowledge: it is AI complete.[2] However, there are many cases where enough information is available in the Japanese input, or the English structure constrains the form of the noun phrase. I describe in Chapter 5 how it is possible to obtain the relevant information from Japanese using only a limited context, and combining it with the known restrictions of English, in order to choose as good a translation as possible with the information available.

The resulting generation is highly accurate, with an error rate below 10%. In my final evaluation, I show that the number of noun phrases with erroneous articles (9.5%) is less than the number of noun phrases that are translated so badly (or not translated at all) that they cannot be evaluated (23.3%). Therefore, the system has reached a level where further research into improving the generation of articles and number should be put on hold and efforts directed at improving the overall quality of machine translation. In particular, more work is needed on the source language syntactic and semantic analysis of long sentences and the relations between clauses.

In conclusion, generating determiners and determining number is a difficult problem, but can be largely solved by combining a deep semantic analysis with the use of sensible defaults. By exploiting robust representations for the referential use and boundedness of noun phrases and combining them with English-specific information on countability and inherent possession it is possible to generate determiners with an accuracy of over 85%. Therefore, even without full understanding, natural language processing has reached the stage where detailed semantic representations can be used to solve difficult problems.

---

[2]A problem is AI complete if it can be solved only by a complete Artificial Intelligence, one that is capable of fully understanding language and making inferences about the real world.

Guide to the Reader

The remainder of this book consists of the following chapters:

2: Background This chapter is a survey of the relevant linguistic issues of reference, countability, definiteness and thematic marking. Impatient readers could skip straight to chapter 4.

3: Determiners and Number in Machine Translation This chapter is a comprehensive survey of work on this problem in the field of machine translation and related areas of natural language processing.

4 Semantic Representation After a preliminary discussion of noun phrase structure, I propose a tractable representation of referentiality, boundedness and definiteness. This forms the basis for a series of algorithms to determine the correct interpretation.

5: Automatic Interpretation This is the most hands-on chapter, in which I introduce the algorithms used to determine values for referentiality, boundedness and definiteness in a machine translation system. It finishes with a description of the algorithm to generate the articles.

6: Evaluation and Discussion In this chapter, I evaluate the implementation of the algorithms in a Japanese-to-English machine translation system. The results are then compared with other systems.

7: Construction of the Lexicon Much of the processing to generate articles and number depends on detailed lexical knowledge. In this chapter I discuss the compilation of the detailed knowledge used in the lexicon. First I define in more detail the features in the lexicon and then give tests to allow the lexicographers determine them.

8: Automatic Acquisition of Lexical Information In this chapter I show how lexical information can be semi-automatically acquired from existing dictionaries and corpora.

9: Conclusion I suggest how the research can be further refined, and applied to other tasks, such as other generation tasks and language learning.

Chapters 2, 4 and 7 are more linguistic in focus, the remaining chapters are more computational.

2

Background

Questions about how to use determiners and number arise in many fields: linguistics, philosophy of language, computational linguistics and second language learning to name a few. In this chapter I bring together some of this literature, concentrating on the factors relevant to determining number and generating determiners when automatically translating from Japanese to English, with special emphasis on computational approaches. Because translation is concerned with how to create a text in the target language with the same meaning as the source language text, emphasis is placed on the semantics and pragmatics of the use of determiners and articles in English as well as syntactic phenomena.

I begin with a brief syntactic account of English and Japanese, concentrating on noun phrases. This is to set the scene for the discussion that follows (§ 2.1). There is a more detailed discussion in the following chapter (§ 4).

The use of number and determiners in English is strongly connected to the concept of **reference**. Accordingly I give a brief overview in Section 2.2. Much of the philosophical and linguistic literature is concerned only with referring noun phrases, especially subjects and objects of sentences, with some discussion of generic noun phrases. However, a natural language processing system must be able to process a wide range of input, so I also consider non-prototypical uses of noun phrases, such as locatives and measure phrases (§ 2.2.4). This is followed by an outline of some of the research on the grammatical phenomena of countability and number, and their relation to sentence meanings (§ 2.3).

Next, in Section 2.4, I look at the use of determiners, focusing on the most difficult determiners to translate: the articles and possessive pronouns. I then look at the related phenomenon of thematic marking in Japanese (§ 2.5).

2.1 Syntax

2.1.1 English Syntax

Because English syntax has been extremely widely studied, I will not attempt to survey the literature comprehensively. Instead, I will very briefly summarize the relevant areas in which it differs from Japanese. In this section I will describe the simpler, more common cases; exceptions will be discussed later on.

The order of elements in an English sentence is highly constrained. The subject precedes the verb, and the object comes after the verb (SVO): *[the dog]$_{Subj}$ [ate]$_V$ [a bone]$_{Obj}$*. With the exception of personal pronouns, the distinction between nominative and accusative case is not marked: the same form of a noun is used for both the subject and object. Instead the relation between a noun and the verb which governs it is characteristically shown either by the position of the noun phrase in the sentence or by the use of a preposition (or both).

English noun phrases are marked for **number**, with a contrast between **singular** and **plural**. This is reflected in two ways. (1) The head noun characteristically inflects for number: e.g. *mammoth* is singular, *mammoths* is plural. (2) There are various types of agreement, in particular, verbs agree in number with their subject. In English, for most verbs, subject-verb agreement is expressed only in a different inflectional form for third person singular subjects of present tense finite verbs: *he goes* vs *I/you/we/they go*. In addition, pronouns agree with their antecedents and some noun phrase dependents show number agreement: *this mammoth* vs *these mammoths*.

Linked to the system of number is that of countability. Nouns which are **countable** typically show the singular/plural distinction, and can take as dependents determiners such as numerals and *many*. Some nouns, however, are **uncountable**. Uncountable nouns typically are either always singular (e.g. *furniture*) or always plural (e.g. *goods*). Uncountable nouns cannot be directly modified by determiners such as numerals (instead to enumerate an uncountable noun a classifier construction is used: *two pieces of furniture*). Many nouns can be either countable or uncountable. Countability is discussed further in Section 2.3.

Another distinguishing property of a noun phrase is that the head noun can take a dependent with the syntactic function of **determiner**: prototypically the articles *a* and *the*. Following Huddleston (1984), Huddleston and Pullum (2002), I make a distinction between the class of words which prototypically functions as determiners, which I shall call **determinatives**, and the syntactic function itself. Other determinatives are the demonstratives (*this/these* and *that/those*), *some*, *any*, *either* and the possessive pronouns (*my*, *your*, . . .). As well as simple determinatives, possessive phrases such as *the king of Spain's* can also function as determiners. The boundary between the determinatives and adjectives is not clear-cut. I will discuss which words and phrases can function as determiners in more detail in Section 4.1.2. The determiner is obligatory for noun phrases headed by singular countable nouns. In modern English there can only be one central determiner.

Noun phrases are not freely omissible. In particular, a **clause** headed by a finite verb must normally have a subject. However, in certain constructions and genres the subject can be omitted even in English: for imperative clauses (*Eat it!*), or in the diary genre (*Jan 12: Went to the beach, mucked around.*), headlines and so on. The subject in a clause and the determiner in a noun phrase show similar properties (they are both largely obligatory and unique). They can be thought of as variants of the same syntactic function: **specifier**.

2.1.2 Japanese Syntax

Japanese syntax is very different from English syntax. One major difference is in word order: in Japanese, dependents normally precede their heads. For example, in a clause the verb is final (SOV): $[inu\text{-}ga]_{Subj}$ $[hone\text{-}o]_{Obj}$ $[tabeta]_V$ "the dog ate a bone (lit: dog bone ate)". Within a clause, the order of the dependents can vary quite freely. The relation between nouns and verbs is shown by postpositional particles (*joshi* in traditional Japanese grammar). Noun phrases are often omitted, particularly in speech.

I take the noun as head, primarily because it cannot be omitted but also to simplify the comparison with English. It is also possible to consider the postposition as head (Gunji, 1987, Siegel, 1998). The choice of head is discussed further in Section 4.2.2.

The postpositions can be divided into three classes: case-markers, semantic-markers and adverbial-markers. Arguments marked by the three case-markers correspond roughly to subject, object and indirect object in English. Arguments marked by the semantic-markers can be complements in clause structure, but are more typically adjuncts. Semantic-markers are thus close to English prepositions in function. As in English, the mapping from semantic-marker to case-role is not straightforward. In addition, the boundary between the case and semantic-markers is not easy to set. For example, *-ni* is variously classed as only a case-marker, only a semantic-marker or both (Ono, 1996).

The case-markers *-ga* "NOM" and *-o* "ACC" can be replaced by adverbial-markers, in particular the focus-markers (*-wa* and *-mo*).

Adverbial-markers normally follow semantic-markers and *-ni* "DAT": *kare-ni-mo* "also to him".

Japanese noun phrases show no number contrast. There is no morphological or syntactic distinction between singular and plural, or countable and uncountable. Japanese noun phrases do not require the presence of a determiner. There is no syntactic equivalent to English determiners, but the semantic equivalents to the English determiners (such as *kono* "this", *watashi-no* "my"), are always omissible and there may be more than one.

Japanese sentences can also have multiple nominative marked arguments, or none. Thus, it has been argued that Japanese has no functional categories equivalent to English specifiers (Fukui, 1995). Some examples are given in (2), where possessive phrases and determinatives co-occur.

(2) *a.* 私の　　　この 本
        watashi-no kono hon
        I-ADN　　　this　book

    This book of mine (lit: my this book)

    b. 太郎 の　　昨日 の　　　話
        Tarō-no　　kinō-no　　　hanashi
        Taroo-ADN yesterday-ADN story

    The story [Taroo gave/about Taroo] yesterday (lit: Taro's yesterday's story)

The final difference mentioned here is with the demonstratives themselves. Where English has only two lexemes *this/these* "proximal" and *that/those* "distal", Japanese has a three-way distinction between *kore* "proximal", *sore* "medial" and *are* "distal".

2.2   Reference

Noun phrases are, characteristically, used to refer to something. Reference is the relationship that holds between expressions and what the expressions stand for (their **referent**s) when they are used. I take a conceptualist view of reference, that is, that "Linguistic expressions refer to entities in [the world as conceptualized by the language user]" (Jackendoff, 1998, 211). Normally, the world as conceptualized by language users models the actual world reasonably well and real world inferences can be and are used to construe meaning. This does not have to be the case: people may misunderstand a given situation, or have a poor grip on reality.

The meaning of a noun considered outside of any particular occasion of use is its **denotation** (also called **sense** or **intension**). For example, *dog* (and the Japanese equivalent *inu*) both denote "a member of the genus *Canis* (probably descended from the common wolf) that has been domesticated by man since prehistoric times"(WordNet, 1997). The denotation can be represented in predicate logic as a one-place relationship: $\text{dog}(x)$.

In order to provide a tractable representation, it is important to cover a wide range of language use. Therefore, I concentrate on empirically-based descriptions of relevant phenomena rather than formal approaches to reference. To date, formal approaches have not yet reached the stage where they can be implemented in large-scale natural language processing systems. Most formal approaches are fragmentary and require more knowledge encoded than is currently available in robust NLP systems. As I show in Chapter 6, a reasonable solution can be found without the use of a full formal theory, but rather with the engineering approach of creating successively more accurate approximate descriptions. As formal approaches become richer, they can be used to create even more accurate models.

In the following sections I will discuss some of the referential uses of noun phrases. I first describe the simplest case of reference: referential noun phrases, and then go on to generic noun phrases. This is followed by a discussion of some less prototypical uses of noun phrases, such as ascriptive noun phrases, noun phrases with locative and temporal reference, and idiom chunks.

The referential use of noun phrases is not marked explicitly in either English or Japanese. In Japanese, referential use is connected with the choice of marker (postpositional particle) and word order. In English, it is closely connected with the use of articles.

2.2.1   Referential Noun Phrases

The most common kind of noun phrase is one that is used to refer to some entity in the discourse world, as in (3):

(3)   *I can see the two dogs*

Referential noun phrases can be modified by the full range of determiners. They can be plural or singular, the grammatical number being linked to the way the referent is conceived: for example, *one dog* to refer to a single animal, *two dogs* to refer to two animals, *some dogs* to refer to a group of more than one animal (see Section 2.3). Referential noun phrases can typically be **pronominalized**: either replaced by a definite pronoun or referred back to by one (4).

(4)   *I saw a dog$_i$ this morning. It$_i$ was white.*

Considering the meaning of a noun to be a first-order relation such as *dog* "dog(x)", then a referential noun phrase headed by *dog* is used to both pick out an entity in the conceptual discourse world, and to say that it must satisfy the relationship dog(x).

2.2.2   Generic Noun Phrases

Noun phrases can also refer to kinds, not just examples of kinds. For example, in (5), the noun phrase *dogs* refers to all members of the class dog (similarly for *inu-wa* in (6)). Referring to a kind is called **generic** reference. However, generic reference is different from universal quantification because it does not necessarily refer to the entire denotation. For example, in (7), the sentence is true only for those female dogs with offspring which do suckle them, not the whole class of dogs, yet *dogs* has generic reference:

(5)   <u>*Dogs*</u> *are mammals*

(6)   犬 は　　哺乳類　　だ
　　　inu-wa　honyūrui da
　　　dog-TOP mammal be

　　　<u>Dogs</u> are mammals

(7)   <u>*Dogs*</u> *suckle their young*

Again, there is a large body of literature on generic reference. Carlson and Pelletier (1996) give a survey of current topics and issues. The most widely adopted approach is to represent generic reference with the generic operator **GEN**, giving sentence (5) the following reading: **GEN**$[x]($dog(x), mammal$(x))$, that is, there is a generic relation between members of the class dog and members of the class mammal. All this does is to say that generic reference exists, without saying much about what it means to refer generically. However, the same generic reference relation exists in both Japanese and English, although it is expressed differently. Therefore, in order to contrast Japanese and English, there is no need to make the exact meaning of the generic operator clearer.

Another useful concept in the discussion of generic reference is that of **characterizing** sentences. Sentences such as *Mary usually smokes a cigarette after dinner* are characterizing, and share some of the same properties as generic noun phrases. For example, the previous sentence is appropriate whether or not Mary smokes after every dinner, in the same way that *Dogs have four legs* can be used despite the existence of a three-legged dog. Noun phrase arguments of a verb in characterizing sentences will often have a generic interpretation: *Toyota is a company that manufactures <u>cars</u>.*

In English, generic noun phrases cannot be modified by the full range of determiners, and their grammatical number is fixed: plural for countable noun phrases with no determiner, and singular otherwise. Generic noun phrases take three forms in English:[3] indefinite singular (generic 'a'), *<u>A mammoth</u> is a mammal*; definite singular (generic 'the'), *<u>The mammoth</u> is a mammal*; and bare plural (and singular uncountable) (generic ϕ), *<u>Mammoths</u> are mammals/<u>Furniture</u> is expensive*. There are some restrictions as to their use, in particular, generic 'a' cannot be used when the predicate holds only over the entire class, rather than over a typical member of some class: **A mammoth evolved into an elephant*.

Interestingly, the preferred form has shifted from definite singular to bare plural during the last century (Krifka et al., 1996, 113). An example of this shift is given in (8: Krifka et al.'s 185), where two English wartime propaganda posters, from the First and Second World Wars, are compared. In the WWI poster the subject is a definite singular *the Hun*, whereas in the WWII poster it is a bare plural *Germans*:

(8) a. *<u>The Hun</u> is a sly and cunning beast! Do not divulge secrets to strangers!*

   b. *<u>Germans</u> are sly and cunning! Do not divulge secrets to strangers!*

Generic noun phrases can typically be pronominalized, as in (9):

(9) a. *<u>Elephants</u>$_i$ like <u>bananas</u>$_j$.*

   b. *<u>They</u>$_i$ pick <u>them</u>$_j$ with <u>their</u>$_i$ trunks.*

In Japanese, generic noun phrases are characteristically marked with the focus marker *-wa* "TOP", although there is no explicit distinction between generic and referential noun phrases. However, Japanese can mark the subject of characterizing sentences with the grammaticalized phrase *-to-iu* "called", followed by a nominaliser and a case-marker, as in (10). Nominalisers include the structural nouns (*keishiki-meishi*) *no* "thing", *mono* "thing", and *koto* "abstract thing", as well as *tokoro* "place" or *jikan* "time". This provides a good test for Japanese sentences; if the subject can be followed by '*-to-iu*-NOMINALISER-MARKER' (e.g., *-to-iu-mono-wa*), then the sentence is characterizing, and the subject will typically be generic:

---

[3] There is also a fourth form: definite plural, which is used for names of some national groups: *the Italians*.

(10)　象 と いう もの が　　　　　バナナ が　　好き だ
　　　zō-to-iu-mono-ga　　　　　　*banana-ga*　*suki-da*
　　　elephant-QUO-called-NOMINALISER-NOM banana-NOM like

　　　[things called] <u>Elephants</u> like bananas.

2.2.3　Ascriptive Noun Phrases

An **ascriptive** noun phrase is used to ascribe an attribute to another noun phrase, which I will call its **predicand**. Typically a noun phrase is ascriptive if it is the complement of a copular verb (such as *be* or *become*), although ascriptive noun phrases can be found in other constructions: in (11), for example, where *tsūyakusha* "interpreter" is the ascriptive noun phrase and *watashi* "I" is its predicand:

(11)　私 は　　　　<u>通訳者 として</u>　　　働く
　　　watashi-wa tsūyakusha-toshite hataraku
　　　I-TOP　　　　interpreter-as　　　　work

　　　I work as <u>an interpreter</u>.

An ascriptive noun phrase is **non-referring**. However, it introduces its denotation into the discourse, and the kind it defines can be referred to, as in (12). As can be seen in this example, the pronoun refers back to the kind `actress`, not to any individual actress, thus the use of *they* (referring to *actresses* in general) rather than *she* (referring to Mary):

(12)　*Mary wants to be an actress because they lead glamorous lives.*

In English, ascriptive noun phrases typically agree with their predicand in number, as in (13) and (14). This agreement is pragmatic rather than syntactic; in particular, if the predicand's referent is conceived of as an **aggregate**[4], and the ascriptive noun phrase is headed by a collective noun, then the ascriptive noun phrase may be singular, as in (15). This kind of discord is not restricted to ascriptive noun phrase agreement (see Section 2.3.1):

(13)　*A computer is <u>a tool</u>*　　　　　　　　　　　(ascriptive NP)

(14)　*Computers are <u>tools</u>*　　　　　　　　　　　(ascriptive NP)

(15)　*The students are <u>a mob</u>*　　　　　　　　　(ascriptive NP)

Not all complements of copular verbs are ascriptive. There are at least two interpretations: **predicational** and **specificational**. Consider a copular sentence of the type NP_1-*wa* NP_2-*de-aru* "NP_1 is NP_2".

---

[4]An aggregate is a collection of heterogenous things taken as a whole.

In the predicational interpretation, NP_2 predicates something of NP_1, as in (16). In this case the complement noun phrase, NP_2, is ascriptive, as it ascribes a property. It will characteristically be indefinite. In English, the order of subject and complement can sometimes be reversed for emphasis, with a special pattern of intonation. In general, generic predicational sentences cannot be reversed: #*A tool is a computer*.

In the specificational interpretation, NP_1 and NP_2 are both referential, with the same referent. If the copular verb is negative, then both noun phrases can be referential and have different referents, as in (19). Typically NP_2 specifies the value of NP_1, that is, it answers the question who or what is NP_1. In this case, the NPs can be reversed without changing the meaning of the sentence, as in examples (17) and (18), although sometimes the nominative case-marker will be preferred for one order in Japanese (Nishiyama, 1990). In English, both the subject and complement of a specificational sentence will characteristically be definite, and the sentence itself conveys a contrastive meaning (Declerk, 1988, 10,19–22,24).

(16) 私 の 　　　指導者 は 　　いい ひと 　で ある
watashi-no shidōsha-wa ii hito de-aru.
I-ADN 　　　advisor-TOP good person be

My advisor is a good man. 　　　　　　　　(predicational)

(17) 私 の 　　　指導者 は 　　X 博士 　　　で ある
watashi-no shidōsha-wa ekkusu-hakase de-aru.
I-ADN 　　　advisor-TOP X-doctor 　　be

My advisor is Dr X. 　　　　　　　　　　(specificational)

(18) X 博士 は 　　　私 の 　　　指導者 　で ある
ekkusu-hakase-wa watashi-no shidōsha de-aru.
X-doctor-TOP 　　I-ADN 　　　advisor 　be

Dr X is my advisor. 　　　　　　　　　　(specificational)

(19) 私 の 　　　指導者 は 　　Y 博士 　では ない
watashi-no shidōsha-wa uai-hakase de-wa-nai.
I-ADN 　　　advisor-TOP Y-doctor 　be-not

My advisor is not Dr Y. 　　　　　　　　(specificational)

2.2.4 Defective Noun Phrases

Non-prototypical noun phrases are common, therefore adequate processing is essential for a wide-coverage natural language processing system. Ross (1995) points out that many noun phrases are **defective**, that is, they do not show the full range of behaviors that prototypical noun phrases do. In particular, they do not exhibit all of the following behaviors (in English):

A Definite pronominalization.

B Modifiability by a full range of determiners and modifiers.

C Pluralizability and the triggering of number agreement.

D The ability to undergo movement (such as passive, topicalization and various dislocations).

Ross (1995) identifies five kinds of **defective noun phrases**: **idiom chunks**, **predicate nominals**, **measure phrases**, **locatives/temporals**, and **cognate objects**. All of them differ in referential use from both generic and referential noun phrases. With the exception of cognate objects, they are all very common, although they are often neglected in linguistic discussions of reference or article use.

Idiom chunks in non-decompositional idioms (such as *the bucket* in *kick the bucket* "die" or *in line*) are non-referring. This explains why they cannot be referred to or replaced by pronouns. Ross's predicate nominals are ascriptive noun phrases, and also non-referring. Measure phrases (such as *twelve dollars* in *It costs twelve dollars*), in combination with their governing verb, predicate an amount and do not refer to an entity or entities. Note, however, that a sentence like *I saw twelve dollars lying on the ground* has two interpretations. In one, the noun phrase is referential and there are twelve dollar notes or coins lying on the ground. In the other it is a measure phrase, in which case there could be 24 fifty cent coins, 12 dollar coins, 6 two dollar coins or indeed any combination that adds up to a value of twelve dollars. In Japanese, measure phrases are defective in that they typically do not take a postposition, even when they are arguments, as in (20):

(20)　それ は 千 円　　掛かります
　　　sore-wa sen-en　kakarimasu
　　　it-TOP　1000-yen cost

　　　It costs 1,000 yen.

Locative and temporal noun phrases functioning as adjuncts (or embedded with prepositional phrases functioning as adjuncts), such as *the city* and *yesterday* in *The man lost his wallet in the city yesterday* refer in a different way to noun phrases functioning as subject and object such as *the man*. Both *the man* and *his wallet* refer to participants in the situation, but *yesterday* picks out the time the event occurred, and *the city* the place.

In English, locative and temporal expressions are prototypically prepositional phrases, with the noun phrase a complement of the preposition. However, they are realized in a variety of ways. They can be bare noun phrases, but only for certain nouns, with certain modifiers: e.g. unmodified deictic day names (*yesterday, today, tomorrow*). In Japanese also, temporal and locative expressions are typically marked with the postpositions *-ni* or *-de* (similar to English prepositions), but may be bare noun phrases. Again this is possible only for certain nouns, with certain modifiers: e.g. unmodified deictic day names (*kinō* "yesterday", *kyō* "today", *ashita* "tomorrow" (§ 5.4.5).

In addition, locative and temporal adjuncts differ from standard arguments such as subject and object in that there can be multiple locative and temporal expressions, as in (21). This is predictable from their meaning: locative expressions denote regions of space rather than entities, and this region can be specified at different levels of granularity.

(21) *I work at NTT in Kyoto in the Kansai region in Japan* .

English time position noun phrases used primarily to refer to time are highly idiosyncratic in their lexical choice, as well as their choice of determiners, typically having no surface determiner, although some take the definite article. These noun phrases are normally adjuncts, but they can also be a complement in some constructions, such as, the subject of *Spring has come*. Noun phrases headed by the same nouns, but not primarily referring to time, behave as do other nouns: *It was a spring to remember*. To handle these lexical and syntactic idiosyncrasies requires special processing for temporal noun phrases.

Some examples of temporal noun phrases lacking articles when unmodified are given in (22). Each example is followed by idiomatic class of its head (Flickinger, 1996, Bond et al., 1997).

(22)			
	a.	today, yesterday, tomorrow	(deictic-day)
	b.	Monday	(day-of-week)
	c.	Christmas	(holiday)
	d.	3 o'clock, 12:15	(numbered-hour)
	e.	February	(month)
	f.	1997	(year)
	g.	dawn	(time-of-day)
	h.	winter	(season)

In contrast with the noun types shown in (22), ordinal numbers denoting the day of a month, on the other hand, normally take the definite article: *the 19th*.

The choice of dependent also affects the choice of determiner, for example, there are some temporal expressions which take no determiner when they are modified by another class of time expressions (23):

(23)   a. Monday morning

        b. yesterday morning

        c. Monday night

        d. February 19

        e. February 19th

2.2.5 Non-referring Noun Phrases

Another non-referring use of noun phrases is to stand for variables that are not linked to referents. One example of this is **negative bound** interpretations: *a car* in (24):

(24) *I don't own a car.*

In this case the noun phrase *a car* is within the scope of the negation and does not refer to any particular car. Therefore it is non-referring and cannot be referred back to by a pronoun.

Another non-referring use is **non-specific** reference. In (25), any good doctor will do. Therefore the reference is not to some specific entity, and is non-specific. The same ambiguity exists in the equivalent Japanese sentence (26):

(25) *I am looking for any good doctor.*

(26) 私は   いい 医者 さん を   探して いる
      watashi-wa ii   isha-san-o   sagashite-iru
      I-TOP   good doctor-HON-ACC look for-be

      I am looking for a good doctor.

2.3 Number and Countability

Number and countability in English are closely linked to meaning, and yet arbitrary, in that whether a noun phrase will be countable is often a matter of convention. The arbitrary realization of number and countability is a problem for non-native speakers as well as for natural language processing systems. Even closely related languages differ in their conventions. To use Allan's (1980) example, there is nothing about the concept denoted by *lightning* that rules out **a lightning* being interpreted as *a flash of lightning*. In both German and French (which distinguish between countable and uncountable uses of words) the translation equivalents of *lightning* are fully countable (*ein Blitz* and *un éclair* respectively).

In general, however, referents that are conceived of as bounded individual entities like *dogs* are referred to by countable noun phrases, while those conceived of as substances, such as *gold*, are typically referred to by uncountable noun phrases. A countable noun phrase will be singular if it refers to one referent (*There is a dog on the lawn*) and plural if there are two or more (*There are two dogs on the lawn*). Here the plural noun phrase reflects the semantic **plurality** of the referents: there are more than one discrete individuals.

2.3.1 Number in English

Every English noun phrase has number, which is manifested in two ways: noun morphology and agreement.

Morphological number

Many nouns have both singular (sg) and plural (pl) forms. The singular is normally the base form, with the plural form typically made by suffixing an *s*: *dog* sg; *dogs* pl. However, there are many nouns with irregular plurals, either with syncretism between singular and plural: *sheep* sg or pl; or where the plural is formed by various morphological changes of low productivity: *ox* sg; *oxen* pl.

Number Agreement

There are several forms of number **agreement**: **verb agreement**, between a verb and its subject; **pronoun agreement**, between a pronoun and its antecedent; **ascriptive agreement**, between an ascriptive noun phrase and its predicand; **appositive agreement** between an appositive noun phrase and its head; and **dependent agreement** between a noun and its modifiers. Some examples are given below:

(27)	*The dog takes a bath.*	(verb agreement: sg)
(28)	*The dogs take a bath.*	(verb agreement: pl)
(29)	*The dog took its time.*	(pronoun agreement: sg)
(30)	*The dogs took their time.*	(pronoun agreement: pl)
(31)	*The dog is a puppy.*	(ascriptive agreement: sg)
(32)	*The dogs are puppies.*	(ascriptive agreement: pl)
(33)	*The dog, a dalmatian, is friendly.*	(appositive agreement: sg)
(34)	*The dogs, dalmatians, are friendly.*	(appositive agreement: pl)
(35)	*This dog looks nice.*	(dependent agreement: sg)
(36)	*These dogs look nice.*	(dependent agreement: pl)

For most English verbs, verb agreement occurs only with the third person singular form. Only the copula *be* has contrasting first person singular and plural forms: *I am*, *we are* and so on. In existential sentences, the verb characteristically agrees with the post-verbal complement (the logical subject), not the dummy subject *there*, as in (37):[5]

(37)　　a.　*There is one apple on my plate.*

　　　　b.　*There are three apples on my plate.*

In the case of pronoun and appositive agreement, the two noun phrases have the same referent. As syntactic number reflects plurality, they should agree with each other. Although pronoun agreement has often been discussed in the literature, to the best of my knowledge, agreement for appositive noun phrases has not been, although they behave in the same way. Ascriptive phrases do not refer at all, but they agree in number in a similar manner.

Finally, some dependents within the noun phrase (typically determiners, but also some adjectives) select for the number of the head noun. For example, the cardinal numeral *one* can select only a singular noun, while all other integers select plural nouns. The demonstratives also agree in number with their heads, and thus have contrasting forms: *this/these*, *that/those*.

Morphological number and verb number do not always agree. There are several situations in which there can be **discord** as in (38) to (41):

(38)　*The Seven Samurai is my favorite movie.*

(39)　The government has/have agreed.

(40)　Two centimeters is enough.

(41)　Every person$_i$ has agreed that they$_i$ take only their$_i$ share.

In all of these cases, the meaning of the noun phrase overrides its grammatical number. In the first case, *The Seven Samurai* is the title of a film, and is used to refer to a single film. In the second, (39), *the government* can be thought of as either a group of people, or as an entity in its own right. Nouns with referents which can be conceived of as either a group or an entity are called **collective nouns**. In (40), *two centimeters* measures a single length, and it is this length which is said to be enough. Finally, in (41), *every person* refers to a set of

---

[5]There is also a construction that has singular agreement even with a plural logical subject: *there's three apples on my plate*. However, this occurs only with the contracted form *there's* not with *there is*, and should be treated as a special construction that shows no agreement.

people, and can therefore be referred back to by the plural *their*. In some dialects *they/their* is used to refer to a single person whose gender is not specified. However, as in this case, the pronoun triggers plural verb agreement (Bender and Flickinger, 1999). There is never discord between the demonstrative and its head: *this two meters [is enough]*.

2.3.2 Number in Japanese

Unlike English, there is no syntactic number in Japanese. Japanese nouns do not have contrasting singular and plural forms, and there is no verb agreement. Nouns and pronouns can be marked with a collectivizing suffix if their antecedent refers to a group, but this is normally done only if the antecedent is animate: *gakusei-tachi* "the students (lit: student-COL)". Japanese does have some noun phrase dependents whose meaning entails that the referent of the noun they modify must consist of more than one individual entity, such as *korera-no* "these". Even in these cases there is no morphological marking or agreement. Most modifiers do not imply anything about the plurality of the referent of their head. For example, demonstratives such as *kono* "this" can be translated as *this* or *these* depending on the context.

Martin (1988, 143–154) gives several ways that Japanese mark the concept of plurality:

Classifiers *kuruma-ga ichi-dai* "one car (lit: car-NOM 1-CL)"
kuruma-ga ichi-dai ichi-dai "each and every car"

Quantifiers *kuruma-ga takusan* "many cars"
kuruma-ga kobetsu-ni "the cars individually"

Collectivizing suffixes *the boys* "otoko-tachi" (also *-ra, -ren, -shū, -zoku*)

Quantifying prefixes *sho-gaikoku* "foreign countries" (not productive) (Also, **Duals** *morote* "both hands" (not fully productive))

Reduplication *hito-bito* "people" (⊢ generic)
(not productive; only a handful of reduplicated words are possible)

Inherent *demo-tai* "demonstrators"
oyako "parent and child"

Verbal implication *atsumaru* "gather", *chirasu* "scatter"

Reciprocals *otagai-ni* "to each other", *niru* "resemble", *aida* "between"

Aspect *kodomo-ga umare-sugiru* "too many children are born"

These are all semantic indicators of plurality, with no overt syntactic effect in either noun morphology or verbal agreement. Pronouns with a plural affix may be used with semantically plural antecedents, particularly if they are animate. More often, an anaphoric classifier or zero pronoun is used instead. Downing (1996, 194) points out that all of these ways of indicating plurality also have some other function: none of them are solely plural markers.

2.3.3 Countability

Countability in English involves two phenomena: whether a noun can be both singular and plural, and what kind of dependents it can take.

Many syntactic accounts treat countability as a binary feature of nouns [±count] (or equivalent) to be marked in the lexicon. There are several properties which depend on countability. Countable nouns [+count] can be singular or plural, while uncountable ones are only singular. Some dependents select only for countable nouns (*many*, *few*) while some select only for singular uncountable nouns (*much*, *little*). Indefinite noun phrases headed by singular countable nouns require a determiner, while those headed by uncountable nouns do not. This binary division does not, however, deal with the full range of possibilities and restrictions on use in English.

Allan (1980) argues that the binary countability distinction applies only at the level of noun phrases. Most nouns in English can appear in either countable or uncountable noun phrases, as in (42):

(42)   a. *I ate too many cakes.*   (countable)

           b. *I ate too much cake.*   (uncountable)

           c. *An oak grew in my garden.*   (countable)

           d. *Oak grows in Britain.*   (uncountable)

Allan (1980) therefore distinguishes between **noun phrase countability** and **noun countability preferences**. A noun phrase is countable if its head is plural or is denumerated: that is the NP reference is quantified by the **denumerator** as a number of discrete entities (Allan, 1980, 541). Some denumerators are *a(n)*, *each*, *every*, *either*, *several*, *many*, *both*, *(a) few* and the cardinal numerals.

Noun countability preferences are lexical properties of the noun. The main advantage of marking nouns in the lexicon with noun countability preferences is that it avoids redundant homonymy. Nouns such as *cake* which can be used in either countable or uncountable noun phrases need only be listed only once. There are, however, genuine homonyms which differ in countability, such as *paper* "substance" which is uncountable and *paper* "article" which is countable. These must be separate lexical entries.

The relationship between countability and meaning is not straight-forward in all cases (§ 2.3). For things that are not obviously conceived of as either individuals or substances, the grammaticalization of number in the noun phrases that refer to them appears arbitrary. The classic example of this is *oats* which is plural, and is not used to head a singular noun phrase,[6] compared to *wheat* which is singular, and is not used to head a plural noun phrase, although both words denote similar kinds of grain. Wierzbicka (1988) holds that there are no arbitrary syntactic differences. All syntactic differences are semantically motivated, although they may not be fully predictable, because they have arisen through historical change and depend on shared conceptualizations that may differ over time or in different regions. Comparing *oats* to *wheat*, *oats* conventionally appears in oatmeal or porridge, where it consists of small particles mixed together. On the other hand *wheat* is only seen as grain by farmers, while most speakers only see it ground as flour, or in a field of wheat. Therefore, in English, *oats* is plural and *wheat* is singular. Unfortunately, such semantic motivations are often not so direct as to be predictable from even a detailed semantic representation, and thus are effectively arbitrary for the purposes of natural language processing.

Wierzbicka (1988) identifies several conceptual properties that may make a referent hard to count, and thus realizable as uncountable. One is homogeneity: homogeneous substances, such as gold, are uncountable. Even referents that are in fact made up of discrete units, but appear homogeneous and are normally treated as a mass, will typically be uncountable: e.g. *sand* or *wheat*. Some normally uncountable homogeneous things can, however, be referred to as countable if a few units are being referred to. Wierzbicka calls this class **singular mostly**. It includes nouns such as like *hair* and *clover*.

Another important concept is heterogeneity: class terms for heterogeneous groups, such as *furniture* or *clothes*, are also uncountable. This is because it is unnatural to count dissimilar objects, but the class terms are used to group together such objects.

As noted earlier, (§ 2.3, page 18), the core conceptual difference is between referents conceived of as bounded individual entities which are countable, and those conceived of as substances, which are typically uncountable. These two classes are often referred to as **count** and **mass** (or **substance**), and there is a well-developed philosophical literature that deals with their interpretation and formal properties (Pelletier, 1979, Link, 1997, Allan, 1998). I will use the terms **bounded** and **non-**

---

[6]The morpheme *oat* can be used in compound words such as *oatmeal*.

bounded, following Jackendoff (1996). An entity that is individuated has a natural boundary, and is thus bounded; a non-individuated entity on the other hand, has no salient boundary.

Prototypically, count referents are bounded units that can be enumerated; mass referents are unbounded substances. Typically, a count referent cannot be divided and remain the same: half a dog is not a dog. Mass referents can: half a lump of gold is still gold. However, as Mufwene (1981) points out, the referents of many uncountable nouns can in fact be naturally divided into units, just as prototypical count referents can: for example, *toast*, *clothes*, *furniture*, *oats*, etc. In this case, it is the classifier that identifies the unit of individuation that is countable.

If the nature of the referent changes, the appropriate countability of the noun phrase that refers to it may also change. A common change is individual to substance, with the countability changing from countable to uncountable. Pelletier (1979, 5–6) suggested thinking of this process as a **universal grinder** that takes any object and chops it into small homogeneous parts. The claim is that one can take any object normally referred to by a count noun, for example, *book*, pass it through the grinder and then say: *There is book all over the floor*. As Pelletier points out, the universal grinder can be employed at will, giving an uncountable sense for any countable noun with a physical object as its extension. Other changes in the referent can also trigger changes in the countability of the referring noun phrase. For example, any substance can be divided into contextually salient portions by the **universal packager**: for example, *two beers*. Other ways of reflecting the nature of the referent are to refer to an aggregate using a **bare plural**: *I like traffic lights*; or to individual elements of a substance: *two grains of wheat*.

There are many similarities between plural countable nouns and uncountable singular nouns. For example, Mufwene (1981, 210) notes that expressions like *enough*, *a lot of* and *an amount of* can take uncountable singular or countable plural nouns: *a lot of equipment*, *a lot of pieces*; but not countable singular nouns **a lot of a piece*. This is also true for many predicates: *I collect equipment*, *I collect pieces*, **I collect a piece*. This makes sense if countability and number are thought of as a continuum, as in Figure 1.

Jackendoff (1991) also makes this distinction, but in a slightly different way. He introduces two conceptual features: **boundedness** ($\pm$b) and **internal structure** ($\pm$i) (Table 1). Nouns whose referents are +b,−i are countable **individuals**. They may be singular or plural. Nouns whose referents are −b,−i are uncountable **substances**. Nouns

$$\begin{array}{c} \dfrac{\text{non-singular}}{} \\ \underline{\text{singular} \quad \leftrightarrow \quad \overline{\text{plural}} \quad \leftrightarrow \quad \text{uncountable}} \\ \text{countable} \end{array}$$

FIGURE 1 Number/Countability Continuum (Mufwene, 1981)

that are +b,+i are **groups** (or **collective noun**s). They are bounded, therefore they can be referred to as single entities. However, they have internal structure as they are made up of individual elements. Therefore, they can have plural agreement even when they are singular. Finally, nouns which are −b,−i are aggregates. They have no salient boundaries, but have an internal structure. This class is made up of plural countable nouns and some plural only. Together the two non-bounded types are the equivalent of Mufwene (1981)'s non-singular nouns. The four classes are shown, with examples, in Table 1.

TABLE 1 Boundedness and Internal Structure (Jackendoff, 1991)

Boundedness	Internal Structure	Type	Example
+b	−i	**individuals**	*a dog/two dogs*
+b	+i	**groups**	*a committee*
−b	−i	**substance**s	*water*
−b	+i	**aggregates**	*buses, cattle*

This analysis is based on conceptual structures rather than morpho-syntactic properties such as singular/plural forms, and ignores most of the irregular classes.

2.4 Determiners and (In)Definiteness

Determiners are characteristically used in English to show the referential status of a noun. From the point of view of translation, many English determiners have relatively straightforward translation equivalents in Japanese: for example, demonstratives and quantifiers.

Japanese bare noun phrases, however, are normally translated into English noun phrases with articles, or occasionally possessive pronouns. The choice of article is not at all straightforward. Therefore, this section will concentrate on the semantics and pragmatics of article use.

2.4.1   Article Use: *a* and *the*

The core use of English articles is to show whether a noun phrase is definite or not. A definite noun phrase is used when a speaker (a) introduces a referent (or referents) to a hearer; (b) instructs the hearer to locate the referents in a shared set of objects; and (c) refers to the totality of the referent (or referents) within the shared set which satisfies the referring expression (Hawkins, 1978, 1991).

Condition (a) says that the referent must exist (at least in the universe of discourse). Condition (b) says the referent must be **locatable**: the hearer must be able to identify the shared set in which the referent exists. The shared set is a set of referents that the speaker believes is accessible to both the speaker and hearer, either through shared knowledge, or from the surrounding situation. Condition (c) says that the referent is **unique**. The concept of **unique** is defined so as to apply to plural and mass reference as well as countable reference. For noun phrases headed by singular countable nouns, the entity referred to is unique (within the universe of discourse). For plural and uncountable noun phrases, there is some unique maximal set of entities or amount of substance to which the noun phrase refers. For example, *the dogs* refers to some contextually unique set of dogs; *the water* to some contextually unique amount of water.

In contrast, an indefinite noun phrase introduces a new potential referent into the discourse (it can be referring or non-referring, see (§ 2.2.5)). If the referent is a member of a shared set, then it has non-inclusive reference. That is, it refers to a proper subset of the shared set.

Hawkins (1978) identifies eight major usage types of noun phrases where the definite article can be used, divided into two main groups, **familiar** and **unfamiliar**. They are summarized in Table 2:

The familiar uses are those that refer to an entity in the set of entities known to both the speaker and hearer. The set of known entities is structured in various ways. Knowledge that makes things familiar includes the identities of the speaker and hearer, their previous conversations and shared knowledge, and their immediate context. If the entity in question has been referred to previously in the conversation, then the reference is **anaphoric**. If the entity can be associated with (or anchored to) a previously referred entity, then the reference is **associative** (or **bridging** (Matsui, 1995)).

Anaphoric and associative definite noun phrases may be marked with a modifier such as *aforementioned* or *in question* (43–44):

(43)   *This is a description. [...] The aforementioned description*

TABLE 2 Definite NP Usage Types (after Hawkins (1978)).

Usage type	Example
Familiar	
Anaphoric	*I caught a taxi. The taxi was red.*
Associative	*I caught a taxi. The driver was tired.*
Immediate situation	*Look at the taxi.*
Larger situation	*The prime minister caught a taxi.*
Unfamiliar	
Establishing rel. clauses	*The taxi I caught yesterday was red.*
Associative clauses	*The driver of the taxi was tired.*
NP-complements	*The fact that taxis exist is interesting.*
Nominal dependents	*The color red signals danger.*
— unexplanatory	*The same taxi was there today.*

should suffice.

(44) *We have been having some problems with a student. The boy in question is incorrigible.*

If the entity is unique by virtue of being perceivable as such in the immediate context, then the usage type is **immediate situation**. Finally, if the noun phrase refers to an entity that is unique in the larger situation of the utterance, that is, something that the speaker considers unique in the context, then it can be referred to with the definite article. This is called the **larger situation** usage. For example, within a company, one can talk about *the president* with the referent being the company's present president, even though both speaker and hearer know that the entire universe contains many presidents.

Unfamiliar uses are those that introduce unique entities which are not available from the situation, are not associates of some previously referred to entity, and are not anaphoric.

There are four major subtypes. The first is **establishing relative clauses**, where the noun phrase is modified by a relative clause which serves to link the referent to a known entity or to something in the immediate situation of discourse. The second is **associative clauses**, where an associative relationship exists between the referent of the head and its modifier (typically a prepositional phrase headed by *of*): e.g. *the driver of the car* or *the car's driver*.

The third is **NP-complements**, where the head noun takes a clausal complement, and is uniquely identified by it: *the fact that (in)definite articles are interesting to some people*. There are two classes of nouns which take complements: the *fact* class and the *rumor* class. The *fact* class always takes a definite article, and noun and determiner can be omitted without changing the meaning. It includes nouns such as *fact*, *conclusion* and *result*. Noun phrases headed by *fact* will be definite even after set-existential predicates[7]. In contrast, the *rumor* class, such as *rumor* or *time*, also takes clausal complements, but can take definite or indefinite articles. Noun phrases headed by *rumor* nouns can appear in indefinite *there* existential constructions, unlike *fact* nouns: *There is a rumor that* ... vs **There is a fact that* ....

Finally, Hawkins considers noun phrases which require a definite article due to the presence of **nominal modifiers**. There are two further subtypes: the first subtype is noun phrases with a nominal modifier such as *the color red*. In these noun phrases the denotation of the head (*color*) subsumes the denotation of the modifier (*red*): "red" is a "color". In the second subtype are those noun phrases made logically unique by their modifier, such as *the same color, the first verse* or nouns modified by superlatives, such as *the brightest color*. In this case the meaning of the modifier guarantees that its head is unique. Hawkins calls these **unexplanatory modifiers**. Several apparent counter-examples to the definiteness of such logically unique phrases are explained as cases where the meaning is not in fact logically unique. An example of this is *a first baby*, where the compound noun *first baby* is used to refer to firstborn children in general, not the first actual baby in some context. There is some discussion of the distribution of the definite usage types in Poesio and Vieira (1998) (see Section 2.4.4).

The properties of the indefinite article can be explained by its use in contrast with the definite article. An indefinite article entails only the existence of its referent, although the referent can be non-specific, that is, its referent can be an arbitrary individual. The indefinite article is less informative than the definite article, and is therefore the default.

The articles form a **Horn scale** $\langle$ *the*, $\{a, some\}$ $\rangle$ (Hawkins, 1991, 425–6). To form a Horn scale $\langle S, W \rangle$, two words (S and W) must satisfy the following conditions:

(i) $A(S)$ must entail $A(W)$ for some arbitrary sentence frame A;

(ii) S and W must be equally lexicalized;

(iii) S and W must be about the same semantic relations, or from the same semantic field.

---

[7]Set-existential predicates are those which define existence within a set. Examples are *[there] be, have, include* and *consist of*. Hawkins (1991) calls these predicates P-defining.

The articles are in paradigmatic opposition syntactically, so they are equally lexicalized; they are from the same semantic field (that of definiteness), and sentences using *the* entail the equivalent sentence using *a* (or *some* for plural or uncountable noun phrases).

Hawkin's analyses account for a wide range of data with a detailed explanation of the meaning and usage of the articles. However, these explanations rely a great deal on the interpretive power of the speaker and hearer. This makes it extremely hard to falsify. In addition, the analyses rely on a large amount of world knowledge about what is stereotypical, such as frames, what can be taken for granted, and the extent of the speaker's and hearer's knowledge of the situation. Exactly how these values are supplied is an open problem. This kind of knowledge is not yet available to large-scale natural language processing systems and is hard to extract automatically.

2.4.2 Article Use: No Article, *some* and *any*

Chesterman (1991) extends the analysis of Hawkins (1978) to include noun phrases with no article. He also compares definiteness in English with Finnish, which, like Japanese, has no articles.

Chesterman (1991) points out that many analyses of English are left with a large grab bag of 'idiomatic' uses of articles, particularly those in which the article is omitted. Some examples are given in (45):

(45)   Idiomatic article omission:

     a. *Come here, <u>boy</u>.* (vocative)

     b. *The meeting is <u>next Monday</u>.* (temporal)

     c. *What about <u>question seven</u>?* (labels)

     d. *<u>Lunch</u> is ready.* (meals)

     e. *I go to <u>church</u> on Sundays.* (institutions)

     f. *Can you get there by <u>bus</u>?* (means-of-transport)

     g. *I play <u>cello</u>.* (musical instruments)

     h. *I play <u>cricket</u>.* (sports)

Himmelmann (1998) points out that there is a cross linguistic tendency to omit articles for noun phrase complements of adpositional phrases, normally where a definite article would be expected. However, even in historically related languages such as English, German, Swedish and Afrikaans, there is considerable variation between languages as to when articles should be omitted. Therefore, although semantic generalizations are possible, language-specific rules must be provided to handle the irregular use of articles. Even within English, there is a great deal of dialectal variation in the omission of articles: for example, American English tends to omit them more than British or Australian (Chander, 1998).

Chesterman proposes that there are two kinds of noun phrases with no articles. For ease of exposition he treats them as non-realized articles: **null** which is definite, and **zero** which is indefinite. Zero is used in uncountable or plural noun phrases, such as *ham* and *eggs* in *I bought ham and eggs*. Null is used in singular countable noun phrases, such as proper names, and the idiomatic uses shown in (45).

Two main arguments are advanced for considering null as a separate usage. The first is that noun phrases headed by singular proper nouns have no article but are semantically definite. That is they refer to unique, locatable individuals. Only under these circumstances can English singular countable noun phrases have no article. The second is that noun phrases with null articles, like proper nouns, cannot be modified by restrictive relative clauses. Some examples are given in (46–50):

(46) **John Smith/A John Smith I used to know once said ...*

(47) *He's not *John Smith/the John Smith I used to know.*

(48) *What about *question seven/the question seven that you answered yesterday?*

(49) *I play *cricket/that cricket that you find so boring.*

(50) **Lunch/The lunch you ordered is ready.*

Chesterman proposes a feature to distinguish the null and zero articles from the others: **extensivity**. Extensivity refers to the degree to which a referent is conceived of as being abstract, and thus the noun phrase refers to the maximum scope of its denotation. Nouns for which there can be only a little difference in extensivity between the idea and its realization will characteristically be realized with no article, such as *mankind* or *nature*. Proper names typically have no variation between the idea and its realization, and therefore they also take no article.

Articles serve to limit the extensivity of a noun's otherwise infinite denotation. Nouns with an article are typically conceived of as more concrete than those without: *Life is short* vs *The life of Brian*.

Chesterman uses the idea of extensivity to argue further that the null article will be used for things which are considered to be completely familiar. In this case, there is no need to use an article to delimit a concept, as the boundary is already known.

The idea of extensivity describes well the cases where there is no article, introduced in (45). There are, however, cases where familiar terms, in particular, technical terms, are used with no article even though they are uncountable. For example, in a stock market report *trading volume* is used with no article, where I would expect it to take a definite article (associative) or even a possessive pronoun, as it is definitely locatable and can be anchored via a very accessible frame to the company about whom the report is being issued. It seems that this use can be captured by saying it appears with the null article, but Chesterman restricts null articles to countable noun phrases.

One way of testing whether an analysis as null articles is appropriate for noun phrases headed by uncountable nouns is to consider the rules used to generate `null` articles for singular count noun phrases in a natural language processing system. If the rules give the correct predictions for the uncountable cases as well, then the null article is applicable to noun phrases of any countability. Here the null article can be thought of as blocking the definite article. This is hard to do looking at only one language, as it involves solving many problems of reference and familiarity, as well as deciding on the knowledge representation used as input. It is a place where looking at bilingual data, and in particular, rules based on that data, can offer some insights.

The differences between the five articles: `zero`, *some*, *a/an*, *the*, and `null` can be explained in terms of four features: [$\pm$`locatable`], [$\pm$`unique`],[8] [$\pm$`extensive`] and [$\pm$`one`]. A noun is [+`one`] if its referent is conceived of as a single bounded entity, that is, it is **bounded** and **singular**. The articles and their features are given in Table 3.

TABLE 3 Chesterman's (1991) Five Articles, and their Distinguishing Features.

Article	locatable	unique	one	extensive
zero	−	±	−	+
some	±	−	−	−
a	±	−	+	−
the	+	+	±	−
null	+	+	+	+

Noun phrases with each kind of article can be glossed as follows (after Chesterman (1991, 73)):

---

[8]Chesterman calls this feature **all**, but equates it with Hawkins's (1978) **inclusive**. In the interest of consistency, I will refer to it as **unique**, following Hawkins (1991).

zero NP	a referent set itself (which must not be a one-member set)
some NP	not-all members of a referent set
a(n) NP	one member of a referent set
the NP	(pragmatically) all (the members) of a locatable referent set [P-membership].
null NP	a locatable, one-member referent set itself

Further, the articles form a cline from most indefinite to most definite as shown in Figure 2. Although zero and null are not realized, and are thus not equally lexicalized with the other articles, they act as though they are part of a Horn scale. I expand this idea further in Section 4.5.

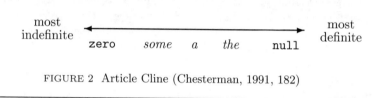

FIGURE 2   Article Cline (Chesterman, 1991, 182)

The article *some* is closely linked to the article *any*. Often they are in paradigmatic opposition, with *some* appearing in positive contexts and *any* in negative contexts (51):

(51)   a. *I bought <u>some</u> bananas*

   b. *I didn't buy <u>any</u> bananas*

The details are more complicated (Lakoff, 1969). Firstly, *some* has quantificational force, with the meaning "a small amount of", and can be used in negative contexts with this meaning. In addition, there are differences between unstressed *some*, the article, and stressed *some* meaning "a certain" as in *some man called to see you*. Be that as it may, *some* and *any* form a pair for at least some of their meanings. Comparing across languages, both *some* and *any* can be used where no equivalent is in the Japanese: the equivalents of *some/any bananas* in (51), for example, is just *banana* "banana". Further, in some languages, a single word is used as an indefinite determiner in both positive and negative environments. For example, Marathi (an Indo-Aryan Language spoken in the region around Bombay) uses the same word for both: *kahi* "some/any" (52):[9]

---

[9]I am indebted to Shipra Dingare for this example.

(52)   a. *Me kahi keli   wicat ghetti*
         I   some bananas buy

         I bought <u>some</u> bananas

      b. *Me kahi keli   wicat ghetti nahi*
         I   some bananas buy   not

         I didn't buy <u>any</u> bananas

2.4.3   Familiarity and Given/New

Another insight into the use of articles is the idea of **given** and **new** information. In general, noun phrases introducing new information are indefinite, while those presenting given information are definite. Of course, there are many exceptions to this: corpus studies show that almost half of the noun phrases determined by the definite article are discourse new (§ 2.4.4).

In an attempt to clarify the meanings of given and new, Prince (1981) introduced a taxonomy of given-new information, under the general term of **assumed familiarity**. This is similar in meaning to Hawkins's (1991) familiarity. The hierarchy is shown in Figure 3; I have added the predicted definiteness to each leaf node. I give a table of examples in Table 4.

The main division is ternary: entities can be **new**, **inferable** or **evoked**. The tree is laid out so that more familiar entities are on the right.

TABLE 4   NP Usage Types (after Prince (1981)).

Usage class	Usage type	Example
New	Brand New — Unanchored	*I caught <u>a taxi</u>.*
	Brand New — Anchored	*I caught <u>a taxi with an old driver</u>.*
	Unused	*<u>The prime minister</u> caught a taxi.*
Inferable	Noncontaining	*I caught a taxi. <u>The driver</u> was tired.*
	Containing	*<u>The taxi I caught yesterday</u> was red.*
		<u>The driver of the taxi</u> was tired.
Evoked	Textually	*I caught a taxi. <u>The taxi</u> was red.*
	Situationally	*Look at <u>the taxi</u>.*

Reference to new entities is further subdivided into **brand-new** en-

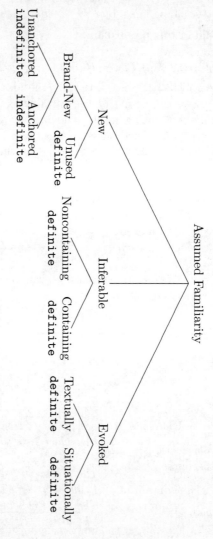

FIGURE 3 Taxonomy of Given-New Information (Prince, 1981)

tities: those that the hearer has no knowledge of at all; and **unused**: those that the hearer may know already, but has no particular reason to have in mind at the time (e.g. *the sun*). The unused subclass is similar to Hawkins' **larger situation**. Brand-new entities themselves are divided into **anchored** — those that are linked to another discourse entity by another NP, contained within themselves; and **unanchored** — those that are not. Typically the anchor will contain at least one NP that is not brand-new, as in (53) (adapted from Prince's (23)):

(53) *a guy {I/John/the plumber/a woman I know/? a woman} work(s) with*

The next subclass is **inferable**s, noun phrases whose referent can be linked to an existing discourse entity by some kind of inference. A special case of these is **containing inferable** where the source of the inference is contained within the NP, as in *one* in *one of these eggs*. This class includes Hawkins's **associative clauses** and **establishing relative clause**s. Those that link back to a separate entity are called **non-containing inferable**s, and are similar to Hawkins's **associatives**.

The last subclass is **evoked** noun-phrases. Noun phrases whose referents have been mentioned before are **textually evoked** (Hawkins' **anaphoric**), those where the referent are obvious from the situation are **situationally evoked** (Hawkins' **immediate situation**).

Because of its hierarchical structure, it is easy to apply this taxonomy to tag noun phrases in discourse, making one decision at each node in the tree. However, it is not specifically designed for predicting or analyzing the use of articles, and does not consider generic or ascriptive uses of noun phrases. It does, however, consider non-article determiners, such as demonstratives. Like Hawkins's analysis, the definitions are quite vague, and there is considerable indeterminacy between classes, a problem that will be discussed further in the discussion of corpus investigations in Section 2.4.4. Nevertheless, it has been widely used, especially in discourse analysis. In particular, it has been used to analyze Japanese (see Section 2.5).

2.4.4 Corpus-based Investigations of Article Use

It is important to test linguistic analyses against large bodies of data. Both Hawkins and Prince divided noun phrases into different classes depending on why they are definite or indefinite. However, they provided no quantitative evidence that these classes are significant, or that people interpret noun phrases differently depending on the various classes.

Poesio and Vieira (1998) tested these two analyses by annotating a corpus with information about definite descriptions. They conducted two experiments, using taxonomies based on those of Hawkins (1978) and Prince (1981). I will report only on the second, improved experiment.

In the second experiment, three annotators were asked to annotate 14 articles from the *Wall Street Journal*, containing a total of 464 definite descriptions. The task was to choose one of four categories for each description, and if the description was judged to be related to an earlier part of the text, indicate which part. The four classes were (i) **coreferential**: the referent had already been referred to before; (ii) **bridging**: the referent could be related to an entity already in the text; (iii) **larger situation**: the referent was new, but presumably known to the average reader and (iv) **unfamiliar**: the entity was new in the text and previously unknown to the average reader. The noun phrases could also be marked as **doubt**, if the annotator was unsure. For coreferential and bridging uses the annotators also identified the antecedent in the text. Guidelines were given as a decision tree, leading through the classes in the order given here, ambiguous cases should therefore be resolved to the lower numbered class.

Their results are summarized in Table 5.

TABLE 5 Coders Classification of Definite Descriptions for 464 NPs (after Poesio and Vieira (1998))

Class	Coder (%)			Average (%)	Agreement (%)	
	C	D	E		Class	Antecedent
Coreferential	44	45	43	44	86	95
Bridging	8.5	6	11	8.5	31	71
Larger situation	25.5	25	20	23.5	71 ⎫ Discourse
Unfamiliar	20	18	26	21	64 ⎭ New
Doubt	2	6	0	3	3	

Overall agreement between annotators was low, the κ coefficient of agreement was 0.58 with the doubts, and 0.63 with them removed.[10] Agreements were also calculated for each class of definite description, and they are also shown in Table 5. In cases where all three coders agreed on coreferential and bridging descriptions, agreement was also

---

[10]The κ coefficient is a measure of how significant the agreement is. $\kappa > 0.8$ is reliable agreement: $0.8 > \kappa > 0.68$ is tentative agreement (Carletta, 1996). See Section 6.1.4 for a definition of the κ coefficient.

measured for the antecedent. The same antecedent was chosen 95% and 71% of the time respectively.

Almost half (44.5%) of all the definite descriptions were **discourse new**, either larger situation or unfamiliar. This shows the importance of this class. Of these discourse new descriptions, roughly half were larger situation and half unfamiliar, although there was considerable variation between coders as to which were classified as which.

Descriptions referring back to previously mentioned entities (subsequent mentions), were mostly coreferential. A comparison with the results of experiment one, where only noun phrases with the same head were judged to be coreferential, shows that two thirds of these (30% of the overall total) have the same head. The remaining one third are hypernyms, synonyms, reference to events and so on (14% of the overall total). The number of bridging references is much smaller again, only around 8.5% of the overall total.

Most of the disagreements were about how to classify the definite description: actual disagreements on meaning, or the antecedent of subsequent mentions were rare. In particular, there were many cases where all three chose the same antecedent, but classed it differently. This could perhaps be avoided by more detailed guidelines for the annotators. Making the annotation task simpler by dividing the descriptions into only two classes, **first mention** (combining larger situation and unfamiliar) and **subsequent mention** (combining coreferential and bridging), improved the κ coefficient to 0.76: the agreement was reasonably good.

More rarely, there were disagreements about the antecedent. In some cases there was not enough information in the text to uniquely identify the antecedent: strictly speaking, the reference failed. This serves to remind us of a minor detail we all know but which may be overlooked in considering machine translation: that text produced by humans for publication is not always perfect.

2.4.5 Possessive Determiners

English also uses possessive pronouns as determiners, in particular, for relational nouns such as `kin, body parts` and `attributes`. Barker (1995) suggests that these nouns have a **valency**[11] greater than one: that is that they take more than one syntactic or semantic argument. For example, being a child implies that there is a parent, and this is part of the lexical structure of *child* in English. Therefore, *child* can be thought of as having a two-place denotation: the extension of *child* will

---

[11]The valency of a word is the range of syntactic elements either required or specifically permitted by it.

be the set of all pairs of entities x and y such that x is the child of y: $child(x, y)$. Using a possessive pronoun fills one slot, leaving the whole noun phrase with a valency of one, like a normal noun phrase. Nouns derived from transitive verbs also have valencies greater than one: for example, *destruction* which has a valency of 3 and can have two extra slots, as in *Rome's destruction of the city*.

Barker (1995) makes a distinction between a possessive relationship that fills a noun's argument slot (LEXICAL possession) and one that does not (EXTRINSIC possession).[12] Lexical possessives can be realized as pre-head or post-head constructions, and their meanings are determined by the role of the slot that they fill. This is not necessarily a possessive relationship as such. For example, *my child* normally means the child I am parent of, not the child I own, and this relationship is part of the meaning of the noun *child*. On the other hand extrinsic possessives are restricted to the pre-head construction, and the exact relationship between the possessor and possessee must be determined pragmatically. Barker (1995, 88) notes that nouns lie on a continuum between the two cases. For example, *pet* is a fully relational noun with a valency of two. The noun *squirrel* has a valency of one. But in English-speaking countries, people typically possess cats, so, in English, *cat* can be thought of as somewhere in between. However, it is not really a continuum. In a given discourse the cat (or cats) being discussed will either be conceptualized as a pet or not. There will normally be a clear distinction.

In general, languages differ as to obligatory features of possession. While Japanese rarely marks kinship terms with possessive pronouns, English usually does, and in some languages these words must be possessed under all circumstances (Nida, 1964, 205). The Japanese equivalents of English noun phrases with lexical possessives are not characteristically modified by possessive constructions. For example, in (54) *saifu* "wallet" is unmodified in Japanese, although its translation equivalent, *my wallet*, has a possessive determiner:

(54) 私は　　　　財布 を　　　落とした
　　　watashi-wa saifu-o　　　otoshita
　　　I-TOP　　　wallet-ACC dropped

　　　I$_i$ dropped my$_i$ wallet

Similar relations in Japanese can be indicated by the use of different levels of politeness. For example, the speaker's wife should be +humble:

---

[12]Gawrońska (1993, 212-213) calls lexically possessed nouns "nouns that are are involved in an inherent possession taxonomy"; Bond et al. (1995) call them trigger-nouns.

gusai "foolish wife" or *tsuma* "(humble) wife"; or the addressee's wife +honorific: *okusama* "(honored) wife" (Shibatani, 1990).

2.5 Thematic Marking in Japanese

Although Japanese does not have the syntactic function of determiner, it is still possible to mark whether the referent of a noun phrase is familiar or not. This is typically done with postpositions (discussed in more detail in Section 4.2.2), in particular, the focus-markers (-*wa* and -*mo*) or with demonstratives, such as *sono* "that".

Kuno (1973) contrasts -*wa* with the case-marker -*ga* "nominative". The postposition -*ga* is used in **neutral descriptions** or for **exhaustive listings**. The neutral description use is the unmarked usage. Exhaustive listings are typically answers to questions, and are used to specify the referents who satisfy the query, as in (55). They are similar in meaning to English cleft sentences.

(55) *a.* 誰 が　　日本語 を　　　知って いるか
       dare-ga　nihongo-o　shitte-iru　ka
       who-NOM Japanese-ACC knows　　Q

       Who knows Japanese?

   b. キム は　　日本語 を　　　知って いる
       Kim-ga　nihongo-o　shitte-iru
       Kim-NOM Japanese-ACC knows

       Kim knows Japanese.

       It is Kim who knows Japanese.

By far the most common marking of subjects in Japanese is with **thematic** -*wa*. Thematic -*wa* is used to mark familiar noun phrases, generic noun phrases and even unfamiliar locatable noun phrases (such as those modified by relative clauses or other adnominal phrases). Generally, its distribution is quite similar to that of the definite article in English, except for the fact that -*wa* is also used with generic noun phrases. Indeed, Iwasaki (1987) explicitly links the thematic use of -*wa* with definiteness (which he calls identifiability).

Contrastive -*wa*, on the other hand, is used to contrast the referent with something else, as in (56). Contrastive -*wa* can be used with accusative noun phrases as well as nominative ones. In general, things being compared must be similar, and are thus locatable (and definite or generic): "In the contrastive use, the contrastive groups (kinds) are always in mind" (Arakawa, personal communication).

(56) 田中 は　　背 が　　　高い が キム は　背 が　　　　低い
Tanaka-wa se-ga　　takai ga Kimu-wa se-ga　　hikui
Tanaka-TOP height-NOM high　but Kim-TOP height-NOM low

Tanaka is tall, but Kim is short.

The main problem with Kuno's (1973) analysis is that there is no clear test for determining whether a noun phrase is neutral or exhaustive (if marked with *-ga*), or whether if it is thematic or contrastive (if marked with *-wa*).

Hinds (1987) uses Prince's (1981) taxonomy of given-new information to analyze the use of *-wa* and *-ga* (see Section 2.4.3 for a discussion of the taxonomy applied to English). The distribution is shown in Figure 4. At the extremes, *-ga* is used exclusively for **unanchored brand-new** referents, which are indefinite in English. On the other side of the hierarchy, *-wa* is used for **containing inferables** and **evoked referents**, which are definite in English. In between are three classes where either *-wa* or *-ga* can be used: **anchored brand-new** (which are indefinite in English), and **unused** and **noncontaining inferable** (which are definite in English).

To explain these uses, Hinds introduces two new concepts. The first is a Japanese syntactic construction he calls syntactic-binding, in which a copular sentence of the form NP_2-*ga* NP_1-*da* (subject-predicate) can be expressed as NP_1-*wa* NP_2-*da* (topic-comment). This can be done only for specificational sentences (§ 2.2.3). Either alternate can be used for referents that are not brand-new. In particular, unused referents marked with *-wa* will often appear in the topic-comment construction, as in (57):

(57)　大統領 は　　　　　　　　　人気 者　　　　だ
daitōryō-{wa/#ga}　　　*ninki-mono*　　*da*
prime-minister-{TOP/#NOM} popular-thing be

The prime minister is popular.

The second concept is **staging**, where a noun phrase is marked with *-wa* to indicate that it is going to be a central character. The concept of staging was not clearly explained, and other studies, such as Clancy and Downing (1987), found that it did not accurately describe the use of *-wa* in oral narratives.

In addition, there are rhetorical floutings of normal usage, where an unknown referent is marked as familiar in order to draw the hearer into a story. This is possible in English as well as Japanese. For example, in a story that starts with a sentence like *The man knew he was in the*

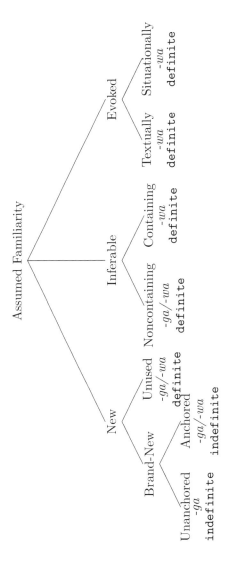

FIGURE 4 Taxonomy of Given-New Information (Hinds, 1987)

wrong place, the man must be discourse new as there is no preceding discourse.

The contrast between *-wa* and *-ga* is also extremely important as a marker of discourse salience. The choice of *-wa* or *-ga* determines how following zero pronouns are interpreted, particularly in complex sentences (Nariyama, 2003, 155-163).

Few studies consider the use of other postpositional adverbial markers. Backhouse (1993, 130–134) contrasts *-wa* with *-mo*. The postposition *-mo* is used when the sentence meaning is applicable to the referent in addition to other items of the same kind (58): it is inclusive. The postposition *-wa* on the other hand is used when other referents of the same kind are not relevant (59): it is exclusive. This explains why *-wa* has both thematic and contrastive uses. In the thematic use, it is used to restrict the sentence meaning to the referent in question: no claims are made about other referents with the same denotation. In the contrastive use, it is used to make a claim about the marked referent exclusive of all other referents.

(58)　彼 も　　行く
　　　 kare-mo iku
　　　 He-FOC　go

　　　 He also will go.

(59)　彼 は　　行く
　　　 kare-wa iku
　　　 He-TOP go

　　　 He [only] will go.

2.5.1 Definiteness in Japanese

In addition to the thematic markers, there are other constructions in Japanese related to definiteness. The formal noun *koto* "thing" is used to mark definiteness in noun phrases of the form *NP-no koto* (Kurafuji, 1998): (60).

(60)　浩巳 は　　　教授 の 事 が　　　　　好き だ
　　　 Hiromi-wa　kyōju-no-koto-ga　　　*suki-da*
　　　 Hiromi-TOP professor-ADN-KOTO-NOM like-be

　　　 Hiromi likes the professor

Ogawa (1996) argues for another definiteness-related choice of case-marker. In Japanese, the thematic object of a stative predicate[13] can be

---

[13]Stative predicates are those that predicate states. They include complex predicates like *nomi-tai* "want to drink", which acts in many ways as a single predicate (Matsumoto, 1996).

marked with the nominative case-marker *-ga*, instead of the accusative, *-o* as in (61). Ogawa claims that this is possible only if the thematic object is definite or generic. For example, if *bīru* "beer" was quantified in (61), only *-o* would be possible:

(61) 博美 が   ビール が/を   飲み たい
      Hiromi-wa   bīru-ga/o   nomi-tai
      Hiromi-TOP beer-NOM/ACC drink-VOLITIONAL

      Hiromi wants to drink beer.

Takano (1995, 387–8), in a discussion of the unquantificational nature of Japanese common nouns, shows that generic noun phrases have similar distribution to proper nouns and definites in Japanese. Nouns marked with the topic marker occur in discourse-initial topic position, and present a non-focus/focus contrast with stative predicates (62, 63; Takano's 16, 17):

(62) *a.* 鯨 は   哺乳動物   だ
            kujira-wa   honyūdōbutsu da
            Whale-TOP mammal   be

            Whales are mammals.

      b. 鯨 が   哺乳動物   だ
            kujira-ga   honyūdōbutsu da
            Whale-NOM mammal   be

            WHALES are mammals.

            It's whales that are mammals.

(63) *a.* 太郎 は   まじめ だ
            Taroo-wa   majime da
            Taroo-TOP earnest be

            Taroo is earnest.

      b. 太郎 が   まじめ だ
            Taroo-ga   majime da
            Taroo-NOM earnest be

            TAROO is earnest.

            It's Taroo who is earnest.

Takano's (1995, 387–8) argument is as follows. Proper nouns are intrinsically definite, and thus can appear in the discourse-initial topic position. Common nouns can have a similar uniqueness implication because they can refer to the 'maximal plural entity', that is the plural entity composed of all other plural entities in the set. A set composed of the maximum plural entity is guaranteed to be a singleton set. If a common noun in a generic noun phrase denotes this maximum plural entity, then it has the same semantic property as a proper noun does: an implication of uniqueness.

This generic reading would explain why the null article is used in English generic noun phrases: when referring to the maximum plural entity they refer to a locatable, one-member referent set itself. However, it is not the case that generic noun phrases refer to the maximum plural entity. Generic reference does not have to refer to every member, only every relevant member. For example, *Dogs suckle their young*, which is true even though males never do and an unknown number of females do not either (recall Section 2.2.2). This is why a generic operator is necessary to mark the meanings of generics, not just a universal quantifier.

2.5.2 Marking in Japanese Compared to Finnish

Although Finnish is not genealogically related to Japanese, it is similar in that Finnish also has no articles. Chesterman (1991) discusses some interesting phenomena related to definiteness in a language without articles in his comparison of English with Finnish.

As in Japanese, definiteness is not explicitly marked in Finnish, so he compares Finnish expressions with their English translations. Chesterman (1991, 131–2) raises an important methodological point: this method gives different results depending on the language of comparison. For example, German and English use definite and indefinite articles differently, so a Finnish noun phrase may correspond to an indefinite article in English, but a definite one in German. In fact, though, in the example he cites (64) the noun phrase *sudet* "wolves" has generic reference. Therefore, a definite article could be used, if the noun phrase was translated as singular in English. Although *wolves* is closer to *sudet* than *the wolf* in that it has the same number, either is an acceptable translation equivalent in the context of the entire sentence. As these problems show, the use of translation equivalents to define something in another language is hard to do consistently, and will depend on the language you choose as its equivalent.

(64) *Sudet*   *ovat petoeläimiä.*
      wolves-NOM are   beasts-of-prey-PARTITIVE

      Wolves are beasts of prey.   (indefinite)

      #The wolves are beasts of prey.   (definite [my addition])

      The wolf is a beast of prey.   (definite [my addition])

> <u>Wölfe</u> sind Raubtiere.   (indefinite)
>
> <u>Die Wölfe</u> sind Raubtiere.   (definite)

There are several kinds of information used in Finnish that can be used to infer definiteness, as shown below.

Word order: Preverbal subjects are characteristically definite, postverbal indefinite.

Intrinsic definiteness: Things considered unique from general knowledge: *aurinko* "the sun" and proper nouns.

Function words: Some demonstratives mark definiteness explicitly; there are also modifiers that force an indefinite reading.

Case marking: The partitive of quantity rules out a referential definite reading.

Context: Context, including previous reference, is the most important thing.

Chesterman (1991) points out that these devices are not equally important. They form an ordered hierarchy, with word order defaults being potentially overruled by intrinsic definiteness, intrinsic definiteness being overruled by function words, and so on down to context, which can overrule anything.

3

Determiners and Number in Machine Translation

This chapter describes various approaches to generating determiners and determining number, focusing mainly on Japanese-to-English machine translation systems. Other systems with similar problems, such as Russian-to-English and Japanese-to-German, are also considered.

The generation of articles is also an important topic in the field of natural language generation. However, the problems are quite different in a system where the input to the system is a reasonably complete description of a known situation. Dale's (1992) EPICURE, for example, has the features given [±], unique [±] and number [sg,pl]. With these known it is reasonably simple to generate *the* for [+given,+unique], *a/an* for [−given, sg] and so on. I shall therefore concentrate on research that considers cases where the input to the generator may be partially under-specified.

The survey shows a progression in two ways. One is the gradual enhancement of rules, from wide-coverage rules with simple features to combinations of more specific rules based on more complicated features. Another progression is from manually producing rules to learning rules from corpora. The two progress in tandem: as the features become richer, it is harder to write all the rules by hand and makes more sense to learn them. At the same time, the machine learning algorithms take advantage of the features identified in the hand-crafted knowledge rich approaches.

3.1 Initial Heuristic Approaches

Early Japanese-to-English machine translation systems did not attempt to determine articles or number correctly, instead leaving the task to a human post-editor. Even so, three approaches were explored: (1) to generate no articles at all; (2) to generate all noun phrases with definite articles; (3) to use the dictionary default associated with the head of each noun phrase (Nagao, 1989).

As machine translation systems became more sophisticated, more complicated approaches were introduced. In general, they were heuristics: simplifications that improved results without guaranteeing optimal, or even (grammatically) correct results.

Ganeshsundaram (1980), in a discussion of machine translation as information transfer across language boundaries, presented techniques for supplying *a/an*, *the* and ϕ for English automatically translated from Russian. The proposed heuristics used a variety of information. Some were based on the English surface structure: for example, noun phrases in the construction 'one of N' should be definite (*one of the tables*). Much use was made of information provided by human pre-editors. For example, noun phrases were given an identification number by the pre-editor such that noun phrases with the same referent would have the same number. The default article was then *a/an* on first use, and *the* on subsequent uses. Special rules to omit articles were suggested for noun phrases used in titles (of sections, chapters etc.). The heavy emphasis on human pre-editing means that their method cannot be used for fully automatic high quality machine translation.

The kinds of heuristic algorithms commonly used in Japanese-to-English machine translation systems are given in Figure 5, as summarized by Kikui and McClure (1991). The rules are applied in the order shown: first the rules for number are applied from top to bottom, and then the rules for articles.

Most commercial systems currently available in Japan use heuristics similar to those outlined in Figure 5, with the addition of many idiomatic rules to handle the omission of the article in idioms such as times of day (*at dawn*), seasons (*in spring*) and meals (*after dinner*). The heuristics generally have the following characteristics:

- Reliance on use of dictionary information as much as possible.
- Binary contrast of countable/uncountable at the dictionary level.
- No analysis of noun phrase reference.
- Possessive pronouns are not considered as alternatives to articles.
- Rules are hand-made and tuned by extensive testing.
- There are many idiomatic rules based on small sets of words. For example, generate *dawn* or *night* without an article if it follows *at*.
- Information is used from both the source language structure (Japanese) and the target language structure (English).

Determination of number	Determination of articles
Dictionary rule 1: If the head is uncountable then SINGULAR	**Dictionary rule 1:** If the noun is normally used without an article then ZERO, if it is normally used with the definite article then *the*.
Dictionary rule 2: If there is a dependent that restricts the number of its head then adjust the number accordingly.	**Dictionary rule 2:** If there is a Japanese element that is translated as a determiner (such as *this*) then ZERO, or if there is an adjective that requires the definite article (such as *previous*) then *the*.
Syntax: Match the number of a noun phrase used predicatively with the number of the sentence subject.	**Syntax 1:** If the head noun is modified by a relative clause then *the*.
Explicit information: If the Japanese noun phrase has a suffix that marks plurality then PLURAL.	**Syntax 2:** If the head noun is modified by a prepositional phrase headed by *of* then *the*.
Default: Use the default value in the dictionary.	**Default:** If the head is plural and countable then ZERO; else if the head is singular and countable then *a/an*; else *the*.

FIGURE 5 General Heuristic Rules for Determining Articles and Number (translated and adapted from Kikui and McClure (1991)).

Kikui and McClure (1991) also proposed an extension to the algorithm based on topic marking in Japanese. Specifically they proposed that for the default article, if the Japanese noun phrase is the topic, that is, if it is followed by the topic-marker -*wa*, then its translation should be definite (*the*). They further pointed out two important factors that their heuristics do not cover: generic reference; and the use of possessive pronouns. However, no immediate solution was proposed.

Nogaito and Iida (1990), proposed another approach, based on three uses of noun phrases. The first is noun phrases whose referent has appeared in the text before (that is, those with anaphoric reference), which are labeled `ident-i`. The second is noun phrases whose referent is identifiable in the domain (and thus can be definite on first use). These noun phrases are labeled `basis`. For example, in the domain considered (conference registration), they assume that the referent of *kaigi* "conference" will be identifiable. The final case is noun phrases whose reference is restricted to a unique referent by a modifier (e.g. *saigo-no kōen* "the last lecture"). These noun phrases are labeled `uniq`. The algorithm for generating articles, assuming that the above three features can be determined, is:

if a noun phrase has a possessive pronoun or quantifier as dependent
    or is marked in the lexicon as taking no article
    then generate no article
else if the noun phrase is labeled as `ident-i`, `basis` or `uniq`
    then generate the definite article: *the*
else generate the indefinite article:*a/an*

No algorithm was given for determining the values of these features, and the only results given were for a simulation on a single dialogue containing 25 noun phrases. In this simulation there were three errors, two due to the need to generate possessive pronouns and one due to a problem with countability.

Ozawa et al. (1990) present a classification of nouns for the purpose of generating articles in a machine-aided English text generation system. Nouns are divided according to four criteria: countability, morphology, agreement and default article use. The combinations used by Ozawa et al. (1990), and the number of occurrences in a Japanese-to-English machine translation dictionary of 50,000 words are given in Table 6.

There are three countability-based criteria: (1) the noun can head a singular noun phrase with an indefinite article (sg); (2) it can head a plural noun phrase (pl); (3) it can head an uncountable noun phrase, where it is singular but cannot take the indefinite article (UC). The

TABLE 6   The 24 Noun Classes proposed by Ozawa et al. (1990)

#	Countability			Morph-ology	Agree-ment	Art-icle	Number in dic.	Example
	Sg	Pl	UC					
1	+	+	+	*0	0	-	4,000	*time*
2	+	+	+	*0	1	-		*youth*
3	+	+	+	*0	2	-		*family*
4	+	+	+	*0	3	-		*work*
5	+	+	+	*0	4	-		*domino*
6	+	+	+	*1	0	-		*sheep*
7	+	+	+	*2	0	-		*focus*
8	+	+	-	*0	0	-	12,000	*book*
9	+	+	-	*0	1	-		*people*
10	+	+	-	*0	2	-		*group*
11	+	+	-	*0	3	-		*mean*
12	+	+	-	*2	0	-		*city*
13	+	+	-	*2	0	the		*backwoods*
14	+	+	-	*3	0	-		*index*
15	+	-	+	*1	0	-	≪300	*knowledge*
16	-	+	+	*0	0	-	≪300	*energy*
17	-	+	+	*2	0	-		*statistics*
18	+	-	-	*1	0	-	≪300	*feel*
19	+	-	-	*1	0	a		*standstill*
20	-	+	-	*1	0	-	≪300	*police*
21	-	+	-	*0	0	-		*thank*
22	-	-	+	*1	0	-	8,000	*information*
23	-	-	+	*1	0	the		*equator*
24	-	-	+	*1	0	ϕ		*Japan*

Morphology: *0 = regular plural; *1 = singular or plural form only; *2 = irregular plural; *3 regular and irregular plural coexist.

Agreement: 0: normal agreement; 1: singular with plural agreement (strong); 2: singular with plural agreement (weak); 3: plural with singular agreement; 4: plural, acts as uncountable.

Number in Dictionary: Ozawa et al. (1990) only give the number of dictionary entries for the larger groupings: 1–7, 8–14 and 22–24. The others are said to total less than 300 in all. The numbers are from an English dictionary of 50,000 lexemes with around 24,300 nouns.

possible combinations of these three criteria yield seven classes, depending on whether a given noun passes one, two or all three tests. These classes are shown divided by lines in Table 6. This is similar to the approach taken by Allan (1980) to determine the countability preferences of English nouns.

Morphology is used to make four subdivisions. Nouns with regular morphology take *(e)s*, another class has irregular plurals, a third class has both regular and irregular plurals, such as *focus*, which has two possible plurals *focuses* and *foci*. These are all straight morphological properties. The other morphological class recognized is nouns with only one form, either singular or plural. Many of their examples, however, are not due to morphology, but to usage. For example, *equator*, which they give as an example of a noun with no plural form, in fact does have a morphologically regular plural form *equators* as in: *one cannot have two equators*. While it is a fact that there can be only one equator,[14] it is not a question of morphology.

Verb agreement mismatches are also used to classify nouns. This includes singular nouns that can head noun phrases with plural verb agreement: *the group have decided*, and plural nouns that can have singular agreement: *dominoes is a fun game*.

Finally, nouns can be marked with default articles. The criteria used are not clear. The examples given of default *the* are either proper nouns: *the Pacific*; or have unique referents in most domains: *the equator*. The examples given of default indefinites are words mainly used in idiomatic constructions, such as *a standstill*. The fact that an indefinite article is associated with *standstill* is a property of the construction (*come to a standstill*), not a property of the word on its own. Examples given of nouns that take no article were mainly proper nouns such as *Jupiter*, which were also marked as being uncountable (and thus have no article by default).

There is no discussion of the use of semantic attributes to separate a noun into different classes, for example, *lamb* "young sheep" is of type 1, but *lamb* "meat" is of type 22 (the types are given in Table 6). Ozawa et al. (1990) classify only the nouns. They do not present an algorithm to decide which of the possible uses is appropriate in a given context. That, they say, is the next step.

---

[14]The equator is defined to be "an imaginary line around the Earth forming the great circle that is equidistant from the north and south poles" (WordNet, 1997). This defines a unique circle.

3.2 Extending Heuristics as Expert-System-like Rules

Murata and Nagao (1993) and Murata (1996) introduce heuristics to determine the referential property (GENERIC, NON-GENERIC INDEFI-NITE or NON-GENERIC DEFINITE) and number (UNCOUNTABLE, COUNT-ABLE SINGULAR or COUNTABLE PLURAL) of Japanese noun phrases. The heuristics are written as separate sets of rules for referential property and number. Each rule is triggered by a condition based on a shallow syntactic analysis of the string and returns both a possibility (POSSIBLE or IMPOSSIBLE) and a likelihood value between 1 and 10 for each of the three choices. The overall possibility and likelihood are calculated for all applicable rules, and then the choice with the highest likelihood is selected from the possible candidates. These rules gave success rates of 68.9% for referential property and 85.6% for number when tested on Japanese texts.

The heuristics, however, have not been incorporated in a complete MT system, so they do not deal with the problems involved with generating English. For example, generic noun phrases may be realized in at least three ways in English; definite noun phrases may take *the* or no article; indefinite phrases may take *a, some* or no article. In addition, the possible use of possessive pronouns is considered only for body-parts, and English idiomatic usages are ignored. This makes it difficult to compare the results with those obtained by a complete machine translation system.

Another problem is that Murata (1996) makes no distinction between referring and non-referring noun phrases. This leaves open the possibility for conflict with their rule that a noun phrase will be definite if it has been presented previously. For example, in the following sentence: *zō-wa honyūrui da-shi, mammosu-mo honyūrui da.* "Elephant-TOP mammal be-and mammoth-ALSO mammal be" *Elephants are mammals and mammoths are also mammals.* This will become *Elephants are mammals and mammoths are also the mammals* using the rules given in Murata and Nagao (1993).

In Murata et al.'s (1996, 41–42) discussion of their results, they state that judging whether a noun phrases is generic or not is very problematic. As examples, they give seven sentences. I would judge at least two of them to include ascriptive noun phrases rather than generic, for example (65):

(65) 有名 な　　シャーロック ホームズ 探偵 の　　　　物語 は
　　　 yūmē-na shārokku　hōmuzu tantei-no　monogatari-wa
　　　 famous　Sherlock　Holmes detective-GEN tale-TOP

たいてい ロンドン 地域 を　　背景 に　　　　　した もの です
taitei　rondon chiiki-o　haikē-ni　　　　shita-mono-desu
usually London area-ACC background-DAT done thing is

The tales of the famous detective Sherlock Holmes normally have the London area as a background.

In this case, *haikē* "background" is non-referential, and ascribes a property to *rondon chiiki* "the London area". Only *the London area* is available as an antecedent for reference. If the noun phrase to which *haikē* "background" ascribes a property is plural, as in (66), then the ascriptive noun phrase should match it:

(66)　*The tales of the famous detective Sherlock Holmes normally have two cities, London and Paris, as* backgrounds/# a background.

In Murata and Nagao (1996), where the processing to find the antecedents of noun phrases judged to be definite (defined as uniquely identified within a context) is extended, they exclude all generic noun phrases from consideration. If, as their examples suggest, all non-referring noun phrases are classed as generic, this removes the problem introduced in Murata and Nagao (1993). It does, however, make the final choice of English articles more difficult, as generic and ascriptive noun phrases are normally realized differently in English.

All the versions of Murata and Nagao's algorithm have the same inherent problem: countability and definiteness are language-specific properties of noun phrases, and are not specified for Japanese (as discussed in 2.5.2). A Japanese noun phrase may well be translated to a noun phrase that is uncountable in English but countable in another language. For example, *jōhō* "information" will normally be translated into English as *information*, which is uncountable, but *renseignement* in French, which is countable. Murata's algorithm, which deals only with Japanese, cannot handle this difference, and must assign an arbitrary value to the interpretation of the Japanese.

3.3　Rule-based Approaches in a Limited Domain

Zelinsky-Wibbelt (1992) uses a fairly deep semantic analysis in the generation of articles in machine translation between English, French and German. She distinguishes between two referential types: **generic** and **identifying** (equivalent to **referential**).

Zelinsky-Wibbelt provides many examples of rules, but there is no quantitative evaluation or discussion of how effective the rules are when used in a machine translation system.

Two relevant algorithms were developed for Japanese-to-German machine translation within the Verbmobil project. One considers only definiteness (Heine, 1998) the other both definiteness and number (Siegel, 1996b). Both approaches ignore noun phrase referentiality, essentially treating all noun phrases as referential, although there is special handling for temporal expressions and number agreement in copular sentences. This simplification is possible because they are designed for a narrow domain (appointment scheduling). Both algorithms are based on the analysis of bilingual dialogues in this domain.

Determination of number	Determination of articles
1. Number information that comes from the Japanese noun [phrase] is copied into the German semantic representation.	1. Known and unique entities in the domain are translated as definite.
2. Known and unique entities in the domain are translated with singular determiner.	2. Noun phrases modified by *kono* "this", *sono* "that", *dono* "which", *onaji-no* "same", *tsugi no* "next" or *kondo no* "this (temporal)" are translated as definite.
3. Number agreement in copular sentences.	3. Previously-mentioned entities are translated as definite.
4. Default: Singular.	4. Default: Indefinite.

FIGURE 6 Preference Rules (from Siegel (1996b))

Even within this domain, however, it appears that considering referentiality is useful. Consider (67), Siegel (1996b) argues that the translation of *shain* "employee" depends on the context. In particular, it depends on whether the company has one or more employees. However, *shain* "employee" refers to the entire group of employees in (67), a generic interpretation, regardless of how many employees the company actually has:

(67) この 日 は　　社員 は　　　　　来ません
    kono-hi-wa　*shain-wa*　　*kimasen.*
    this day-TOP employee-TOP come not

    Employees do not come on this day.

Siegel (1996b) uses transfer rules and preference rules. They are shown in Figure 6. Rules are applied on under-specified semantic representations during the transfer stage.

The rules are similar to the methods employed by Kikui and McClure (1991). There are two major differences. First, the rules are much simpler, a reflection of the limited corpus used in developing the rules. Second, they include a discourse check for previous mention.

Siegel argues that the transfer stage is the best place to determine number and definiteness because it allows the integration of source and target language information with domain and discourse information.

> It is not an adequate solution to transfer an under-specified representation to the German generation module, because the information that is needed to decide on the definiteness and number of the noun phrase partly comes out of the Japanese surface, partly from German lexical restrictions, and partly out of domain and discourse restrictions. Not all of this information is available at the generation phase. (Siegel, 1996b, 44)

Information from both the source and target languages is needed, along with domain and discourse restrictions. This is not, however, an argument for doing everything during the transfer stage. While it is simpler to do so, it is not easily extendable to other language pairs. A more general solution is to enrich the representation of the source language analysis, so that it can represent all the information that can be obtained. The transfer stage should pass all relevant information to the generation module. It can then be combined with information about the target language for the final generation process. Ideally, the enriched representation of the source language should be useful for other tasks, including purely monolingual ones. Further, keeping target-source independence makes it easier to port to new language pairs, as well as to test the analysis and generation components separately.

Heine (1997, 1998) presents similar heuristic rules for determining definiteness. Like Siegel (1996b), the rules apply during the transfer stage. The rules are divided into four sets depending on which syntactic level they trigger: noun-rules, clause-rules, NP-rules and a rule for floating quantifiers.[15] Each rule-set is checked in turn: if a rule matches, then the definiteness is determined and the processing ends. If none of the rules match, they are followed by context checking.

Noun-rules are triggered by those noun phrases that can be marked as definite or indefinite because of their lexical properties. These can be due either to the nature of the head itself, such as indexicals (for

---

[15] A **floating quantifier** is a quantifier whose surface position is not next to the noun phrase it quantifies: for example, *all* in *They had all finished the exam.* Japanese floating quantifiers are discussed further in Section 4.2.3.

example, proper names), or due to the presence of restrictive modifiers. Heine has nine noun-rules.

Clause-rules depend on the governing verb. For example, the subject of *hairu* "enter" is typically indefinite, while the subject of *owaru* "finish" is definite, at least in the domain considered. Similarly, the subject of an existential question or a negated sentence is indefinite. For example, NP_1 will be indefinite in NP_1-*wa arimasu-ka* "Is there an NP_1" or NP_1-*wa arimasen* "There is no NP_1". There are nine such clause-rules.

The NP-rules are based on the type of Japanese postposition. These rules are considered to be weak, because they are considered only if no rules from the preceding two levels are triggered. Four NP-level rules are given: NPs marked with one of -*wa* "TOP", -*kara* "from", -*made* "to" or -*no* "ADN" are all considered definite. It is not generally true that any noun phrase marked with the adnominal marker is definite, although there are no counterexamples in Heine's (1998) corpus.

There is only one rule: a noun phrase quantified by a floating numeral-classifier combination is indefinite. The default is indefinite anyway, this rule is useful only because it prevents the context checking. For example, in (68), there is no need to check whether *kaigi* "meeting" has been previously mentioned or not, as it is made indefinite by the application of the floating quantifier rule:

(68) 二十 八 日 が 午後 に 会議 が 一件 入って
nijūhachi-nichi-ga gogo-ni kaigi-ga ikken haitte
28-day-NOM afternoon-in meeting-NOM 1-CL entered
おります
orimasu.
is

I have a meeting on the afternoon of the 28th.

If no rules match, then context checking will take place. If an antecedent is found during context checking then the noun phrase will be definite, otherwise it is indefinite. Antecedents are checked for by a simple string match. If an identical noun phrase had appeared earlier in the dialogue, it is taken to be the antecedent. In the published results, this phase had not been implemented.

The rules (excluding the context checking) have been implemented and evaluated, with an accuracy of 90.2% for determining the definiteness of Japanese noun phrases to be translated into German. The accuracy for noun phrases for which the algorithm returns a result is 98.9%, but it only returns a result for 79.5% of the noun phrases. Treating the remainder as definite, the overall accuracy is 90.2%.

3.4 Use of Context to Generate Articles

Gawrońska (1990, 1993) proposes and implements a method for generating articles in machine translation between Russian or Polish and English or Swedish. The Slavic input languages have no articles, like Japanese, although they do show number/countability distinctions. English and Swedish both mark number and definiteness: Swedish uses an affix on the head noun of a definite noun phrase, or a definite article, or both.

In the implementation, sentences are parsed into a functional (semantic) representation. The functional representation of noun phrases includes a slot for definiteness, with the values `definite`, `not definite` (equivalent to indefinite), `possessive pronoun` or no value (under-specified). The functional representation for most Slavic noun phrases will have no value for the definiteness slot. In order to generate an English or Swedish noun phrase from these representations, a value must be supplied. This is done during the transfer phase.

In an isolated sentence, or the first sentence of a paragraph, default rules are used, similar to those for Japanese given in Section 3.3. One major difference is that information about aspect is used in the rules: for example, the lexical individuation rule "positive+plural+marked imperfective aspect = default: no definite article: P[olish] *Czytuję* (imp.) *gazety* ⇒ E[nglish] *I read newspapers*" (Gawrońska, 1993, 211).

Gawrońska's (1993, 212) system also has two rules to generate possessive pronouns, an important task that has been neglected by most of the other systems. The rules are: (f) an **inherently possessed noun** in an argument with instrumental role will be definite in Swedish, and generated with a possessive pronoun in English (69); (g) an **inherently possessed noun** in an argument with participant role or 'sem_object' will be generated with a possessive pronoun (70):

(69) *Sobakada*   *viljala*   *xvostom*   (Russian)
      dog   wag   tail-INSTRUMENTAL

      Hunden viftade med svans<u>en</u>   (Swedish: definite)

      The dog wagged <u>its</u> tail   (English: possessed)

(70) *Spotkałem*   *sąsiada*   (Polish)
      meet-1ST-SG   neighbor-ACC

      Jag träffade <u>min</u> granne   (Swedish: possessed)

      I met <u>my</u> neighbor   (English: possessed)

The system uses complicated rules to determine coreference, for both objects and events. These were implemented only in a small prototype, and no quantitative results were given for their success.

Another context-based approach is that of Cornish et al. (1994). A context monitor dynamically processes contextual information on a shallow level to supplement the information used by a conventional Japanese-to-English machine translation system. The context monitor is designed to supply information about noun phrase reference, in particular, noun phrase anaphora. This enables the system to differentiate between first reference (which defaults to indefinite) and subsequent reference (which defaults to definite). In addition, information about number and gender is inherited from previous references, so that a noun phrase's number can be successfully determined if it shares the same referent with a noun phrase whose number is known. Because of the complexity of the analysis and the richness of the augmented semantic network used, the system has been implemented only as a model system, with a lexicon of about 300 words. It remains to be seen whether it will be possible to use the context monitor with a large-scale machine translation system.

3.5 Statistical Approaches

In addition to creating rules by hand, NLP research is moving towards automatically learning methods, mainly using annotated data. Recently several approaches have appeared which are relevant to the problem of generating articles. As there is little bilingual data, current approaches have focused on either source language analysis (Arakawa, 1998, Vieira and Poesio, 2000), or target language generation/post-editing (Knight and Chander, 1994, Chander, 1998, Langkilde and Knight, 1998).

3.5.1 Source Language Statistics

Arakawa (1998) introduces a method for recognizing the referential use of Japanese noun phrases, using only monolingual information. The method differs from the previously discussed methods in that it divides the use of articles into a finely grained collection of 3 types and 19 subtypes. The method uses a combination of background probabilities, as well as lexical, syntactic and contextual clues. The method achieves both recall and precision of 86.3% in a closed test, that is, on the same data used to train the rules. It achieves 79.9% recall and precision in an open test, using five-fold cross validation on the training data.[16]

---

[16]In n-fold cross validation data is divided into n parts, and each part in turn is used as test data while the system trained on the other n-1 parts. The n results are normally averaged together.

He distinguishes between three major usage types. The first is **definite** which is divided into six sub-types, then **indefinite** with three subtypes (including non-specific NPs), and finally **other** with eight subtypes. This division into three types seems to be motivated according to which article should be used when translating the NP to English: definite, indefinite/zero, or idiomatic (none if the NP is not translated as an NP, predictable from the construction for idioms, or null otherwise) respectively. The complete set of Arakawa's (1998) usage types is given in Table 7, with examples and descriptions. The types are used for tagging Japanese text, although most examples are given in English.

Noun phrases headed by common nouns were manually marked in a corpus of 200 Japanese dialogues in the travel domain. There were 5,200 common nouns in 7,560 utterances. The frequency of each type of usage is also given in Table 7.

TABLE 7 NP Usage Types (from Arakawa (1998))

Type	Usage	Description or Example	Freq. (%)
Definite:	(38%)		
X	Indexical	*today* (non-personal)	2.2
D	Deictic	*this room* (Immediate Situation)	0.1
T	Anaphoric	having antecedents	14.0
F	Referent identified	via background knowledge (Larger Situation)	11.0
f	Referent identified	via modifiers	10.7
d	Other definite	reference to something in the speaker's mind	0.1
Indefinite:	(35%)		
U	Non-specific	*I'd like to reserve a room*	29.5
P	Predicative	*. . . is a twin room*	4.2
n	New object	introducing new objects	1.0
Others:	(27%)		
G	Generic	*We are closed on Sundays*	0.2
Q	Interrogative	*which book*	3.4
p	Adjectival	*gogo* "p.m."	8.0
q	Numerative	*two cups of coffee*	0.6
s	Symbol	*A, B*	0.04
V	Verbal	verb derivatives	1.1
x	Idiomatic	*for the sake of . . .*	1.0
C	Complementizer	*koto, no*	12.9

This list of types includes NPs not translated as nouns in English, such as noun dependents (p) and complementizers (C). These made up over 20% of the examples in the corpus, and were not included in the calculations of results by most other researchers.

The tagged corpus data revealed some interesting trends. The ratio of definite noun phrases to indefinite noun phrases for several (Japanese) features is given in Table 8. As can be seen, some features appear far more often with either definite or indefinite noun phrases, although none were perfect discriminators.

TABLE 8   The Definite/Indefinite Ratio of Some Types of NPs (Arakawa, 1998)

Feature	Label	Ratio
NP marked with topic marker -*wa*	TOPIC	2.58
NP governed by past tense verb	PAST	2.29
NP modified	MODIFIED	1.64
NP governed by intentional verb	INTENTIONAL	0.93
NP quantified	QUANTIFIED	0.37
Average $\frac{\text{No. of definite NPs}}{\text{No. of indefinite NPs}}$	all	1.26

Arakawa's algorithm proceeds as follows. First, all nouns heading noun phrases are marked with relevant features. This is done automatically by the parser. The features include both syntactic and semantic features ($\pm$), such as ANAPHORIC, MODIFIED, TOPIC, PAST, INTENTIONAL; semantic attributes; probabilities of being a certain type, marked for verbal (=V), modifier (=p), known object (=F), non-specific (U or P), specific (F or f or T or n), idiom (x) or complementizer (C); and existence of candidate antecedent (classified into four ranks from string match to semantic attribute match). These were then used to calculate the probability of each type of noun usage for each combination of features. The resulting probability distributions were used by a Naive Bayes classifier (Manning and Schütze, 1999, 126) to classify the usage type of each noun.

Results were given for four sets of features as follows: Baseline: 29.5% (all non-specific); non-probabilistic markers only: 51.1%; probabilistic markers only: 66.3%; all markers: 79.9%. As can be expected, using all the information available, a combination of syntactic, semantic and pragmatic knowledge with statistical defaults, gave the best results.

Most of the features used by the algorithm had already been considered by Murata (1996), although the INTENTIONAL feature (e.g. NP is any argument of a volitional sentence) is new. The main novelty lies in the explicit calculation and use of domain-based probabilities. All the non-statistical methods use default values for noun phrases headed by certain nouns. For example, a noun phrase headed by *taiyō* "sun" will be marked as definite. Arakawa's approach puts emphasis on the fact that these defaults are domain dependent, and gives a method for learning them.

A breakdown of the results with or without a given feature was included for seven features. Use of any of the ANTECEDENT, MODIFIED and PREDICATIVE features gave gains of around 5%. The TOPIC, PAST, INTENTIONAL and QUANTIFIED features all gave little or no gain. This was not predicted by the corpus data, which showed a greater deviation from the average for TOPIC, QUANTIFIED and PAST than MODIFIED (Table 8). Arakawa (1998) suggests that these features are not good discriminators due to the sparsity of the data.

Another possibility is that some features always appear with others. If so, ceasing to use one of the features will have no effect, as the others are still there. Thus, the feature in question does not need to be tested. Looking at one feature at a time is not necessarily a reliable test of the importance of a given feature.

Unfortunately, the cost of tagging, particularly with such a rich set of noun phrase usage types, is high, and there is a limit to human tagger accuracy: Poesio and Vieira (1998) report cross-tagger agreement of around 61% for a simpler set of features (see Section 2.4.4). This means that this method is hard to extend to wider domains and different genres, as it is not feasible for one person to tag all the text.

One possible solution, for those domains where bilingual text aligned at the noun phrase level is available, would be to use the English determiners to mark definiteness on the Japanese noun phrase equivalents: if an English NP is definite then mark its translation equivalent as definite. Even in this case, the distinction between `zero` and `null` would be hard to make automatically. Further, this would not give the same fine set of types used by Arakawa (1998).

3.5.2 Target Language Statistics

Knight and Chander (1994) take a different approach to generating articles. They proposed the use of an automated post-editor to correct articles in the machine-translated text. Their prototype was automatically trained on an English corpus to replace *a/an* and *the* when they have been removed. The corpus consisted of 400,000 noun phrase instances and a window of two words on either side of the phrase. They constructed decision trees to choose the article for the 1,600 most frequent nouns. For noun phrases headed by these nouns, the accuracy is 81%. By guessing *the* for the remainder of the nouns, they achieve an overall success rate of 78%. Their task is slightly artificial: replacing articles in original English text, with the knowledge that an article is required in a given position. Post-editing machine translation is a much harder task than this for the following reasons. First, a practical system needs to not just choose between *a/an* and *the* but between *some*, *any*, *a/an*, *the*, possessive pronouns and no article. Second, the typical output of a machine translation system is not very close to text written originally in English. Therefore, it is likely that rules learned from natural English text will not all be applicable. In particular, state of the art systems only determine number correctly 80-90% of the time.

This research was extended by Chander (1998), who made a stand-alone posteditor which inserts articles {*a/an*, *the*, zero} into text without articles. Rules were calculated using a window of 12 words on either side of the position in question. In addition, the text was POS (part of speech) tagged, chunked into noun phrases, and the countability of the head determined from a dictionary to give more information. This was done both when learning and when applying the rules. Rules were learned using a standard decision tree learning algorithm: ID3 (Quinlan, 1993).

The posteditor did well on good English text with the articles removed, with a maximum accuracy of 96% for test data from the same genre (Wall Street Journal). Here, the accuracy is counted per word in the sentence, as an article can be inserted before any word. This means that zero is almost always the best choice, and that the results appear much higher than systems that calculate the accuracy per noun phrase: the baseline is 92%. When the system was tested on text from a different genre (Computer Science Text) the accuracy fell to 94%. On raw MT output the accuracy was only 88%, lower than the MT system's built-in rules, which gave 95% accuracy (using the per word metric). If the posteditor was integrated into the MT system, so that it used the system's knowledge of where an article could be inserted, the accuracy rose to 95.5%, slightly above the MT system's existing accuracy. It seems therefore, that learning rules from English text is not so useful as a posteditor, but can be useful to learn rules to include in a generation component.

Langkilde and Knight (1998) have introduced a more general method to use target language statistics in generation, in the NITROGEN system. It avoids most of the problems of the earlier approach, but introduces a new limitation. In this system, all candidate sentences not ruled out by constraints are generated in a lattice. For example, *inu* "dog" would produce (*dog*, *a dog*, *the dog*, *dogs*, *the dogs*). The entire sentence is then evaluated using bi-gram probabilities calculated from a corpus, and the most likely candidate chosen. This produces smooth output, and can also handle common idiomatic constructions. However, it still has no way of distinguishing between first mention and subsequent usage. In addition, the automatically acquired rules in this system are based only on bigrams (pairs of adjacent words). This means that they use only information about the word itself and the words on each side, not the entire noun phrase and two words on each side, so they must be less accurate than those in Knight and Chander (1994).

Minnen et al. (2000) also use a corpus to decide which article to generate, but assume that the structure of the noun phrase is known. They extract all base noun phrases from the Penn Treebank Wall Street Journal data (Taylor et al., 2003, Bies et al., 1995). This gave a total of 300,000 NP instances, where the distribution with respect to articles is: *the* 20.6%, *a/an* 9.4% and 70.0% with no article. They trained a memory-based learner with eight features:

- NP head word
- NP head POS
- Functional tag of the NP: text category, grammatical function and semantic role or NONE
- Category of the constituent embedding the NP: e.g., PP for *the problem* in *to the problem*.
- Functional tag of the constituent embedding the NP
- Other determiners of the NP
- NP head countability
- NP head semantic classes (not disambiguated)

The accuracy (tested with 10-fold cross validation) was 83.0%: significantly better than the baseline of generating no articles (70.0%) or using only the head of the NP for training (79.9%). However, the results are based on a large, relatively homogeneous corpus. Furthermore, information about the noun phrase number is taken as given. For many applications there is neither a large amount of homogeneous training data nor information about number.

Han et al. (2004) took a similar approach, but using a different feature set and learning method, with a much larger, diverse corpus. The eleven features were:

- Word and POS of the word two words before the NP
- Word and POS of the word just before the NP

- Word and POS of the word just before the NP and NP head word and POS
- Word and POS of the word just after the NP
- Word and POS of all awords in the NP
- POS of all words in the NP
- Word and POS of the initial word in the NP
- POS of the initial word in the NP
- NP head word and POS
- NP head POS
- NP head countability

Training and testing on 6,000,000 NPs using 4-fold cross validation and a maximum entropy learner got an impressive accuracy of 87.99%. Relatively shallow cues work well with a large enough corpus. Like Minnen et al. (2000), they assume knowledge of the noun phrases' number and countability. Han et al. (2004) apply the system to correct errors in English learners' essays, and found it agrees with human corrections 94–95% of the time.

⋆ ⋆ ⋆

In the next Chapter (§ 4), I will present a semantically-motivated description of the use of number and determiners in English and the equivalent for Japanese. The description is detailed enough to be useful in a machine translation system, without being so detailed that it cannot be produced by current natural language analysis techniques.

4

Semantic Representation of Reference, Countability, Number and (In)Definiteness

In this chapter I outline a representation of the structure and meaning of noun phrases that gives enough information to generate determiners and to determine number in English generation. The representation satisfies two criteria. First, it has a wide coverage, in that it is able to describe both common cases and exceptional ones (the core and the periphery). Second, the representation is machine-tractable: "there exist computer programs which can derive it from a text and generate text from it" (Raskin and Nirenburg, 1998, 136). That is, it is realizable, not just descriptively adequate. I will demonstrate the tractability further in Chapters 5 and 6.

4.1 Noun Phrases in English

The descriptions follow the structural approach of Huddleston (1984), and I will keep the same clear distinction between syntactic functions (such as subject in English) and forms (such as noun phrases). Indeed, the syntactic description of English noun phrases largely follows Huddleston (1984, 1988), although with the emphasis placed differently. Unfortunately, there is no comparable descriptive grammar of Japanese. I have generally followed the grammar developed for natural language processing by Miyazaki et al. (1995), which follows the broad tradition of Miura's (1967) constructive process theory, which is, in turn, based on the work of Tokieda (1941).

4.1.1 English Noun Phrase Syntactic Structure

I take the traditional position that nouns head noun phrases. This is because nouns are in general obligatory within the noun phrase (although they can be elided), and they carry those features that are subject to selectional constraints, either semantic or via subcategorization. A noun phrase can consist of just a head noun, or a head noun and dependents (with the head possibly elided).

A noun phrase can have many dependents, as in (71): *the long thesis, my life-work*. Here, the noun and modifier make an intermediate constituent, the **nominal**, to which the determiner adjoins to make a noun phrase. The nominal is the equivalent of N′ in an X-bar structure (Jackendoff, 1997). Peripheral dependents adjoin to the noun phrase to make another noun phrase. A noun phrase consisting of a single noun: *gold* still requires some syntactic machinery to make it into a noun phrase. For nouns with no determiner, two approaches are possible. The first is to use a non-branching rule to satisfy the empty determiner slot, as in (72). The second is to add an empty determiner, as in (73). Both cause roughly the same ambiguity for generation: one adds an extra syntactic rule, another a lexical item. Throughout this discussion, the structure with the empty determiner (73) is assumed, but it could equally well be replaced by a non-branching rule.

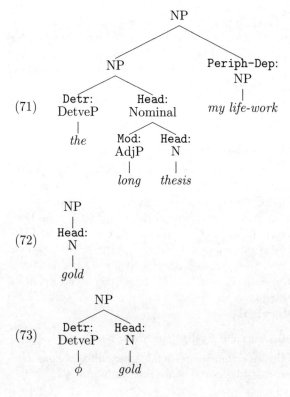

For the sake of simplicity, I will often omit the intermediate levels and treat all dependents as adjoining at the same level as in (74). Differences in status within the noun phrase will be indicated by the syntactic function associated with each element. This is a major simplification, and hides some of the structure, but it is sufficient for most of the following exposition.

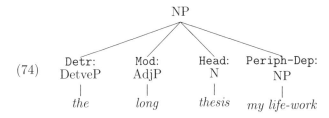

The syntactic function of **determiner** is used only within noun phrases. Many syntactic theories treat the determiner as a **specifier**, bringing out its similarity to subjects in clauses or degree modifiers in adjective phrases. However, as this is peripheral to the problems of generating determiners and determining number, I shall not be concerned with such similarities here.

There can be only one determiner in a noun phrase, although the determiner may have internal structure of its own. I will discuss determiners in more detail in the following section.

Modifiers can also have internal structure of their own. In particular, a noun can be pre-modified by a nominal, as in the following: *a [5 kg] apple, the [first place] winner*. In this case, even though the nominal is of the form `numeral head`, there is no morphological marking of number. Number agreement occurs only in full noun phrases. The modifying nominal places no special restrictions on the number of the noun phrase it is embedded in. Peripheral dependents adjoin to complete noun phrases. They are typically adverbs or prepositional phrases.

4.1.2 Determiners

In this section, I will clarify what words or phrases can function as determiners. There are two ways of dividing determiners: according to their meaning, or according to the order and co-occurence restrictions between them. Despite several efforts to predict all order and co-occurence restrictions from semantic groupings (Chase, 1983, Hockey and Egedi, 1994), it has not proved possible to do so.

Determiners are characteristically the first element in the NP. Following Huddleston (1984), I further divide the syntactic function of determiner into three classes, depending on the linear order: **pre-**

determiners, **central determiners**, and **post-determiners**. Order is defined relative to the central determiners, which include the articles. Central determiners are those which are in paradigmatic contrast with the articles: that is, those that cannot be used together with the articles, only instead of them. Pre-determiners must precede the central determiners, and post-determiners follow the central determiners. I list the expressions that can fill the three functions in Figure 7. None of the classes are closed: each has potentially infinite members, due to the presence of fractions, multiples, cardinal numerals and possessive phrases.

It is not clear where the distinction between post-determiners and adjectives should be drawn. This function is filled mainly by quantifiers such as *many* and numerals. Post-determiners differ from adjectives in that they can select for the number or countability of the head (e.g., *many* must have a countable plural head). However, *many* is like an adjective in that it is gradable: *very many*, and there are some adjectives that select for the number of their head (e.g., *various*). I take as post-determiners the cardinal numerals, fixed numbers such as *score* and *dozen*, the quantifiers *every, many, few, little*, the special possessive word *own*, and *such*. It is convenient to group them with determiners because (1) some of them can complete a countable singular noun phrase: *one, every*; (2) several select for the number and countability of their head; (3) several are closely related to central determiners *much/many, few/little, a few/a little, each/every*. However, the distinction between post-determiners and adjectives is not essential for the algorithm I introduce in Section 5, which could equally well be applied if the post-determiners are treated as adjectives.

A noun phrase can have a pre-determiner, central determiner and post-determiner (e.g., *all the many books, all my many enemies*), although such noun phrases are rare in modern English.

There are some combinations that are frozen, such as *a little* or *many a*. I treat these as single determiners made up of two words, with a fixed internal structure.

The status of *such* as in *There are many such people here* is problematic. I classify it as a post-determiner, because it follows central determiners such as *two* or *another*: *another such victory would ruin us*. It has the idiosyncratic property that it precedes the indefinite article *a* when they co-occur: *such a victory would ruin us* (Siegel, 1994, 484). I also classify *own* as a post-determiner, as it must follow a central determiner (e.g., a possessive: *my own son*) and precedes all other modifiers.

Another approach to classifying determiners is by their meaning, into

pre-determiners
- quantifiers: *all, both*
- fractions: *half, one-third, . . .*
- multiples: *double, twice, three times, . . .*
- *what* (exclamative: *What a great party!*)

central determiners
- articles: *the, a(an), some, any*
- demonstratives: *this/these, that/those*
- possessive pronouns: *my, your, his, her, its, our, their*
- possessive phrases: *the king's, his friend's, . . .*
- quantifiers *no, some, any, either, neither, another, each, enough, much, more, most, less, a few, a little, many a, several*
- *which, what* (interrogative: *What sound is that?*)
- pronouns: *we, us, you*

post-determiners
- cardinal numerals: *one, two, three, . . .*
- fixed-numbers: *dozen, score, . . .*
- quantifiers: *every, many, few, little*
- emphatic possessive: *own*
- *such*

FIGURE 7 Determiners Grouped by Linear Order

quantifiers, whose meaning relates to the quantity of a noun phrase's referent; possessives, whose meaning is largely related to possession; and the determinatives, whose meaning is largely related to reference. The three groups are shown in Figure 8. I group *such* with the determinatives, although it does not fit clearly into any of the three groups.

---

quantifiers

- cardinal numerals *one, two, three, ...*
- other quantifiers *all, both, no, some, any, much, many, few, a few, little, a little, either, neither, another, enough, more, most, less, many a, several*
- fractions: *half, one-third, ...*
- multiples: *double, twice, three times, ...*

possessives

- possessive pronouns: *my, your, his, her, its, our, their*
- possessive phrases: *the king's, his friend's, ...*
- emphatic possessive: *own*

determinatives

- articles: *the, a/an, some/any*
- demonstratives: *this/these, that/those*
- *which, what* (interrogative)
- *what* (exclamative)
- *such*
- pronouns: *we, us, you*

FIGURE 8 Determiners Grouped by Meaning

Quantifiers occur equally readily in both Japanese and English, and are thus less of a problem for translation than determinatives and possessives. Possessive phrases, in addition to functioning as determiners, can also function as modifiers in NP structure: e.g. *men's* in *the men's room* "the toilet". There is a clear distinction between *[the men]'s room* "the room owned/used by the men" where the noun phrase *the men* plus the clitic *'s* is the determiner of *room*, and *the [men's] room* "the male toilet", where *the* is the determiner of *men's room*. This is shown by the different number agreement. If a plural quantifier is added, it agrees with *man* in the first case and *room* in the second: *[the two men]'s room* vs *the two [men's] rooms*. This possessive modifier construction is not very productive: **two desk's chairs* cannot be used to mean *two chairs for desks*. The existing possessive modifiers can therefore be treated as single lexical units. Information about a noun's countability is more semantic than syntactic and will be discussed in Section 4.4.

4.1.3 Distribution of Determiners in English

To examine the distribution of determiners in English, I looked at which words filled the determiner slot in noun phrases in the Penn Treebank Wall Street Journal data (Taylor et al., 2003, Bies et al., 1995).[17] All **base noun phrase**s were extracted — that is, all simple non-recursive noun phrases, more specifically all noun phrases which either do not dominate a noun phrase themselves or dominate only a possessive noun phrase. This gave a total of 301,170 noun phrase instances.

The distribution of words filling the determiner slot (or if it was empty the post-determiner slot) are given in Table 9. The Penn Treebank does not uniquely identify a determiner slot, so I took the first word tagged either as determiner (`dt` equivalent to my determinative) (skipping pre-determiners), pronoun (`prp`), cardinal number (`cd`), wh-interrogative (`wp`) or *such* (which is tagged as an adjective: `jj`). If the word in question was the only word in the noun phrase (which was common for pronouns (7.0%), demonstratives (1.0%) and cardinal numerals (1.1%)), I judged it not to be a determiner, but a pronoun or number in its own right.

This data was taken using the Penn Treebank part of speech tags, with no corrections. There are some errors in the tagged data: for example, almost all of the pronoun cases are erroneous: *he and others* was tagged as a single noun phrase, with *he* as determiner. Moreover, the Treebank classes all instances of *much, more, most, less* and *little* as degree adverbs, whether they are determiners or not. In this case I have not counted them. Many of the post-determiners are also tagged as adjectives: for example, *many* and *few/a few* — *many* is tagged as a determiner only 5 times, but as an adjective 643 times.

Even with these problems, the distributional data shows some interesting facts. The first is that not having a determiner is the most common choice over all noun phrases (59%). There are a number of factors that cause this. One is that noun phrases headed by pronouns (about 8% of the total) do not take articles, and neither do most proper nouns (about 19%). This will be discussed in more detail after presenting a breakdown according to the part of speech of the head noun in Table 10.

The second fact is the importance of possessive pronouns: 3.5% of the noun phrases have a possessive pronoun. Because the text is all from

---

[17]This work was done with Guido Minnen, who extracted the base noun phrases, and Ann Copestake. Some of the data also appears in Minnen et al. (2000).

TABLE 9 Distribution of Determiners in the Wall Street Journal

Class	Determiner	Number	Percentage
No Determiner (59.2%)	ϕ	177,833	59.047
Articles (29.2%)	a/an	27441	9.111
	any	846	0.281
	some	1,459	0.484
	the	58,164	19.313
Demonstratives (1.2%)	this	1,950	0.647
	these	616	0.205
	that	798	0.265
	those	382	0.127
Possessive Pronouns (3.3%)	my	292	0.097
	your	242	0.080
	his	2,045	0.679
	her	416	0.138
	its	4,399	1.461
	our	444	0.147
	their	2,072	0.688
Possessive Phrases (3.5%)	PossP	10,474	3.478
Quantifiers (3.5%)	another	436	0.145
	each	350	0.116
	either	34	0.011
	every	205	0.068
	many	5	0.002
	neither	18	0.006
	no	749	0.249
	Cardinal numerals	8,660	2.876
Such (0.2%)	such	528	0.175
	such a	56	0.019
Interrogatives (0.1%)	what	38	0.013
	whose	184	0.061
Pronouns (0.01%)	you	6	0.002
	he, him	7	0.002
	she	1	0.000
	it	7	0.002
	we,us	10	0.003
	they,them	3	0.001

newspaper articles, 3rd person pronouns are by far the most common. In comparison, a search in a much smaller collection of 500 sentences of Japanese newspaper text found no pronouns at all. Another interesting fact was the extremely low frequency of the articles *some* and *any*, which together occurred in only 0.76% of the noun phrases.

I have taken a less detailed grouping of the determiners and shown their distribution against the part-of-speech of their heads in Table 10. All demonstratives are collapsed together (Demve), as are all the quantifiers (Quant); *any* is grouped with *some*. Possessive pronouns, pronouns and possessive phrases are treated as one group (PossP). Interrogatives and *such* are combined with no determiner. The part of speech codes are those of the Penn Treebank (Bies et al., 1995). There is still some noise in the results: for example, the constituents marked as NPs but headed by prepositions (0.12%) and so on.

For all parts of speech except singular common nouns, the most likely choice is to have no determiner. For singular common nouns, the definite article is the most common choice. Pronouns, demonstrative pronouns, existential *there*, *which*, *whatever* and *who(ever)* almost never take determiners. Noun phrases headed by numerals typically take other numerals as determiners, or no determiner at all.

Considering only noun phrases headed by common nouns, determiners are unevenly distributed over singular and plural. Singular nouns are 1.8 times as common as plural nouns. The indefinite determiner *a/an* occurs almost only with singular nouns: the exceptions are either cases of number discord like *a good 12 inches* or mis-tagged complex determiners such as *a dozen* or *a few*. The other indefinite determiners *some/any* appear more often with plural noun phrases. The definite determiner is 4.17 times as likely to appear with a single head. Demonstratives and possessives are over twice as likely to be with a singular head than a plural one, slightly more than the ratio of 1.8 expected if there was no correlation with number.

4.2   Noun Phrases in Japanese

Most modern grammars of Japanese concentrate on the verb phrase, with limited discussion of noun phrase structure (Kuno, 1973, Gunji, 1987, Tsujimura, 1996). In this section, I will describe the structure of noun phrases, in particular, the relation of the noun to the postposition, and then discuss some possible markers of plurality.

4.2.1   Japanese Noun Phrase Syntactic Structure

In Japanese, as in English, I take the noun to be head of the noun phrase, and for the same reasons: nouns are obligatory within the noun

TABLE 10 Distribution of Determiners with Part of Speech of NP Head

Part of Speech	None	a/an	some	the	Demve	Poss(P)	Quant	%
nn (N sg)	36,225	26,478	956	40,180	2,698	13,021	4,471	41.18
nns (N pl)	46,339	352	1,282	9,635	994	6,067	4,693	23.03
nnp (Prp N sg)	46,758	257	2	6,775	33	1,122	62	18.27
nnps (Prp N pl)	1,258	2	6	528	2	47	24	0.62
prp (Pronoun)	21,229	0	0	0	0	12	12	7.05
cd (Numeral)	12,287	168	34	374	10	20	1,049	4.63
dt (Demve)	3,030	0	4	18	0	8	4	1.02
ex (there)	1,075	0	0	0	0	0	0	0.36
in (Preposition)	502	0	0	0	0	0	1	0.17
jj (Adj)	826	121	3	370	5	79	51	0.48
jjr (Adj-er)	294	1	5	10	0	1	11	0.11
jjs (Adj-est)	275	0	0	179	0	12	0	0.16
rb (Adverb)	473	41	1	15	2	2	20	0.18
wdt (which, . . .)	4,808	0	2	2	0	0	3	1.60
wp (who(ever))	2,758	0	1	0	0	0	8	0.92
Misc:	527	21	9	78	2	18	40	0.23
Total:	178,664	27,441	2,305	58,164	3,746	20,041	10,449	100%

Misc includes: cc, fw, md, pdt, pos, prp$, rbr, rbs, rp, sym, to, uh, vb, vbd, vbg, vbn, vbp, vbz and wrb.

phrase (they can never be elided within the NP); and they are the bearers of the features needed for semantic selectional restrictions.

A minimal noun phrase normally consists of a noun and a postposition: *kin-ga* "gold-NOM". The postposition is often omitted in speech. I shall discuss postpositions further in the next section (§ 4.2.2).

Nouns can be pre-modified by special adnominal-modifiers (*rentaishi*) such as *aru* "certain"; finite adjective and verb phrases; other nouns, either directly or with an adnominal modifier; and certain prefixes (such as *shin-* "new"). Nouns can be post-modified by some suffixes (such as *-tachi* "and others" or *-chū* "during"). The postposition always follows other dependents. I shall refer to the syntactic function of the postposition as that of **marker**, because one of its important function is to mark the case of the noun phrase. A complex noun phrase is shown in (75):

(75)

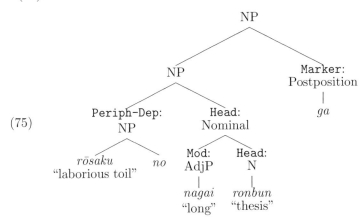

Unlike English, there is no syntactic or orthographic difference between common nouns, proper nouns and pronouns in Japanese. Proper nouns and pronouns can be pre-modified by the full range of noun dependents, so long as there is a reasonable interpretation.

Two subclasses of nouns that will be mentioned in later discussion are **verbal nouns** (§ 5.2.2) which can combine with the light verb *suru* "do", to form a verb phrase, and **numeral classifiers** (§ 4.2.3), which must follow numerals.

4.2.2 Postpositions

Japanese verbs typically select for a constituent formed by at least a noun and a postposition. These postpositions are **adpositions** according to Huddleston's (1988, 123) universal criteria:

a They serve to mark the semantic role and/or grammatical function in the clause of their NP complements. They include words expressing the spatial relations "at", "to" and "from".

b They show no inflectional contrasts.

c They head[18] phrases functioning as dependents of verbs, nouns and adjectives.

d They prototypically take an NP complement.

Postpositions can be further subdivided into three classes: case-markers, semantic-markers and adverbial-markers, listed in Table 11 (Ono, 1996).

TABLE 11 Japanese Postpositions (Ono, 1996)

Type (Number)	Examples
case (3)	*-ga* "nominative", *-o* "accusative", *-ni* "dative"
semantic (8)	*-ni* "locative/goal" *-e* "locative-goal", *-de* "locative/instrumental", *-to* "commitative", *-kara* "source", *-made* "goal", *-yori* "source/comparative", *-no* "adnominal"
adverbial (10)	*-wa* "topic", *-mo* "emphatic", *-nado* "such as", *-dake* "only", *-made* "even", *-bakari* "only", *-sae* "even", *-demo* "even", *-shika* "only", *-sura* "even"

There are three case-markers: *-ga, -o* and -ni. In noun-postposition constructions, where the postposition is one of the case-markers, *-ga* and *-o*, the postpositions are freely omissible in speech or casual use such as email. Because of this omissibility, the noun is best treated as the head in these constructions.

In noun-postposition constructions where the postposition is a semantic-marker, the postposition is not omissible, and is often analyzed as the head (Tsujimura, 1996, 135), giving a structure parallel to English prepositional phrases: *tōkyō-e* "to Tokyo". A major argument proposed for this analysis is that these postpositions are inherently meaningful. Meaning, however, is not necessarily a good guide to syntactic analysis. Unlike English prepositions, Japanese postpositions never appear on their own, and cannot be stranded, they are very tightly linked to their noun phrases. Rather than posit different structures, Gunji (1987) and Siegel (1998) treat all noun-postposition

---

[18]Or mark, as I shall argue below.

constructions uniformly as postpositional phrases. This has the advantage that all phrases can be analyzed as head-final.

Another analysis, that of Yoshimoto (1998, 36-37), instead treats the noun as head of a noun-postposition construction, citing the omissibility of the postposition as evidence. He assigns the postpositions to the category specifier, due to the "similarity to the English specifiers in delimiting the range of applicability of the maximal projection."

Postpositions do not, however, agree with their heads in the way English determiners do: there is no equivalent contrast to that between *these three books* and *this one book* with Japanese postpositions. On the other hand, there is no syntactic agreement of any kind in Japanese, so lack of head-dependent agreement is not surprising. Another, more telling objection to treating postpositions as specifiers is the fact that a phrase can have more than one postposition, as in (76), although only one of them can be a case-marker:

(76) 東京 から が 　三 時間 　　かかる
　　Tōkyō-kara-ga　　*san-jikan*　*kakaru*
　　Tokyo-SOURCE-NOM 3-hour-period take

It takes three hours from Tokyo (lit: "From Tokyo takes three hours")

Because of their omissibility, I do not analyze postpositions as heads. However, rather than analyze them as specifiers, I will instead treat them as markers. I will also adopt a uniform structure for all noun-postposition constructions, treating the differences between the various kinds of markers as lexical.

I give a type hierarchy of the various marking types in Figure 9 with examples of postpositions shown on the lowest level. Within the case-markers, neither of the postpositions *-ga* or *-o* can be followed by an adverbial-marker, therefore they form a subclass of their own. Within the semantic markers, adnominal *-no* is the only postposition that marks phrases which modify nouns, so it is also in a class of its own. This classification is similar to the hierarchy proposed by Siegel (1999).

There are fewer Japanese postpositions (around 20) than English prepositions (around 50). Both languages have complex constructions that function like prepositions: for example, *-no ue-ni* "on top of (lit: -ADN top-LOC)" or *-ni kan-suru* "with regards to (lit: -GOAL regard-do".

4.2.3 Numeral Classifiers

In this section, I will discuss Japanese **numeral classifier**s in more depth. Most Japanese nouns cannot be directly modified by numerals.

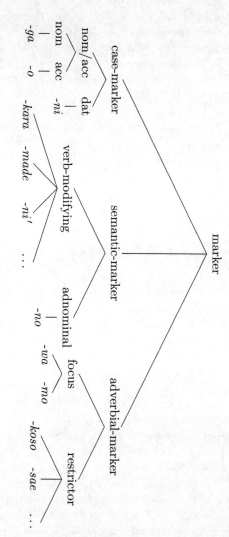

FIGURE 9 Case-Markers

Instead, when it is necessary to count a number of referents, a noun is modified by a numeral-classifier combination, similarly to the way uncountable nouns are counted in English: (77):

(77) 二 枚 の　紙
      ni-mai-no kami
      2-CL-ADN paper

      2 pieces of paper

Syntactically, numeral classifiers are a subclass of nouns. The main property distinguishing them from prototypical nouns is that they cannot stand alone. Instead, they postfix to numerals, forming a quantifier phrase. Japanese also allows them to combine with the quantifier *sū* "some" or the interrogative *nan(i)* "what" (78):

(78) *a.* 二匹　*ni-hiki "2 animals"*   (Numeral)

      b. 数匹　*sū-hiki "some animals"*   (Quantifier)

      c. 何匹　*nan-biki "how many animals"*   (Interrogative)

Numeral classifiers form a closed class, although a large one. According to Koiso (1994), more than three hundred numeral classifiers are identified in a typical Japanese dictionary. Typically individual speakers use far fewer, somewhere between 30 and 80 (Downing, 1995, 346).

Numeral-classifier combinations can also function as noun phrases on their own, with anaphoric or deictic reference, when what is being quantified is recoverable from the context. For example, (79) is acceptable if some letters have already been referred to, or are clearly visible:

(79) [context in which some letters are salient]

      二通 を　　読んだ
      ni-tsū(-o)　yonda
      2-CL(-ACC) read

      I read two (of the) letters

Classifiers (80) have the following semantic structure (Paik and Bond, 2002). The classifier has two semantic arguments: (x) the numeral (or quantifier or interrogative) represented by `numeral+`; and (y) the **target**, the thing being classified. Because the noun being classified can be omitted if it is recoverable from the context, it is a default argument, one which participates in the logical expressions in the lexical semantic structure, but is not necessarily expressed syntactically.

(80)
$$
\text{CL} \begin{bmatrix} \text{ARGSTR} & \begin{bmatrix} \text{ARG1} & \text{x:numeral+} \\ \text{D-ARG1} & \text{y: ?} \end{bmatrix} \\ \text{QUANT} & \text{quantifies(x,y)} \end{bmatrix}
$$

Classifiers differ from each other in the restrictions they place on the quantified variable, y, and in the kind of quantification that takes place. I group classifiers into five major types, according to both the kind of selectional restrictions, and the kind of quantification involved. These are: **sortal** which classify the kind of the noun phrase they enumerate (such as -*tsu* "piece"); **event** which are used to enumerate events (such as -*kai* "time"); **mensural** which are used to measure the amount of some property (such as *senchi* "-cm"); **group** which refer to a collection of members (such as -*mure* "group"); and **taxonomic** which force the noun phrase to be interpreted as a generic kind (such as -*shu* "kind"). Sortal classifiers can be divided further into at least two kinds: **kind** classifiers, which select for a target's taxonomic type; and **shape** (or **property**) classifiers, which select for a target's spatial representation. Mensural classifiers can be divided into three types: **portion** classifiers, which divide an entity into portions; **container** classifiers, which package a substance into containers; and **measure** classifiers, which measure the amount of a substance. Measure classifiers have the interesting property that the units of measure can be substituted without changing the meaning: *2 meters = 200 centimeters = 0.002 kilometers.*

Kind classifiers are characteristically used for complex objects and tend to be specific. However, depending on which aspect of a noun's meaning is salient, different classifiers may be used to classify the same thing. There is a major distinction in the type of quantification: **enumeration** where the number of individuals is quantified; and **measurement** where the amount of a substance is quantified. Examples of the types of quantification in English are given below:

(81)   *2 cakes*   (enumeration)

(82)   *200 grams of cake*   (measurement)

In Japanese, nouns are conceptually under-specified with respect to boundedness, and almost all of them act the same as English non-bounded nouns. Semantically, common nouns in Japanese, and mass nouns in English, can be treated as the name of a kind. Proof of this is that they can be used, as is, for kind reference with generic predicates, as in (83). This can be coerced to an individual reading, typically by the use of classifiers, as in (84).

(83) 私は　　　　ケーキ が 好き だ
　　　watashi-wa kēki-ga　　suki-da
　　　I-TOP　　　cake-NOM like

　　I like cake.

(84) 私は　　　　一 つ の　　ケーキ を 食べた
　　　watashi-wa hito-tsu-no kēki-wo　　tabeta
　　　I-TOP　　　1-CL-ADN　 cake-ACC ate

　　I ate one cake.

English count nouns, however, have an individual reading by default. This difference between Japanese nouns and English nouns correlates with a difference in conceptualization between substance and object, as shown by Imai and Gentner (1997), where Japanese speakers tend to take substance as more basic than object. The effects of the different kinds of classifiers on the interpretation of countability are discussed further in Section 4.4.2.

Numeral classifier combinations appear in several major patterns of use as shown below (**T** refers to the quantified noun phrase, **Q** to the numeral-classifier and **m** is a case-marker):

Type	Form	Example
pre-nominal	Q-no T-m	*ni-hiki-no inu-ga* "two dogs"
appositive	TQ-m	*inu ni-hiki-ga* "two dogs"
floating	T-m Q	*inu-ga ni-hiki* "two dogs"
	Q T-m	*ni-hiki [. . .] inu-ga* "two dogs"
partitive	T-no Q-m	*inu no ni-hiki-ga* "two of the dogs"
anaphoric/deictic	T-m	*ni-hiki-ga* "the two dogs"

TABLE 12 Types of Quantifier Constructions

Pre-nominal, appositive and floating constructions are generally indefinite. The floating and appositive constructions have the same quantificational meaning as the pre-nominal, although there are pragmatic differences (Downing, 1996, Kim, 1995). Pre-nominal constructions are typically used to introduce important referents, with non-existential predicates, while floating constructions typically introduce new number information about a known referent. In addition, floating constructions are used when the nominal has other modifiers, and are more common in spoken text. It is possible for a knowledge-based NLP system to robustly identify the target of floating quantifiers (Bond et al., 1998).

In the partitive construction the quantifier restricts a subset of a known amount: e.g., *tegami-no 3-tsū* "three of the letters". This is a very different interpretation to the pre-nominal construction. In this construction, the quantified N will be definite. Anaphoric/deictic numeral classifiers combinations are, by definition, definite.

4.2.4 Japanese Collectivizing Suffixes

The closest that Japanese has to number marking on nouns is a suffix which can be added to nouns with multiple individual referents. I will refer to it as a **collectivizing suffix**, following Martin (1988, 143–154). In fact, there are four suffixes; apart from the difference in politeness (the degree of respect that the speaker holds for the referent of the noun phrase), they all have the same interpretation. They are listed in Table 13.

TABLE 13 Japanese Collectivizing Suffixes

Japanese	Gloss	Politeness
-*kata*	and others	Very Polite
-*tachi*	and others	Polite
-*ra*	and others	Neutral
-*domo*	and others	Humble

The collectivizing suffixes differ from English plural inflection in the following ways. First, collectivizing suffixes are not obligatory. A noun can refer to multiple individual referents and not be marked with the collectivizing suffix. Indeed, if a noun is pre-modified by a numeral-classifier combination then it is almost never modified by the collectivizing suffix. Collectivizing suffixes are generally used with pronouns, or common nouns and proper nouns referring to humans, or personified animals. Finally, Japanese collectivizing suffixes can be used only with noun phrases with locatable individuated referents (corresponding to English countable definite noun phrases). Typically the noun phrase will be anaphoric, but it may also be locatable from the immediate or larger situation.

A pronoun marked with the collectivizing suffix is used only if the antecedent's plurality is salient, for example, if the referents are of different types. If the plurality is not salient, as in (85), then it will not be used. Even if the antecedent has an individuated interpretation, the collectivizing suffix is not obligatory for the pronoun, and is normally not used, as in (86). It is more natural if there are different kinds of the same referent being referred to, as in (87). However, in normal usage a zero pronoun would be used in all these sentences, and the question of using or not using a collectivizing suffix does not arise. This makes it hard to obtain robust judgments for any of these sentences.

(85)   a. 私 は   ケーキ を 食べた
       watashi-wa kēki-o   tabeta
       I-TOP   cake-ACC ate

       I ate some cake(s)

    b. それ は   美味し かった
       sore-wa   oishi-katta
       that-COL-TOP delicious-PAST

    c. * それ ら は   美味し かった
       sore-ra-wa   oishi-katta
       that-COL-TOP delicious-PAST

       [It was]/[They were] delicious.

(86)   a. 私 は   ケーキ を 三 個   食べた
       watashi-wa kēki-o   san-ko tabeta
       I-TOP   cake-ACC 3-CL   ate

       I ate 3 cakes

    b. それ は 美味し かった
       sore-wa oishi-katta
       that-TOP delicious-PAST

    c. ?? それ ら は   美味し かった
       sore-ra-wa   oishi-katta
       that-COL-TOP delicious-PAST

       They were delicious.

(87)   a. 私 は   ケーキ を 一つ ずつ   食べて 見た
       watashi-wa kēki-o   hito-tsu-zutsu tabete-mita
       I-TOP   cake-ACC one-CL-each   eat saw past

       I tried each cake

    b. それ ら は   美味し かった
       sore-ra-wa   oishi-katta
       that-COL-TOP delicious-PAST

    c. ??   それ は   美味し かった
       sore-wa oishi-katta
                that-TOP   delicious-PAST

       They were delicious.

In contrast, pronouns referring back to humans are normally marked for number (and gender):

(88) 私 は　　　女性 を　三 人　　見た
     watashi-wa josei$_i$-o san-nin mita
     I-TOP   girl-ACC 3-CL   saw

     I saw 3 girls

(89) 彼女 たち は/*彼女 は　　　　笑って いた
     *kanojo$_i$-tachi-wa/*kanojo-wa waratte-ita*
     she-COL-TOP/*she-TOP   laugh PAST

     They were laughing

Second, collectivizing suffixes differ from English number in that they do not mark plurality (one or more discrete entities of the same kind), but rather a group of entities, with the one referred to by the noun being salient. The members of the group do not have to be of the same kind. Depending on the context *sensei-tachi* "teacher and others" can refer to a group of teachers, or a teacher and an associated group (such as the teacher's students). English *teachers*, on the other hand, can refer only to a group of teachers. In practice, the groups referred to by Japanese noun phrases with collectivizing suffixes are typically homogeneous, and they therefore act like plural markers. Because the noun marked with the collectivizing suffix must be salient, the resulting noun phrase is normally interpreted as definite.

4.3 Types of Reference

In order to handle the various referential properties a noun phrase can have, I propose a feature USE, with four possible values: `referential`, `generic`, `ascriptive`, and `idiom-chunk`. These correspond to the four major types discussed in Section 2.2.

referential is the default value, used to cover all uses that are neither idiomatic, generic or ascriptive. **referential** noun phrases are those that refer to some referent in the discourse, or introduce a potential referent (a variable). Because the distinction between referential and quantified noun phrases is not overtly marked in either English or Japanese, and noun phrases are translated the same way irrespective of whether they are specific or non-specific I do not distinguish between them but use the value **referential** for both.

generic noun phrases refer to a kind. **ascriptive** noun phrases do not refer; instead they ascribe a property to some referent. Finally, **idiom-chunk** is used to mark those noun phrases where the NP has no referential status on its own, but can be interpreted only as part of a larger idiom. Many different idioms can assign the value idiom-chunk. It is used whenever the idiom gives enough information to determine the number and determiner. The analysis to determine the appropriate value for USE is given in Section 5.2.

4.4 Boundedness, Internal Structure, Countability and Number

In this section, I describe the features for noun countability preferences and the interpretiation of boundedness.

4.4.1 Noun Countability Preferences

Countability and number are semantic features. However, whereas they influence morphology, determiner (and modifier) selection and agreement in English, they have far less effect in Japanese. Therefore, in this section, I will initially concentrate on countability preferences for English nouns. However, in the final section, I will show that noun countability preferences are also relevant for Japanese.

Noun number and countability are semantically motivated, not arbitrary, as discussed in Section 2.3.3. However, due to the impossibility of fully predicting countability from meaning, I propose that English nouns are divided into five major countability preference classes: `fully countable`, `strongly countable`, `weakly countable`, `uncountable` and `plural only`. Two of these classes have subclasses: `collective` are a subclass of `fully countable` and `semi-countable` of `uncountable`. Default values for **number** and classifier (`cl`) should also be considered. These classes and additional features are summarized in Table 14.

TABLE 14 Noun Countability Preferences

Noun Countability Preference	Example	Default Number	Default Classifier
fully countable	*knife*	sg	—
fully countable	*noodles*	pl	—
fully countable	*shoes*	pl	*pair*
-- collective	*group*	sg	—
strongly countable	*cake*	sg	—
weakly countable	*beer*	sg	—
uncountable	*furniture*	sg	*piece*
uncountable	*rice*	sg	*grain*
-- semi-countable	*knowledge*	sg	*piece*
plural only	*clothes*	pl	—
plural only (bipartite)	*scissors*	pl	*pair*

The two most basic types are **fully countable** and **uncountable**. Fully countable nouns such as *knife* have both singular and plural forms, and cannot be used with determiners such as *much, little, a little, less* and *overmuch*. Uncountable nouns, such as *furniture*, have no plural form, and can be used with *much*.

Between these two extremes there are a vast number of nouns, such as *cake*, that can be used in both countable and uncountable noun phrases. They have both singular and plural forms, and can also be used with *much*. Whether such nouns will be used countably or uncountably depends on whether their referent is being thought of as made up of discrete units or not. As it is not always possible to determine this explicitly when translating from Japanese to English, I divide these nouns into two groups: **strongly countable**, those that refer to discrete entities by default, such as *cake*, and **weakly countable**, those that refer to non-bounded referents by default, such as *beer*.

In fact, almost all English nouns can be used in uncountable environments, for example, if they are interpreted as substances after being ground (§ 2.3.3). The only exception is classifiers such as *piece* or *bit*, which refer to quanta, and thus have no uncountable interpretation. There is some evidence that language users are sensitive to relative frequencies of variant forms and senses of lexical items (Briscoe and Copestake, 1999, 511). The division into `fully, strongly, weakly` and `uncountable` is a coarse way of reflecting this variation for noun countability.

The last major type of countability preference is **plural only**: nouns that have only a plural form, such as *clothes* or *scissors*. They can neither be denumerated nor modified by *much*. Plural only nouns are further divided depending on what classifier they take. In particular, **bipartite noun**s take *pair* as a classifier when they are denumerated: *a pair of scissors*. This is semantically motivated, bipartite nouns refer to entities with bipartite structures: that is they are made up of two parts. Bipartite plural only nouns have only a singular form when used as modifiers (*a scissor movement*). Plural only nouns such as *clothes* use the plural form even as modifiers (*a clothes horse*). In this case, the base (un-inflected) form is *clothes*, and the plural form is zero-derived from it. The word *clothes* cannot be denumerated at all. If clothes must be counted, then a countable word of similar meaning is substituted, or *clothing* is used with a classifier: *a garment, a suit, a piece of clothing*.

The two minor types are subsets of fully countable and uncountable nouns respectively. Unless explicitly indicated, they will be treated the same as their supersets. The **collective** nouns share all the properties of fully countable nouns. In addition, they can have singular or plural verb agreement with the singular form of the noun, depending on whether the reference is distributed among the members of the group or treats the group as a unified whole: *The committee has/have decided*. The **semi-countable** nouns share the properties of uncountable nouns, except that they can be determined by *a*; for example, *a knowledge [of Japanese]*.

The types could be further divided on semantic lines: for example, meat-producing and fur-producing animals will all be `strongly countable` (with the animal sense countable and the meat/fur sense uncountable). Wierzbicka (1988) offers several other subdivisions. Allan (1980) had others. However, many of the subtypes do not show substantial difference in behavior. While there is definitely a difference in meaning between, for example, "names of substances composed of particles, not too many for anyone to be able to count but too many for anyone to want to count" (*oats, coffee-grounds*) and "names of groups of objects and/or 'stuffs' " (*leftovers, groceries*), nouns from these classes will almost always appear in the same expressions: bare plural noun phrases. I have, however, made finer distinctions than Allan (1980), whose classification I am closest to, in particular, because I specify the default classifier when necessary. This is because this information is essential when generating an uncountable/plural only noun which is quantified in some way.

The divisions I have made are also close to those proposed by Ozawa et al. (1990) (§ 3.1). Unlike them, I do not consider irregular morphological forms, as I consider it should be left to the morphological component. One major difference is that I list classifiers for uncountable nouns. I do not include Ozawa et al.'s (1990) class for words such as *dominoes*, where the plural can be used to refer to the game itself, with singular agreement. Instead, I posit separate entries in the lexicon for *domino* the piece, which is fully countable, and *dominoes* the game, which is uncountable, with the classifier *game*. The game is uncountable because it has singular verb agreement, and co-occurs with *much*: *I don't play much dominoes these days*. At present, there is no way of showing that these entries are related in the lexical representation I propose, although ideally they should be related by a lexical rule.

Another group that has not been discussed in the literature is the class I shall call **paired nouns**. This is the class of things which come naturally in twos, such as *shoes*, and are normally talked of as pairs: *I bought a pair of shoes*, but are in fact fully separable. They will be entered in the dictionary as fully countable nouns with the default number of plural and a default classifier *pair*. They differ from bipartite nouns in that two separate entities make up the pair — for bipartite nouns a single entity is made up of two sub-parts.

In translation, an English word that is a paired noun will typically take *pair* unless it is countable and explicitly made single (*kata-hō-no* "one-of", *migi-no* "right", *hidari-no* "left"). A sortal Japanese classifier for a paired noun is normally translated as *pair*. Some examples of paired nouns are: *chopsticks, shoes, earrings, legwarmers, gloves* and *contact lenses*.

Information this detailed about noun countability preferences cannot be found in standard dictionaries. The tests used to determine a given noun's countability preferences and the distribution in the dictionary are described in more detail in Chapter 7, where I also introduce two methods for acquiring countability from semantic classes (§ 8.2), and from corpus evidence (§ 8.3).

Countability in Japanese

The basic distinction between countable and uncountable also applies to some extent in Japanese, with the vast majority of nouns being `uncountable`. Because Japanese has no number feature, there can be no further split into singular and plural only.

Semantically, it has been shown that Japanese speakers tend to give nouns a `substance` interpretation (Imai and Gentner, 1997), like uncountable nouns in English. Further, most Japanese nouns are used in a bare noun phrase to refer to the class they denote, again like English uncountable nouns. Syntactically, they cannot be directly modified by numerals, just like English uncountable nouns.

However, there are a significant number of Japanese nouns which are `fully countable`: all numeral classifiers, words that denote times, wins, losses and draws and many others (Bond and Paik, 2000). Semantically, these nouns refer to discrete enumerable individuals. Syntactically, they can be directly modified by numerals.

4.4.2 Countability, Boundedness and Number

In order to model the semantic plurality and finally select the countability and number of English noun phrases, I propose a noun phrase feature **interpretation**, with seven values, all shown in Table 15. Each interpretation is given along with the countability values that it is compatible with; whether the noun phrase will be interpreted as bounded or non-bounded; and the number of the head noun. Countability is marked as CO: countable (compatible with fully, strongly and weakly countable); US: uncountable singular (compatible with strongly and weakly countable and uncountable); and UP: uncountable plural (plural only).

The interpretation of the noun phrase can be influenced by a variety of factors, including the role a noun phrase plays in a verb's argument structure, the dependents it has, what other noun phrases it is coreferential with, and so on. The interpretation interacts with a noun's countability preference to determine the final countability and number; it may also serve as a trigger to embed the noun phrase in a classifier construction.

TABLE 15 Noun Phrase Interpretation

Interpretation	Count-ability	Bound-edness	Internal Structure	Number	Example
Individuated-sg	CO	+	−	sg	*a dog*
Individuated-pl	CO	+	−	pl	*two dogs*
Non-Bounded-1	US	-	−	sg	*gold*
	CO, UP	-	+	pl	*dogs, cakes, scissors*
Non-Bounded-2	US	-	−	sg	*gold, cake*
	CO, UP	-	+	pl	*dogs, scissors*
Substance	US	-	−	sg	*dog, cake, gold, ?scissor*
Depends	US	-	−	sg	*gold, cake*
	CO, UP	-	+	pl	*dogs, pairs of scissors*
Unknown	any	±	±	any	

There is a basic split between the **bounded** interpretations, where the referent is conceived of as one or more bounded individuals and the **non-bounded** interpretations, where the referent is conceived of as a substance or aggregate (see Section 2.3.3). For noun phrases with a bounded interpretation, the number of the individuals (singular or plural) must be specified: **individuated-singular** and **individuated-plural**.

There are three non-bounded interpretations: **non-bounded-1**, **non-bounded-2** and **substance**. The two **stuff** interpretations can be realized as singular or plural noun phrases (substances or aggregates), depending on whether they are conceived of as having any internal structure. The third interpretation, **substance**, allows only an interpretation with no internal structure and can be realized only by singular, uncountable noun phrases. I have added a special value depends, for lexeme pairs such as *much/many*, where the form of the modifier itself depends on the interpretation. The interpretation can also be unknown, in which case number and countability will be decided directly from the noun countability preferences of the head noun.

These seven interpretations do not have any direct syntactic status.

They are almost certainly epiphenomena, and could maybe be done away with given a more complete semantic analysis. However, they provide a level of granularity that covers the interpretations of most noun phrases, and yet is simple enough to be used by lexicographers in building large-scale lexical resources.

Values for `interpretation` can be given to elements that modify nouns or noun phrases (for example, *kaku* "each" has the interpretation `individuated-singular`) or that govern them (e.g., *kire* "slice (of)" has the interpretation `substance`; the first argument of transitive *atsumaru* "gather" has the interpretation `non-bounded-1`). How this effects the countability of the entire noun phrase will be discussed in detail in Section 5.3.

NP Countability and Number (Bounded)

There are two bounded interpretations, which differ only in the number of the noun phrase. The interaction of the interpretation with the noun countability preferences is shown in Table 16.

If the noun can be countable, then it will be: the number is determined by the interpretation (`individuated-singular` ⇒ singular); (`individuated-plural` ⇒ plural). If the noun cannot be denumerated (`uncountable` or `plural only`), then the noun phrase must be embedded in a classifier construction (*a* CL *of NP*). Which classifier is used is part of the lexical information for uncountable nouns (the default classifier (§ 4.4.1)). If there is no default classifier, for example, for *clothes* or *goods*, then a different word has to be chosen: *clothes* cannot be individuated.

TABLE 16 NP `Interpretation` (Bounded)

Noun Countability Preference	NP `Interpretation`	
	`individuated-singular`	`individuated-plural`
Fully Countable	1 dog	2 dogs
	1 noodle	2 noodles
Strongly ~	1 cake	2 cakes
Weakly ~	1 beer	2 beers
Uncountable	1 piece of information	2 pieces of information
Plural Only	1 pair of scissors	2 pairs of scissors
	1 set of scales	2 sets of scales
	*1 piece of clothes	*2 pieces of clothes

Bounded interpretations are most commonly triggered by the presence of a **denumerator**: a dependent which entails that the referent of its head is quantified as a number of discrete entities (§ 2.3.3). These will typically be determiners in English (more specifically quantifiers), but can also be adjectives such as *multiple*. In Japanese, they are typically quantifier phrases (either premodifying or floating), such as *ono-ono* "each" or *san-ko* "three (things)" or prefixes such as *kaku-* "each".

Not all quantifying expressions force a bounded interpretation. There are some which have a `stuff` interpretation, such as *subete* "all" and some whose translation may depend on the countability and number of their head, such as *takusan* "much/many" (see also Section 5.3.3).

There are some subtle distinctions among the quantifiers. Whereas the referent of the noun modified by *takusan* "much/many" may be bounded or non-bounded, *kazukazu* "many" implies that the referent of the head it modifies is made up of discrete entities, that is, it is bounded (and should be marked as `individuated-plural`). Murata et al. (1996) claim that a noun phrase with the head modified by *takusan* is plural, but this is clearly not so, as is shown in (90). The noun phrase in question should be non-bounded, which means it will only be plural for noun phrases headed by countable nouns, not all nouns. This shows the importance of using a fine-grained set of interpretations, and combining them with English-specific countability preferences.

(90) ビールを たくさん 飲んだ
     bīru-o   *takusan* *nonda?*
     beer-ACC lot-of   drunk?

Did you drink a lot of beer/much beer/many beers?

NP Countability and Number (Non-Bounded)

Three values are provided for non-bounded interpretations, as shown in Table 17. The most common (`non-bounded-1`), is translated as plural only for fully, strongly countable and plural only heads. A typical example of a noun phrase with a `non-bounded-1` interpretation is the object of *atsumeru* "collect". There is another similar interpretation, (`non-bounded-2`), where the noun phrase is plural only if the head is fully countable or plural only. A typical example of this is the complement of *-sei* "made of". In this case, the noun phrase is conceived of as a substance, and the internal structure will only be expressed for nouns which, in English, are conceived of as having inherent boundaries. The interpretation `non-bounded-2`, is also used for bare generic noun phrases (§ 4.4.3).

There is no hard and fast boundary between `non-bounded-1` and `non-bounded-2`, and their names were chosen to reflect this. Considering translation equivalents, in many cases either could be used. The difference comes out only when the head is a strongly countable noun, and even in this case there is often little to choose between translations: e.g., *I like all chocolate* vs *I like all chocolates* for *chokorēto-ga suki-da* "chocolate-NOM like-be".

TABLE 17 NP Interpretation (Non-Bounded)

Noun Countability	NP Interpretation		
Preference	non-bounded-1	non-bounded-2	substance
Fully Countable	dogs	dogs	dog
	noodles	noodles	noodle
Strongly Countable	cakes	cake	cake
Weakly Countable	beer	beer	beer
Uncountable	information	information	information
Plural Only	scissors	scissors	? scissor
	scales	scales	? scale
	clothes	clothes	? clothes

The last non-bounded interpretation (substance) is used in cases where there is no internal structure, for example, the complement of the portion classifier *-kire* "slice", or the output of the universal grinder (see page 24). Nouns whose conceptualization in English includes some internal structure, such as bipartite nouns (e.g., *scissors*) do not make sense heading noun phrases in this environment. If you grind a pair of scissors so that they lose their shape, then they are no longer scissors, they are just metal. Fortunately, because of the inherent semantic incompatability, over many years of translating large samples of text, I found that plural only nouns never turned up in substance interpreting environments outside of NLP test suites.

The substance interpretation also predicts the forms for prenominal modifiers, such as *scissor* in *scissor kick*, where the *scissor* refers to some abstract concept of scissor. For nouns which appear to be plural even in this environment (e.g. *goods* in *goods train*), I assume that their plural and base (un-inflected) forms are in fact the same: *goods*.

NP Countability and Number (Unknown and Depends)

Finally there are noun phrases for which there is no information about their interpretation. These are translated based on the inherent countability of their heads, as given by the noun countability preference of the head noun.

TABLE 18 NP Interpretation (Unknown and Depends)

Noun Countability Preference	NP Interpretation unknown	depends (non-bounded)
Fully Countable	a dog	many dogs
	noodles	many noodles
Strongly Countable	a cake	many cakes
Weakly Countable	beer	much beer
Uncountable	information	much information
Plural Only	scissors	many (pairs of) scissors
	scales	many (sets of) scales
	clothes	many clothes

The interpretation of depends has almost the same effect on countability and number as non-bounded-1. It was kept separate because it was useful to mark translations whose choice of lexical realization may change depending on the countability of their head. Also, for some speakers, plural only with default classifiers, such as *scissors*, must use the classifier after quantifiers such as *many*, making the environment slightly different from non-bounded-1.

NP Countability and Number (Classifier Constructions)

The number and countability of noun phrases embedded in classifier constructions is largely determined by the classifier type (defined in Section 4.2.3). Sortal classifier are denumerators, and thus the noun phrase they quantify will be bounded. The classifier itself will only be translated for uncountable or plural only heads.

The embedded noun phrase in a mensural classifier construction will be given a non-bounded-2 interpretation: *a box of cake*. In general, mensural classifiers do not specify whether the referent of the measured noun consists of individuals or not. As a translation of *kēki-no hako* either *a box of cake* (non-bounded-2) or *a box of cakes* (non-bounded-1) is possible. The non-bounded-2 interpretation is more suitable as a default, because it is more general: the referent of a *a box of cakes* can always be referred to as *a box of cake*, but not vice versa.

A subtype of mensural classifiers, **portion** classifiers, forces an interpretation with no internal structure, for example, *-kire* "slice". The classifier is always translated, and the embedded noun phrase has the substance interpretation: *hito-kire-no-inu* "1 slice of dog".

Group classifiers combine with plural or uncountable noun phrases to make a countable noun phrase representing a group or set. A Japan-

ese noun phrase of the form *XC-no-N*, where C is a group classifier, will
be translated into English as *X C of N*, where N will be plural if it is
headed by a fully or strongly countable noun or a plural only: this is the
`non-bounded-2` interpretation. This is generalized to all such partitive
constructions in English, regardless of the original form in Japanese.
Thus, noun phrases of the form *A-no-C*, where C is a group classifier (but not a Japanese numeral classifier) will also be translated as
a C of N, where N will have the `non-bounded-2` interpretation. This
makes possible a uniform treatment of noun phrases such as (91) and
(92) during English generation, even though their Japanese structure
is very different:

(91)   二 箱 の   ペン (XC-*no*-N)
       ni-hako-no pen
       2 box-ADN pen

       2 boxes of pens

(92)   ペン の   箱   (N-*no*-C)
       pen-no   hako
       pen-ADN box

       a box of pens

The last type of classifier is **taxonomic** classifiers. Taxonomic classifiers are partitives of quality and can occur with countable or uncountable noun phrases. The embedded noun phrase will agree in number
with the head noun phrase if fully or strongly countable: *a kind of car,
2 kinds of cars; a kind of equipment, 2 kinds of equipment*. This sets
them apart from the other classifier constructions. Examples of taxonomic classifiers with embedded noun phrases of various noun countability preference are given in Table 19.

4.4.3   Countability and Number for Generic Noun Phrases

An English generic noun phrase can generally be expressed in three
ways: indefinite singular (generic 'a'), *A mammoth is a mammal*, definite singular (generic 'the'), *The mammoth is a mammal*, and bare
plural (and singular uncountable) (the bare generic), *Mammoths are
mammals/Furniture is expensive*, as was discussed in Section 2.2.2.

Generic 'a' is restricted in use to countable noun phrases. Generic
'the' takes the `substance` interpretation: *the scissor is a useful device*
vs #*the scissors are useful devices*. It is not normally used with uncountable nouns: *gold is a precious metal* vs #*the gold is a precious
metal*.

The bare generic, in contrast, can be used with any countability,
taking the `stuff` interpretation. I choose the `non-bounded-2` inter-

TABLE 19 Taxonomic Classifiers

Noun Countability Preference	Taxonomic (Singular)	Taxonomic (Plural)
Fully Countable	1 kind of dog	2 kinds of dogs
	1 kind of noodle	2 kinds of noodles
Strongly Countable	1 kind of cake	2 kinds of cakes
Weakly Countable	1 kind of beer	2 kinds of beer
Uncountable	1 kind of information	2 kinds of information
Plural Only	1 kind of scissors	2 kinds of scissors

pretation as default, although either is possible:{*Cake is/Cakes are*} *delicious*.

4.5 Definiteness and Topicalization

I extend the Horn scale of articles introduced by Hawkins (1991) (and discussed in Sections 2.4.1 and 2.4.2) to include the two types of missing article introduced by Chesterman (1991) and the possessive pronouns. The resulting scale is given in (93):

(93) ⟨ *null, the, PossPro,* {*a,some*}, *zero* ⟩

To form a Horn scale the words in question must be equally lexicalized; they must be from the same semantic field; and sentences using one word must entail any sentences using a word on its right (Hawkins, 1991, 425–6).

Strictly speaking, the zero and null article are not equally lexicalized with the other articles. However, they are in paradigmatic contrast: a noun phrase can either have an article or no article: it cannot have both. In addition, all the articles, and the possessive pronouns, are short words of one syllable, normally unstressed. They are as close as possible to being unrealized and still being a word. Therefore, they are very close to being equally lexicalized. All the articles, and the possessive pronouns, are from the same semantic field: that of definiteness.

A singular countable noun with no article (null) has the most restrictive reference of all: it is both definite and extensive, and therefore is the leftmost member of the Horn scale. The definite article implies only that the noun phrase it modifies is definite: that is, unique and locatable. Possessive pronouns, on the other hand, only mark a noun phrase as locatable; they do not entail uniqueness. Possessive pronouns also entail a possessive relation of some kind, which a sentence using

	null	extensive, unique, locatable, exists
⊢	*the*	unique, locatable, exists
⊢	PossPro	locatable, exists (possessed)
⊢	*a*	exists, singular
⊢	*some*	exists
⊢	zero	

FIGURE 10   Entailments in the Definiteness Horn Scale

the definite or null article does not entail, although this entailment is outside of the semantic field.

There are two problems with using information about extensivity, uniqueness, locatability, possession or even existence as semantic features in machine translation. The first is that the realization of this information can be very language-specific, particularly when a noun phrase should be conceived of as extensive (and thus requiring no article) or inherently possessive (and thus requiring a possessive pronoun). For example, Swedish and English differ in some constructions, as shown in (69) (page 58). They are not, therefore, good candidates for semantic primitives that can be transfered from the representation of one language to the other.

The second problem is that it is not possible to obtain enough useful information about extensivity, uniqueness, locatability or even existence from parsing the Japanese input. None of these features are explicitly represented in Japanese, which makes it extemely difficult to determine them automatically. Therefore, I use a smaller, more easily determined set of values: topicalized, which is defined only for the Japanese representation but is passed to the English generation as part of the semantic representation; and null, definite, indefinite, which are defined only for the English representation.

In Japanese, topicalized is used to represent noun phrases marked with the focus markers *-wa* or *-mo*.

In English, indefinite is the default value, and may be realized as an indefinite article *a* for singular countable noun phrases, or zero for uncountable or plural phrases. It may also be replaced by a possessive pronoun for **inherently possessed nouns**. definite is used for noun phrases which are locatable and unique, either within a text or within a wider context. In the implementation, this is determined from more general syntactic cues. Locatability and uniqueness are not directly determined.

The **null** feature is used for extensive definite nouns which will require no article. It is mainly used for proper nouns and nouns in defective noun phrases, especially in idiomatic constructions, such as those discussed on page 29. Indefinite and definite have been used as features by most researchers in this area. Explicit use of a null marker is an important innovation that is essential to cover non-core constructions. More details of how these values are determined are given in Section 5.4.

As was shown in Section 2.4.5, English conventionally uses a possessive pronoun to indicate a relationship such as ownership, as in *my wallet*, or a family relationship, as in *my father*. Japanese does not. This usage is tied to the meaning of particular words. In particular, words which denote **kin, body parts, work, personal possessions, attributes** and so on are commonly translated with possessive pronouns. Such nouns are marked in the lexicon with a flag. I call them **inherently possessed nouns**.

Finally, I also mark in the lexicon several small classes of nouns that appear in constructions with idiomatic article use. These are described in more detail in Sections 5.4.5 and 7.1.4.

I have not introduced a feature that distinguishes *some/any* from *zero*. There were two reasons for this. The first is that, because *some* also functions as a quantifier, there are several translation equivalents for *some* in Japanese: *ikutsuka-no, ikuraka-no*, ... It is thus generated already by the normal transfer process. The second is that *some* is comparatively rare: it appears less than 3% as often as *the* in the British National Corpus (Burnard, 2000); only once every 500 words for speech, and once every 600 words in the written corpus. In the Wall Street Journal, it is used less than once in every 200 noun phrases (Taylor et al., 2003). Therefore, as they occur relatively seldom, I have excluded *some* and *any* from my algorithm.

5

Automatic Interpretation of Reference, Number and Determiners

In this chapter, I give a detailed description of my method for generating articles and number in Japanese-to-English machine translation. The essential idea is to determine the meaning of the Japanese input, as far as this is possible, and then use this as a base to generate the English. For a perfect translation, the meaning should include the pragmatic information about usage: what did the speaker intend the utterance to convey? However, I shall focus on the level of semantic analysis, which is sufficient for most descriptive text, such as newspaper reports and manuals.

Even with a deep semantic analysis, it is not possible to obtain all the information needed to generate determiners and to determine number for English noun phrases for two reasons. The first is that Japanese does not make explicit definiteness, number and countability. Therefore, the input is inherently under-specified for the task of generating English. The second is that automatic analysis of natural language is imperfect. This makes the input to the generation component even more under-specified. Accordingly, it is important that the system provide graceful defaults: it must supply a reasonable answer even if there is insufficient information. Providing such defaults is an important part of the algorithms described.

Before I introduce the algorithms, I describe very briefly the machine translation architecture it is embedded in. Then, I introduce the three algorithms that make up my method: determination of referentiality (§ 5.2), determination of number and countability (§ 5.3), and determination of definiteness (§ 5.4). After a brief discussion of generic noun phrases (§ 5.5), I describe the actual generation of determiners (§ 5.6).

5.1 Machine Translation Architecture

The processing described in the following sections assumes a standard transfer system. Input text is parsed to a shallow semantic representation. This is transfered to a shallow target language semantic representation. The target text is generated from this. The system can access the representations of previous text, but there is no reordering of sentences.

Japanese sentence

1 Source Language Analysis

⇒ Japanese Case Frame

2 Transfer

⇒ English Case Frame

3 English Generation

⇒ *English sentence*

FIGURE 11 The Translation Process

The semantic structure is an augmented case frame. Each sentence is represented as a hierarchy of case frames, with each **case frame** consisting of a predicate and optionally its arguments (the **case elements**). All elements can be augmented by descriptive features.

For example, the English case frame after transfer for the translation of the sentence *zō-wa hana-ga nagai* "elephant-TOP nose-NOM long" is as shown in (94) (not all information is shown). The predicate is listed first, followed by its arguments. Words are not inflected. The representation contains both semantic elements (such as case roles and semantic classes) and syntactic elements (part of speech and countability). This makes them both available to processing. The words are disambiguated during transfer: *trunk* "a long flexible snout" is distinct from *trunk* "main stem of a tree".

After transfer, the referential status is resolved, appropriate articles and number are selected, and words are inflected and reordered (95). Finally, the sentence is given appropriate capitalization.

(94) English case frame:

$$
\begin{bmatrix}
\text{TYPE} & \text{Sentence} \\
\text{TENSE} & \text{present} \\
\text{ASPECT} & \text{stative} \\
\text{REFERENTIALITY} & \text{characterising} \\
\text{PREDICATE} & \begin{bmatrix} \text{TYPE} & \text{verb} \\ \text{ORTHOGRAPHY} & \textit{have} \end{bmatrix} \\
\text{CASE} & \begin{bmatrix}
\text{CASE ROLE} & \text{subject} \\
\text{TYPE} & \text{common noun} \\
\text{ORTHOGRAPHY} & \textit{elephant} \\
\text{SEMANTIC-CLASS} & \text{537:animal} \\
\text{COUNTABILITY} & \text{fully countable} \\
\text{REFERENTIALITY} & \text{generic} \\
\text{FOCUS} & \text{focused}
\end{bmatrix} \\
\text{CASE} & \begin{bmatrix}
\text{CASE ROLE} & \text{object} \\
\text{TYPE} & \text{common noun} \\
\text{ORTHOGRAPHY} & \textit{trunk} \\
\text{SEMANTIC-CLASS} & \text{564:nose} \\
\text{COUNTABILITY} & \text{fully countable} \\
\text{REFERENTIALITY} & \text{generic}
\end{bmatrix}
\end{bmatrix}
$$

(95) *Elephants have long trunks.*

5.1.1 The Semantic Class Hierarchy

A thesaurus is used to make generalizations over semantic classes of words. This allows rules to be stated at an abstract level. The ontology used in the implementation, and discussed in this and following chapters, classifies concepts to use in expressing relationships between words. The meanings of common nouns are given in terms of a semantic hierarchy of 2,710 nodes (Ikehara et al., 1997). Each node in the hierarchy represents a semantic class. Edges in the hierarchy represent **is-a** or **has-a** relationships, so that the child of a semantic class related by an **is-a** relation is subsumed by it. For example, organ **is-a** body-part. The top four levels of the semantic hierarchy are shown in Figure 12. In addition to the 2,710 classes (12-level tree structure) for common nouns, there are 200 classes (9-level tree structure) for proper nouns and 108 classes (5-level tree structure) for predicates. After some trials, it was found that a classification into at least 2,000 classes is necessary to distinguish between various verb senses (Ikehara et al., 1993).

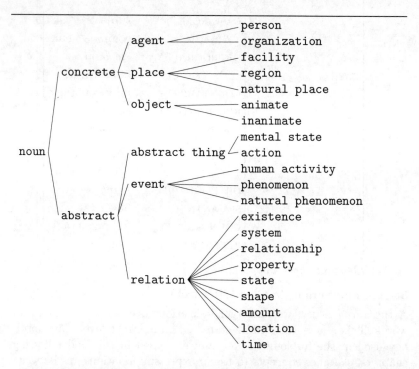

FIGURE 12 The Top Four Levels of **ALT-J/E**'s Semantic Hierarchy

5.1.2 Case roles

Each case element, in both the Japanese and English representations, has a **case role** associated with it (also known as deep cases or θ-roles). The current set of case roles is given in Table 20, along with the most commonly associated case-markers in Japanese, and prepositions or grammatical functions (gf) in English. There are 14 cases and 3 adverbials. The cases can also be used for adjuncts, along with 10 other more specific cases, of which I list only the three temporal cases (TN1, TN2 and TN3).

What is the best set of case roles is still an unsolved problem, or even whether case roles should be replaced by more abstract thematic roles or more concrete participant roles. Whatever the ultimate conclusion, they have proved to be extremely useful in natural language processing and are used in most machine translation systems.

TABLE 20 Case Roles

Label	Name	Case-marker	Preposition (Function)
N1	Agent	ga (kara, towa) [wa]	Subject (gf)
N2	Object-1	o (nitsuite) [ga]	Object (gf)
N3	Object-2	ni (...)	Indirect-Obj (gf)
N4	Loc-Source	kara, yori	from
N5	Loc-Goal	ni, e, made	to (until)
N6	Purpose	ni	for
N7	Result	ni, to	as
N8	Locative	ni, o, de, e, kara	in/at/on
N9	Comitative	to	with
N10	Quotative	to	
N11	Material	kara, yori, de	with, from
N12	Cause	kara, yori, de	for
N13	Instrument	de	with
N14	Means	de	by
QUANT	Amount	—	—
TIME	Time	—	—
ADV	Adverb	—	—
TN1	Time-position	ni	at/in/on
TN2	Time-source	kara	since/from
TN3	Time-goal	made	until

5.2   The Algorithm for Determining NP Referentiality

The first step is to determine the referential property of each noun phrase, that is, whether each noun phrase is generic, referential, or ascriptive. In this section, I describe the proposed algorithm in some detail. An outline of the algorithm is shown in Figures 13 and 15.

---

1. Clause level rules:
   - The complement of the copula in a **predicational** sentence is **ascriptive**: (§ 5.2.1)
   mammosu-wa dōbutsu de-aru. "Mammoths are animals."
   - The subject of an **analytic** sentence (a subtype of predicational) is **generic**: (§ 5.2.1)
   mammosu-wa dōbutsu de-aru. "Mammoths are animals."
   - The subject (and direct object) of a **characterizing** sentence is **generic**: (§ 5.2.1)
   kikai hon'yaku-to-iu-no-wa konnan de-aru. "Machine translation is difficult."
   - The subject of a **specificational** sentence is **referential** (and definite): (§ 5.2.1)
   mondai-wa konnan de-atta. "The problem was difficult."
2. Case element level rules:
   - The complement of *toshite* "as" is **ascriptive**:
   sore-o mammosu-toshite atsukau. "Treat it as a mammoth."
   - Locative noun phrases are **referential**: (§ 5.2.2)
   kūkō-ni itta. "I went to the airport."
   - The appropriate argument of a kind-referring predicate is **generic**: (§ 5.2.2)
   mammosu-wa zetsumetsu-shita. "Mammoths died out."
   - The appropriate argument of an **emotive action** or **emotive state** predicate is **generic**: (§ 5.2.2)
   watashi-wa mammosu-ga suki de-aru. "I like mammoths."

FIGURE 13   Determination of Noun Phrase Referentiality (part 1, continued in Figure 15)

The algorithm is applied to the Japanese case frame during the transfer phase. There are constructions that are syntactic noun phrases in Japanese, but which translate as adjectives or prepositional phrases in English, such as *behind* "ushiro" in *kuruma-no ushiro-ni* "behind the car (lit: car-ADN back-LOC)". As the ultimate concern is with the form

of English noun phrases, there is no need to determine the referentiality
of such Japanese noun phrases. Neither is there any need to determine
the referentiality of a noun phrases that appears as part of a larger
idiomatic expressions as it is given in the lexical entry for the idiomatic
expression. All proper nouns and pronouns are assigned the value **referential**.

The algorithm presented is based on single sentences. It only partially uses information from outside the clause being considered, as described in Section 5.2.3.

Rules are applied top-down, in the order shown in Figures 13 and 15, with later rules over-riding earlier ones. Thus, the rules triggered by elements within the noun phrase are stronger than those triggered by modifiers outside the noun phrase, which are stronger in turn than case element based rules, which are stronger than clause level rules. For example, in (96), the demonstrative *kono* "this" overrides the clause level rule: "the subject of a characterizing sentence is generic":

(96) *a.* 象 は　　　　鼻 が　　　長い
         zō-wa   *hana-ga*   *nagai.*
         elephant-TOP nose-NOM long

      Elephants have long trunks. (characterizing, predicational)

     b. この 象 は　　　　鼻 が　　　長い
         kono zō-wa   *hana-ga*   *nagai.*
         this   elephant-TOP nose-NOM long

      This elephant has a long trunk.   (predicational)

5.2.1   Clause Level Rules

There are four rules to determine reference that are applied at the
clause level, based on four sentence types: specificational, predicational,
analytic and characterizing (§ 2.2.2, 2.2.3). These can all be overridden
by subsequent rules. Analytic sentences are a subtype of predicational
sentences, and a sentence can be both predicational and characterizing.
These rules identify only a few sentence types; the majority of sentences
are not affected by them. A more complete inventory of sentence types
could be defined within some framework of discourse structure. If this
becomes available, further sentence types, and better tests for the four
now considered, can be added as necessary.

Predicational Sentences

All non-specificational copular sentences are taken to be predicational.
In these cases, the complement of the copular verb is set to ascriptive.

Analytic Sentences

The subjects of analytic sentences, that is, sentences that are always true due to the meanings of the words involved, are generic. The test to determine this is whether the semantic class of the subject of a copula is subsumed by the semantic class of the complement. If the complement is headed by a proper noun or measure phrase, then it is a specificational sentence, otherwise it is analytic. Analytic sentences are a subtype of predicational sentences.

Specificational Sentences

Specificational sentences are another subtype of predicational sentences. They specify a value for the referent of the subject noun phrase, which will typically be definite.

There are two tests to identify specificational sentences:

1. If the subject is topicalized (the Japanese source noun phrase was marked by one of the focus markers -*wa* or -*mo* (§ 4.5)) and the verb is past tense.

2. If the semantic class of the subject of a copula is subsumed by the semantic class of the complement, and the complement is a proper noun or measure phrase.

For example, in (97), the semantic class of *kaijō* "meeting place" is `actual place`, which is subsumed by the semantic class of *aoi-kaikan*, `public place`, but *aoi-kaikan* "Aoi Hall" is a proper noun, so the sentence is specificational, not analytic:

(97)　会場 は　　　　　葵会館　　。
　　　kaijō-wa　　　　*aoi-kaikan* Φ.
　　　meeting place-TOP Aoi hall　　is

　　　The meeting place is the Aoi Hall.　　　　　(specificational)

　　　* Meeting places are the Aoi Halls.　　　　　(analytic)

Characterizing Sentences

A sentence that passes one or more of the following tests is characterizing:

1. If the subject is marked by the the marker -*towa* or the complex marker -*to-iu-no-wa*.

2. If the subject is marked by one of the focus markers -*wa, -mo*, and the verb has non-past tense.[19]

---

[19]The following tense distinctions are made for Japanese: non-past tense is the -*u* form; past is the -*ta* form and continuative is the -*te* form followed by *iru* "be" (past or non-past).

3. If there is an adverb with habitual meaning such as *ippan-ni* "generally", then the sentence it modifies will be characterizing.

The subject and, if it exists, direct object of a characterizing sentence will be **generic** as a default. It may be the case that other arguments licensed by the verbs should also be generic, but this depends on the verb meaning in a non-trivial way and has been left for future work.

Other Sentences

Sentences which do not fit any of the above tests are not assigned a value for sentence type, and the referential values of their noun phrases remain unknown.

5.2.2 Case Element Level Rules

There are various types of rules that apply to case elements, mainly licensed by predicates. Verbs that trigger these rules, such as *evolve* and *die out*, are so marked in the lexicon.

Noun phrases marked by the pseudo-marker *-toshite* "as" are assigned ascriptive by default. However, if a noun phrase is modified within the noun phrase in such a way as to be judged as referential, for example, *kono-zō* "this elephant", then this will overwrite the verb marking, and the noun phrase will not be considered to be generic.

Locative Noun Phrases

Locative noun phrases are assigned the value referential (and definite). They are identified in two ways. First, noun phrases which are the complement of locative prepositional phrases (normally marked by a semantic marker such as *-kara* "from" or *-made* "to" or a relational noun) and are headed by a noun that denotes `place` are judged to be locative. Second, some verbs explicitly mark their argument as locative: NP_{LOC}]-*o tatsu* "leave NP_{LOC}".

Noun Phrases Governed by Predicates that Affect Referentiality

Kind-referring Predicates: Predicates which predicate over a whole class, such as *evolve, die out, be extinct*, can take generic ϕ or 'the': *Mammoths evolved into elephants*; *The mammoth evolved into the elephant*. For these verbs, the subject must refer to the entire class as a whole. For example, the definition of *evolve*, in the sense being considered, "the sequence of events involved in the evolutionary development of a species or taxonomic group of organisms", must apply to a whole population: individuals do not evolve. Individual mammoths are not the class as a whole, so generic 'a' cannot be used. Accordingly, #*A mammoth evolved into an elephant* is unacceptable. Some kind-referring predicates whose object is generic, such as *invent*, favor the generic 'the' for countable noun phrases: *Bell invented the telephone.*

Emotive Predicates: The default interpretation of the appropriate argument of verbs which predicate `emotive action` or `emotive state` is generic (Zelinsky-Wibbelt, 1992). Some examples are: *respect, like, loathe* and most of Levin's (1993, 191, type 31.2) *admire* verbs.

Quantificational Predicates: It is also convenient to class the subjects of quantificational predicates such as *be common, be widespread, be rare* and *be scarce* as **generic**, although, strictly speaking, they do not refer to kinds (Carlson and Pelletier, 1996, 95–98).[20] However, they have the same range of forms as generic NPs in English, and are best generated as bare generics when translating from Japanese to English, so it is simpler to treat them as generic for the time being. One would need to be more precise in a system with more detailed semantics.

Encoding in the Lexicon: Each noun phrase argument in the verb valency dictionary can have an optional attribute, USAGE, with one of three values: `generic`, `referential` or `ascriptive`. A further distinction is made between bare generics (ϕ) which are marked in the lexicon as DEFINITENESS = `null` and definite generics (*the*) which are marked in the lexicon as DEFINITENESS = `definite`. Because of the limited acceptance of generic 'a', it is not generated at all. If `definiteness` is not specified, then it will be treated as `null`. The difference in the way these are generated is described in Section 5.5.

Kind-referring, emotive and quantificational predicates have the appropriate noun phrase marked as `generic` in the lexicon. Those where a definite generic is better, such as *exterminate*, are in addition, marked as DEFINITENESS = `definite`. The three possible types are shown in Table 21 followed by some examples.

TABLE 21 Restrictions placed by Verbs.

Type	Example	Subject	Object
kind (Subj)	evolve	generic (ϕ)	—
kind (Obj)	invent, like	—	generic 'the'
emotive	like	—	generic (ϕ)
quantificational	is common	generic (ϕ)	—

(98) *Kind-referring:*

---

[20]The same adjectives used with other copular verbs (such as *seem*) are also quantificational.

  a. *Mammals evolved from reptiles.*   (generic ϕ)

  b. *Who invented the telephone?*   (generic 'the')

(99) *Emotive:*

  a. *I like traffic lights.*   (generic ϕ)

  b. *I loathe suits.*   (generic ϕ)

(100) *Quantificational:*

  a. *Gnus are common in Kenya.*   (generic ϕ)

  b. *GNU software is less widespread.*   (generic ϕ)

A simplified example of the lexical entry for *zetsumetsu-suru* "die out" is given in Figure 14. The English subject is marked as `generic`.

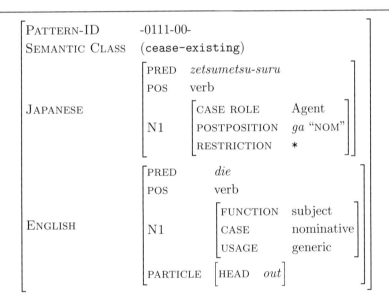

FIGURE 14 Japanese-English Verb Lexical Entry (*zetsumetsu-suru* ⇔ *die out*)

Derived Nominals and Verbal Nouns

Verbal nouns such as *handan* "decision" in *shinpan-no handan* "judge-ADN decision" ⇒ *the judge's decision*, where the adnominal noun phrase *shinpan* "judge" is an argument of the verb, also trigger case element level rules.

In the adnominal construction *A-no-B* "A-ADN B", if B is a verbal noun or derived nominal, A may be one of B's arguments, rather than an external modifier. Whether this is the case or not is found by testing whether A has an appropriate semantic class for the verb's case frames. This is done as part of the Japanese semantic analysis, and the results are passed to the English case frame during the transfer stage.

As a default, if the adnominal noun phrase A is the subject of the derived nominal B, then both A and B will be **referential**. If A is the object of B, then it will be **generic**.

---

3. Modification of and within the noun phrase:
   - A noun phrase whose head is modified by a restrictive relative clause is **referential**: (§ 5.2.3)
   kinō kita otoko "the man who came yesterday"
   - The complement of function words such as *muke* "aimed at", *yō* "for" ... is **generic**: (§ 5.2.3)
   josei-muke-no zasshi "A magazine for women"
   - Context and World Knowledge (§ 5.2.3)
   - A noun phrase with a 'unique' referent is **referential**:
   chikyū "the earth"
   - Two noun phrases judged to be co-referential have the same referentiality:
   denwagaisha-no NTT "NTT, a telephone company"
   - A noun phrase whose head is modified by a demonstrative or numeral is **referential**: (§ 5.2.3)
   kono otoko "this man", *futari-no otoko* "two men"
   - A noun phrase whose head is modified by the possessive construction is **referential**: (§ 5.2.3)
   hana-no saki "the tip of my nose"
4. Noun phrases still undetermined are treated as **referential**.

FIGURE 15 Determination of Noun Phrase Referentiality (part 2, continued from Figure 13)

5.2.3 Modification of and within the Noun Phrase

The final level of rules considers modification of and within the noun phrase itself. The rules are applied in the order shown. If there is conflict between the rules, the later one will override the earlier. An example of such a conflict is given in (101).

Relative clauses

This algorithm uses a simple heuristic: a noun phrase modified by a restrictive relative clause is **referential**.

Typically, noun phrases modified by restrictive relative clauses are non-generic, either ascriptive or referential. Japanese, however, makes no phonological, morphological, or syntactic distinctions between restrictive and non-restrictive relative clauses (Kuno, 1973, 235). For example, the noun phrase *watashi-ni ēgo-o oshiete-iru kimu* "I-DAT English-ACC teaching Kim" could have either a restrictive reading (*the Kim who is teaching me English*) or a non-restrictive reading (*Kim, who is teaching me English,*). The Japanese gives no clue as to which is the preferred reading. Because restrictive relative clauses are more common, the system treats all relative clauses as restrictive and mistranslates the non-restrictive ones.

Function words

Some Japanese function words can be used to deduce a noun phrase's referential use. For example, some Japanese suffixes imply that their complement is **generic**, as in (101). In this case, the noun phrase would normally be interpreted as referential, as it is modified by a relative clause. This is overridden by the effect of the function-word *muke* "aimed at":

(101) 働く　　女性　　向け の　　　　雑誌
　　　　hataraku josei　muke-no　　　zasshi
　　　　working　woman　aimed-at-ADN magazine

　　　　a magazine aimed at <u>working women</u>

The information to trigger this rule is stored in the lexical entry for the suffix *muke*. It requires its head to be **generic**.

Context and World Knowledge

Two rules have been implemented that use context and world knowledge.

The first rule is that noun phrases headed by nouns that are marked in the lexicon as having a unique referent, such as *chikyū* "the earth", are assumed to be **referential**. Whether a noun phrase has a unique referent is, of course, dependent on the context. At present, words whose referent is typically unique are marked in the system dictionary (e.g. *tsuki* "the moon"); others can be defined in domain and user dictionaries. This is the large situation use of Hawkins (1978) (see Section 2.4.1).

The second rule is that noun phrases judged to be co-referential will have the same value of referentiality. This is the classic anaphoric use. In the system used for testing, **ALT-J/E**, co-referentiality is only recognized in two cases: zero pronouns replaced by their antecedent (Nakaiwa and Ikehara, 1995), and apposition. There is no mechanism in place to identify cases of noun phrase anaphora and bridging in Japanese, to handle cases such as (102):

(102)　タクシー に載った。運転手 は　　女性　　だった
　　　　takushī-ni notta.　untenshū-wa josei　　datta.
　　　　taxi-LOC　rode.　driver-TOP　　woman was

I got into a taxi. The driver was a woman.

The subject of the second sentence is, however, translated with a definite article because it is specificational (§ 5.2.1): the subject is marked topicalized and the sentence is past tense. Because the machine translation system can use cues from the source language, it is not always necessary to do full blown anaphoric processing.

Poesio et al. (2004) implemented rules to identify bridging relations using semantic relations in WordNet and information about discourse structure. They found that they could identify the antecedent with 75% accuracy, assuming they knew that a noun was involved in a bridging reference.

Other Noun Phrase Internal Modifiers

Other noun phrase internal modifiers are also considered, for example, demonstratives, numerals or the possessive construction, *A-no B* "B of A". Noun phrases modified by *no* "of" which are judged to be possessive are **referential**. Partitive constructions such as *ōkami-no-mure* "wolf-ADN pack" ⇒ *a pack of wolves* and nouns in a predicate argument relationship (§ 5.2.2) do not trigger this rule. The possessive construction may be translated into English in a variety of ways including a prepositional phrase headed by *of*, a possessive phrase with the clitic *'s* in the determiner position, or a possessive pronoun.

Although most dependents within the noun phrase that affect referentiality also force a definite reading, there are some that force an indefinite reading, such as *aru* "a certain". Just as for the affixes, this information is part of the lexical entry of the dependent. That is, the entry for *aru* "a certain", selects for a **referential** (really a non-specific) head.

If there is no usage specified, the default assumption is that a noun phrase will be used to refer to some specific entity or entities in the discourse world: that it is **referential**.

5.2.4 Summary of Determination of Reference

These rules are all based on a wide-coverage, robust analysis, suitable for use in a large-scale machine translation system. The algorithm has been designed, however, to give enough information to be re-used (with suitable modifications) in a system with more detailed analyses that are capable of integrating syntax, semantics and pragmatics.

The rules are organized as a top-down hierarchy, because the implementation takes the Japanese syntactic-semantic parse as input, and is applied top-down. The rules are defeasible, so that a later rule will over-ride an earlier one. All the higher elements have to be traversed to reach the noun phrases, so it is an efficient implementation. As will be shown in Sections 5.3 and 5.4, there are similar hierarchies for determining the countability, number and definiteness of referential noun phrases. In the implementation, these are all handled together: there is no need for several separate passes.

A similar hierarchy would be needed for any language, with different rules, but the same kind of defeasible structure. Chesterman (1991) gives one for determining definiteness in Finnish, using case information, stress, word order and function words (§ 2.5.2). The three-way distinction in noun phrase referential use has been defined language independently, and should be useful for other natural language processing tasks, in particular, translating between other languages without articles and number (such as Korean or Thai), to other languages with them (such as German or Italian).

5.3 The Algorithm for Determining Noun Phrase Countability and Number

The algorithm for determining the interpretation of countability/number is given in Figure 16. In the implementation, the interpretation is determined during the transfer phase, along with the noun phrase referentiality and definiteness. The algorithm itself is simple, but is based on a large amount of lexical information, described in detail in Section 4.4.2.

Values for the feature `interpretation` (defined in Section 4.4.2) generally come from the lexicon, either as part of the selectional restriction of the predicate, or as part of the semantic information for the noun phrase dependent.

5.3.1 Case Element Level Rules

For some verbs the default interpretation of their subject, object or indirect object should be non-bounded. For example, verbs such as *gather* and *collect* imply that a (possibly unspecified) number of objects

1. Case element level rules:
   - Determine according to verb:
   wadai-ga *tsukita*. "I ran out of topics/* a topic."
2. Modification of and within the noun phrase:
   - Determine according to dependent:
   zenkoku-no *gakkō* "schools/* a school all over the country"
   - Context & world knowledge:
   - A noun phrase judged to be co-referential matches its antecedent:
   Two men, strangers, came in.
   - Some lexical items are marked as plural by default:
   men "noodles"
   - Specific function words that mark plurality:
   If the Japanese is marked as plural:
   tachi ⇒ plural and countable
   - Determine according to classifier:
   hito-kire-no *kēki* "a slice of cake";
   hito-yama-no *kēki* "a pile of cakes"
   - Determine according to quantifier:
   ono'ono-no *kēki* "each cake";
   ryōhō-no *kēki* "both cakes"
3. Determine number and countability by combining the **interpretation** with the head noun's countability preference

FIGURE 16 Determination of Noun Phrase Countability.

(or amount of a substance) is being collected. This is true of the subject for intransitive verbs: *Mammoths collect around water holes*; and the object for transitive verbs: *I collect mammoths*. This implication is a part of the meaning of the verb; a collection must contain two or more members for it to be a collection. Therefore, if I collect something, then I characteristically collect more than one. Thus, the noun phrase referring to the substance being collected will generally be plural if possible — the `non-bounded-1` interpretation. It is possible to collect a single mammoth, but in that case the fact must be explicitly specified, for example, *I only collected one mammoth*.

Some examples of these verbs are Levin's (1993, 253–5) 'verbs of group existence' (*swarm* verbs, *herd* verbs and *bulge* verbs). The *with* variant of *swarm* and *bulge* verbs has a 'holistic' (`non-bounded-2`) interpretation: *The garden was crawling with ?a man/men. A {man was/men were} crawling in the garden.* The *herd* verbs imply a collective (`non-bounded-1`) interpretation.

A similar case arises when a verb's meaning implies that a noun phrase is a substance, (the `substance` interpretation) such as the complement of *of* in the phrasal verb idiom *run out of*. There are many predicates not listed in Levin (1993), who did not consider phrasal verbs, such as *run out [of]*, that must also be marked in the lexicon.

Some examples of patterns marked are given below. Guidelines for identifying relevant verbs are given in Section 7.2.

(103)   *N1-は N2-を 集める   N1-wa N2-o atsumeru*

     ⇒ N1 collect N2 (N2: `non-bounded-1`)

     e.g. *watashi-wa kēki-o atsumeta* "I collected cakes"

(104)   *N1-は N2-を 切らす   N1-wa N2-o kirasu*

     ⇒ N1 run out of N2 (N2: `non-bounded-2`)

     e.g. *watashi-wa kēki-o kirashita* "I ran out of cake"

5.3.2   Modification of and within the Noun Phrase

There are many cases of modification of and within the noun phrase. For example, some dependents, such as those that specify location, give clues as to the interpretation of the noun phrase they modify. The relation that holds between a noun phrase and its dependent is normally unspecified. However, when it is known, the information can be used as a trigger. For example, distributed locations, such as *gakkō* "school" in *zenkoku-no gakkō* "schools all over the country" will be `non-bounded-2`.

Contextual and world knowledge are both used: noun phrases judged to be co-referential match in number and countability, and default knowledge is available for lexical items.

The algorithm also uses specific function words, for example, Japanese collectivizing suffixes such as *-tachi, -domo* or *-ra*. They imply that the noun phrase so marked is bounded and typically plural, as discussed in Section 4.2.4.

If a noun phrase is modified by a Japanese/English pair that is translated as a denumerator (a determiner that may only occur with a countable head) or a classifier (§ 4.4.2), the modifier may have an interpretation listed for its head. For example, a noun modified by *ono'onono* "each" is `individuated-singular`, while one modified by *ryōhō-no* "both" is denumerated and plural. Uncountable and plural only nouns in bounded environments are translated as the complement of a classifier. A default classifier is stored in the dictionary for uncountable nouns and plural only.

During analysis, floating quantifiers are anchored to their (Bond et al., 1998), and denumerate it, as in (105).

(105) 家具 は　　　ふた つ 壊れた
　　　kagu-ga　　　*futatsu kowareta* .
　　　furniture-NOM two-CL broke　　　.

　　　Two pieces of furniture broke .

5.3.3　Countability, Boundedness and Lexical Choice for Modifiers

Sometimes the choice of the English translation of a dependent will depend on the countability of the noun phrase. For example, *ōku-no* can be translated as *many* or *much* depending on the countability and number of the noun phrase that it is in (106). Such dependents are specially marked in the lexicon as `depends` (§ 4.4.2). After the determination of countability is finished, the dependent's form is decided: *many* for countable noun phrases and *much* for uncountable ones. This is done for *much/many, little/few, a little/a few, less/fewer* and *overmuch/too many* (see also Section 7.2). Because the default interpretation of a Japanese noun is non-bounded, these dependents are entered in the transfer lexicon as *much, less, ...*, they will be changed to *many, few, ...* as required:

(106)　*a.* 多く の 情報　*ōku-no jōhō*

　　　　much information

　　　b. 多く の 犬　*ōku-no inu*

　　　　many dogs

The word *less* is often used with a countable plural head (*less problems*) in modern english, and has been in use since at least 899 AD (Mish, 1993, 667). The conservative choice for generation is, however, to follow the prescriptive grammarians and generate *fewer* in such cases.

In addition, English demonstratives agree in number with their head: *this/these, that/those*. These are translated as singular, but also flagged during transfer with **depends** to be checked after the number of their head has been determined. If their head turns out to be plural, then they will be changed appropriately.

The procedural method used by our system requires this backtracking, but only occasionally. In practice, it has a negligible impact on the overall speed of the system.

5.3.4 Countability, Boundedness and Lexical Choice for Heads

There is a more serious problem with a procedural implementation in that the target translation is selected in the transfer stage before countability is determined. In fact, noun phrase boundedness can be used to select lexical items: if the Japanese word *fuku* "clothes" has a bounded interpretation, for example, modified by a numeral classifier, then it should be translated as *clothing*, as *clothes* resists individuation in English (107):

(107) 服 を   ふたつ 買って も いい
     fuku-o   *futatsu katte-mo ii*
     clothes-ACC two   buy-FOC good

    You may buy two items of <u>clothing</u>

    * You may buy two (items of) <u>clothes</u>

This is a weakness of the current implementation, where the system commits to a noun's translation before it generates its dependents. As boundedness is determined, as far as possible, during the source language analysis, it can be used at any stage of the target language selection. If the lexical selection was more underspecified, it would be possible to apply constraints during generation to eliminated impossible alternatives (similarly to Langkilde and Knight (1998), Section refsec:targ-lang-stat). This allows more flexibility at the cost of greater ambiguity.

5.4 The Algorithm for Generating Determiners for Referential Noun Phrases

After the referentiality has been decided in the transfer phase, it is necessary to generate the determiner. Sometimes an element in the original Japanese is translated as a determiner (such as *kono* "this"). More often the system must determine the appropriate English determiner, either a possessive pronoun or an article. The main heuristics used are summarized in Figure 17. The rules are applied in the order shown.

The rules are similar to those used to determine referentiality and countability/number, so I shall not describe them all in the same detail. The major difference is the addition of special processing to generate possessive pronouns, which I shall describe more fully. The heuristics presented in Figure 17 form a pragmatic hierarchy of defeasible rules for interpreting the 'definiteness' of a Japanese noun phrase.

5.4.1 Clause Level Rules

There are three rules for determining definiteness that are applied at the clause level.

The first is a very general rule which makes focus-marked subjects of past and progressive sentences **definite**. This rule captures the intuition that focus-marked sentences are mainly about locatable entities, and so should be realised as definite noun phrases.

The second, triggered at the same time and in the same way as the referential rule in Section 5.2.1, makes the subject of a specificational sentence **definite**.

The third rule, omitted from Figure 17, is tied to a particular construction, and makes the predicand of a resultative predicative complement **definite**, as in (108), where *wall* is the subject of *blue*:

(108)   彼 は   壁 を   青く   塗った
          kare-wa *kabe-o*   *aoku*   *nutta*
          he-NOM wall-ACC bluely painted

          'He painted the/#a wall blue'

An indefinite noun phrase is grammatical in the English translation shown in (108), but is not a good translation of the Japanese in most situations. This rule is, therefore, a useful default.

5.4.2 Case Element Level Rules

There are various types of rules that apply to case elements, mainly licensed by predicates. Verbs that trigger these rules, including idioms such as *kick the bucket*, are so marked in the lexicon.

1. Clause level rules:
   - The subject of a past tense or progressive sentence marked with the marker *wa* or *mo* is **definite**:
   gunshū-wa teikō shita. "The crowd resisted."
   - The subject of a specificational sentence is **definite**:
   kakaku-wa ni-hyaku-en de-aru. "The price is 200 yen."
2. Case element level rules:
   - `place` nouns heading locative noun phrases are **definite**:
   kūkō-ni itta. "I went to the airport."
3. Modification of and within the noun phrase:
   - A noun phrase whose head is modified by a relative clause is **definite**:
   kinō kita otoko "the man who came yesterday"
   - Context and World Knowledge
   - An NP with a 'unique' referent is **definite**:
   chikyū "the earth"
   - If the noun phrase refers to an entity known to be previously mentioned (directly or indirectly) it is **definite**
   - An NP made logically unique by a dependent is **definite**:
   ichiban hayai otoko "the fastest man"
   - An NP modified by a possessive construction is **definite**:
   hana-no saki "the tip of my nose"
   - An NP whose head is modified by a demonstrative is **definite**:
   kono otoko "this man"
   - An NP whose head is modified by a marked modifier is **indefinite**:
   aru otoko "a certain man"
4. If an indefinite noun phrase is headed by an inherently possessed noun and is not the direct object of a verb with meaning `possession` or `acquisition`, then generate a **possessive pronoun**
   saifu-o nakushita. "I lost my wallet."
5. Noun phrases still undetermined are treated as **indefinite**.

FIGURE 17 Determination of an Appropriate Determiner for Referential Noun Phrases

There is one general case element level rule for definiteness: Locative noun phrases are assigned the value **definite**.

5.4.3 Modification of and within the Noun Phrase

The final level of rules considers modification of and within the noun phrase itself. The rules are applied in the order shown. If there is conflict between the rules, the later one will override the earlier.

Relative Clauses

This algorithm uses a simple heuristic: a noun phrase modified by a relative clause is **definite**.

Context and World Knowledge

Three rules have been implemented that use context and world knowledge.

The first rule is that noun phrases headed by nouns that are marked in the lexicon as having a unique referent, such as *chikyū* "the earth", are assumed to be **definite** in addition to being referential (§ 5.2.3).

The second rule is that a noun phrase which modifies another in an appositive relation will be **indefinite**: *NTT, a telephone company*. This can, like all such rules, be overidden by a subsequent one: *NTT, the largest telephone company in the world*.

The final rule is that noun phrases with anaphoric reference to some antecedent will be **definite**, either as a pronoun or a definite noun phrase as in (109):

(109) タクシー を見た。　　汚 かった
      takushī$_i$-o mita. Φ$_i$ *kitana-katta.*
      taxi$_i$-ACC saw. Φ$_i$ dirty-PAST

      I saw a taxi. The taxi was dirty.

Other Noun Phrase Internal Modifiers

An NP made logically unique by a dependent or modified by a possessive construction is **definite**. As was noted in Section 5.2.3, although most dependents within the noun phrase that affect referentiality and definiteness force a definite reading, there are some that force an indefinite reading, such as *aru* "(a) certain".

5.4.4 Generation of Possessive Pronouns

In order to generate possessive pronouns, inherently possessed nouns are marked in the transfer lexicon. These are nouns which typically head noun phrases where English conventionally uses a possessive pronoun but Japanese does not; for example, to indicate a relationship such as ownership, as in *my wallet*, or kinship, as in *my father*, as

discussed in Section 2.4.5. A noun phrase headed by an inherently possessed noun will be generated with a default possessive pronoun if it is
referential, has no other determiner, and is not the direct object of a
verb of possession or acquisition. If the noun phrase is the subject
of a sentence, then the generated possessive pronoun will have deictic
reference, otherwise its antecedent is the subject of the sentence the
noun phrase appears in. The algorithm is outlined in Figure 18.

---

1. A noun phrase that fulfills all of the following conditions will be
   generated with a default possessive pronoun with deictic reference
   determined by the modality of the sentence it appears in.
   (a) The noun phrase is headed by an inherently possessed noun
       that denotes kin or body parts
   (b) The noun phrase is the subject of the sentence
   (c) The noun phrase is referential
   (d) The noun phrase has no other determiner
2. A noun phrase that fulfills all of the following conditions will be
   generated with a default possessive pronoun whose antecedent is
   the subject of the sentence the noun phrase appears in.
   (a) The noun phrase is headed by an inherently possessed noun
   (b) The noun phrase is not the subject of the sentence
   (c) The noun phrase is referential
   (d) The noun phrase has no other determiner
   (e) The noun phrase is not the direct object of a verb of pos-
       session or acquisition

FIGURE 18 Generation of Possessive Pronouns

If the noun phrase's determiner slot is already filled, then it cannot
have a possessive pronoun. Finally, if the noun phrase is headed by an
inherently possessed noun and is neither the subject of the sentence nor
the direct object of a verb with meaning possession or acquisition,
then it will be generated with a possessive pronoun whose antecedent
is the subject of the sentence.

The special rules for kin and body parts reflect the special importance they have to human beings. Special processing for these phenomena is reasonable, considering that it has been argued that humans
themselves have a special faculty for social cognition (Jackendoff, 1992,
Chapter 4).

If the predicate itself shows that the subject is the possessor of the object, then the object noun phrase is typically translated with an indefinite article rather than a possessive pronoun even when headed by an inherently possessed noun. Examples of such predicates are verbs that express possession, such as *own, have* or *possess*; and verbs that express that the object has just been acquired, for example, the direct object of *buy, acquire* or *steal*. With these predicates a possessive pronoun is not needed to show the possessive relation. If a possessive pronoun were to be generated, it would especially emphasize the fact that the subject's referent possesses the referent of the object: e.g. *I bought my car [it wasn't given to me by my parents]*.

Using this algorithm, it is possible to generate appropriate possessive pronouns with an accuracy of 81% (number correctly generated over number needed) and a precision of 88% (number correctly generated over number generated) (Bond et al., 1995).

5.4.5   Defective Noun Phrases

There is some additional processing for defective noun phrases, which is omitted from Figure 17. Defective noun phrases are generally licensed locally (Ross, 1995, 433). Predicate nominals (ascriptive noun phrases) appear after copulas (§ 2.2.3), or are licensed by certain constructions. Idiom chunks are licensed by their predicates. Idiom chunks have a special referential status (§ 2.2.4).

Locative/temporal noun phrases are licensed by locative and temporal case roles (§ 5.1.2), either on the noun phrase itself or on the prepositional phrase that governs it. Measure phrases are also marked at the same level as case roles.

Idiom Chunks

Idiom chunks can have determiners, including articles and `null`, marked explicitly. In such cases there is no need to generate anything. For example, *tōkon* "at present" will always be translated as a PP with an embedded NP headed by a noun with no determiner.

There are also several classes of nouns marked in the lexicon that are more productive and require special article processing, usually the use of the `null` article. The complete list of these classes, with a short description of their use, is given in Section 7.1.4.

One such class is **means of transport**. If an unmodified means-of-transport noun, such as *bus*, follows the preposition *by*, then it will have a `null` determiner, that is, no article. There are two special means-of-transport nouns, *foot* and *horseback* which will also be `null` following *on*.

Another class is **institutions** such as *school* which will be `null` after the preposition *to*: *I am going to school*, or when they are unmodified, and follow a locative preposition *in/on/at*. These determinerless PPs are reasonably common (0.2% of tokens in the British National Corpus) and pose a challenge for any natural language processing system (Baldwin et al., 2003).

Ascriptive Noun Phrases

In English, an ascriptive noun phrase is usually indefinite, and agrees in number with its predicand. If one of the noun phrases has a collective interpretation, such as one headed by *group*, it is counted as plural for purposes of agreement.

Ascriptive noun phrases are typically singular count nouns. They are translated as uncountable only if the noun phrase is headed by an uncountable noun, and even then they will be made countable if their predicand is countable:

(110)   *Cancer is a sickness.*

(111)   *The modem used was a piece of communications equipment.*

(112)   *The communications equipment we used was a modem.*

(113)   *The children are angels.*

Articles are generated in the same way as for indefinite referential noun phrases: countable singular noun phrases will, therefore, take the indefinite article, *a/an*; and countable plural and uncountable noun phrases will take the zero article, ϕ.

Role nouns such as *chairman* in *chairman of the committee* are a special kind of ascriptive noun phrase. These noun phrases occur as the predicative complements of verbs like *elect* and *become*, or as the complement of the preposition *as*, or complement of the preposition of nouns like *role*, *part* or *position*. They have the special property that they can occur with null determiners in the singular: *We elected him chairman*. These are different from normal ascriptive nouns in that they do not agree with their predicand: *We elected them both vice-chairman*.

Measure Phrases

Noun phrases headed by measure classifiers act as singular for verb agreement: *100 metres of cable is a lot* or *24 kms is a long way*.

This is handled by having a special noun phrase feature `agreement`. Normally, it has the same value as the `number` feature of the head noun, but it can take a conflicting value. This is simple to add, but ends up requiring a lot of dedicated code to deal with in the implementation.

A more complete analysis of measure noun phrases has been developed within the HPSG framework. It adds a specific construction for measure noun phrases which accounts for both the syntactic and semantic facts (Flickinger and Bond, 2003). The advantage of this approach is that it requires no extension to the underlying machinery for parsing or generation. The disadvantage is that it requires a more precise English grammar than the one used here.

Locative and Temporal Phrases

As described earlier, locative phrases are translated as definite by default. The handling of temporal expressions is described by special rules specific to temporal expressions.

To handle such cases, a special structure is used: the special compound noun phrase. It is also used for noun phrases where there is no obvious head, such as person and company names, and addresses. This structure is used for time position noun phrases which include the following elements: `year`, `day-of-month`, `month` and/or `numbered-time`. In these noun phrases, there is no obvious semantic head and there are many possible representations in English. Some examples of the choice of expressions for a single date are given in (114). The choice of representation is mainly a question of style. In particular, it does not depend on the Japanese source noun phrase, which has only two possible forms: *2-gatsu-19-nichi* "2 month 19 day" and *2-gatsu-no 19-nichi* "2 month GEN 19 day".

(114)   February the 19th *vs* February 19 *vs* February 19th *vs* the 19th of February

By establishing a set of special structures for noun phrases that behave atypically, and thus have to be treated atypically anyway, we are able to preserve a uniform structure for all other noun phrases (with a single, although potentially phonologically empty, specifier). Although the grammar is consistent with 'purebred' noun phrases, the choice of determiner is not, which is why a separate module is used.

Complex temporal noun phrases require complicated rules. I show the rules for the combination of a noun phrase denoting `deictic-day` or `day` with one denoting `period-of-day` (*morning, afternoon, evening*) or *night* in Figure 19. The Japanese will be of the form α-*no* β "α-GEN β" where α is headed by a `day` or `deictic-day` noun and β is headed by a `period-of-day` noun or *night*, that translates into English noun phrase B.

These transfer rules capture the lexical and phrasal idiosyncrasies of the temporal noun phrases, and are relatively easy to test and expand. The rules are all specific to temporal noun phrases; no generality has been lost by putting them in a separate module.

B is `period-of-day` (*morning, afternoon, evening*) or *night*:
if A is `deictic-day`
    if A = *issakusakujitsu* "the day before the day before yesterday"
      ⇒ *the B before the B before last* (3 before)
    if A = *ototoi* "the day before yesterday"
      ⇒ *the B before last* (2 before)
    if A = *kinō* "yesterday"
      if B = *night*
        ⇒ `null` *last night*
      else
        ⇒ `null` *yesterday* B (1 before)
    if A = *kyō* "today" or *honjitsu* "today"
      if B = *night*
        ⇒ `null` *tonight*
      else
        ⇒ *this B* (today's)
    if A = *ashita* "tomorrow"
      ⇒ `null` *tomorrow* B (1 after)
    if A = *asatte* "the day after tomorrow"
      ⇒ *the B after next* (2 after)
    if A = *shiasatte* "the day after the day after tomorrow"
      ⇒ *the B after the B after next* (3 after)
    if A = *yanoasatte* "the day after the day after the day after tomorrow"
      ⇒ *the B after the B after the B after next* (4 after [rare])
if A is `relative-day`
    if A = *zenjitsu* "the previous day"
      ⇒ *the previous B*
    if A = *yokujitsu* "the following day"
      ⇒ *the following B*
if A is `named-day`
    ⇒ `null`*A* B (Christmas morning)
if A is `day-of-month`
    ⇒ *the B of the A* (A must be ordinal)

FIGURE 19 Rules for `day`, `deictic-day` and `period-of-day`

These rules do not necessarily preserve the Japanese structure. In particular, many temporal expressions made up of two noun phrases with an adnominal marker in Japanese are often most naturally translated as appositive noun-noun expressions. For example, *ashita-no akegata* "tomorrow-GEN dawn" could possibly be translated as *tomorrow's dawn*, but is generally translated as *dawn tomorrow* where *tomorrow* post-modifies dawn.

5.5   Translation of Generic Noun Phrases

Because the bare generic is acceptable for all environments, it is the default choice. Bare generics have no article, and the number and countability depends on the noun countability preference of the head. If the noun phrase is marked as `definite` (such as the object of *hatsumei-suru* "invent"), then the noun phrase will be coerced to be uncountable and singular. Definite articles will be generated for all countability preferences except weakly countable and uncountable, which will instead be generated bare. The possible noun phrases are shown in Table 22.

TABLE 22   Translation of Generic Noun Phrases

Noun Countability Preference	Bare Generic	Generic 'the'
Fully Countable	*pens*	*the pen*
Strongly Countable	*cakes*	*the cake*
Weakly Countable	*beer*	*beer*
Uncountable	*furniture*	*furniture*
Plural Only	*scissors*	*the scissor*

5.6   The Actual Generation of Articles

Finally, articles will be generated according to the number and definiteness of the noun phrase. In the final stage of processing, definite noun phrases take either no article: `null`, or the definite article: *the*. Indefinite countable singular noun phrases will take the indefinite article, *a/an*; while indefinite countable plural and uncountable noun phrases will take the zero article: ϕ. Ascriptive noun phrases are always indefinite.

Generic noun phrases will be generated with no determiner (`null`), unless explicitly marked definite, in which case they will be generated with the definite article *the*.

Articles are generated as shown in Figure 20 for referential noun phrases. There are two ways to get no determiner: either as a definite `null` marked noun phrase or as an indefinite plural or uncountable noun phrase.

If the NP has no determiner and is not `null` then
  if the NP is definite then
    generate *the*
  else (indefinite)
    if the NP is countable and singular then
      generate *a(n)*
    else
      do nothing (`zero`)

FIGURE 20 Generation of Articles

5.6.1 Linear Order and *a/an*

The actual generation of the articles, and thus the choice between *a* and *an*, is done at the very end of the generation process, after the sentence has been produced and the word order fixed. This allows us to look at the start of the word following the article to determine which variant to use. Entries in **ALT-J/E**'s English dictionary are marked with a flag that says whether a preceding indefinite article should be *a* (the default) or *an*. If the word is not in the dictionary then *an* will be generated if either (i) the first letter is a vowel and the next letter is not capitalized; or (ii) the first two letters are capitalized, and the first letter is one of *A, E, F, H, I, L, M, N, O, R, S, X*. The latter case is a check for acronyms (such as *NTT*) and product names (such as *XWindow*) where the first letter is pronounced as an individual letter.

5.6.2 Special Cases

Linear Order Tweaks

Finally, there are two special cases of linear order mismatches that are checked for. First, if *an* is followed by *other* then they are merged to form *another*. Second, if *a* is followed by *such* then they are swapped, changing *a such man* to *such a man*.

Choosing between *one* and *a*

Numeral classifier combinations such as *ichi-mētōru* "1 meter" normally sound better as *a meter*. A special rule has been implemented which changes *one* to the indefinite article for noun phrases headed by mensural classifiers. This rule is triggered during generation.

Ideally, the rule should fire only in non-contrastive environments: that is, it should not fire in cases such as *We only need <u>one meter</u>, not six meters*. However, information as to whether something is being contrasted was not consistently available from the Japanese parse. Therefore the rule as implemented will fire even in contrastive environments. Because contrastive environments are relatively rare, the rule gives a net improvement.

Generation of Markup for Post-Editors

One of the worst errors for a machine translation system is to generate a translation that is grammatically correct and plausible, but different in meaning to the original. This is especially a problem for the generation of possessive pronouns, which will almost always be grammatically correct and plausible, and are occasionally generated wrongly. Other constructions likely to be dangerously mistranslated are unknown proper nouns, supplemented zero-pronouns, and transliterated words.

To make it easier to check for these during post-editing, it is possible to tag them in the output by setting a special flag. The tagged elements can then be marked when presented to a post editor (for example, in a different color or font) for special attention. The tagging of such potentially dangerous elements has been implemented as an option: setting a flag marks all such elements in the output. The flags are marked with tags, which can then be highlighted in some way for the post editor, for example, using a different font. An example with an unknown proper noun and possessive pronouns is given in Sentence 115.

(115)　豪ボン社は、　　　　　　　本部を　　　　　移動した。
　　　　gō-bon-sha-wa　　　　　　*honbu-o*　　　*iten-shita*
　　　　Australia Bon Company-TOP headquarter-OBJ moved

　　　　<u>Australia's Bond Corp</u> moved its headquarters.

```
<seg ana=unknown>Australia Bon Corp</seg> moved <seg
ana=possp>its</seg> headquarters.
```

Australia Bon Corp moved *its* headquarters.

6

Evaluation and Discussion

In this section, I present and discuss the results of testing the algorithms presented in Chapter 5. The tests were done on the implementation in **ALT-J/E**, although the algorithms could be implemented in other systems with similarly detailed semantics.

The rules were initially designed and tested using data from a set of test sentences constructed from linguistic examples. They were then refined by testing on other data sets, especially Ikehara et al.'s (1994a) functional machine translation test set of 3,718 Japanese/English sentence pairs (`http://www.kecl.ntt.co.jp/icl/mtg/resources`). These sentences were designed to fully test a Japanese to English machine translation system, including the morphological analysis, parsing, transfer and generation. Neither countability, number nor article use are specifically tested for by this test set, partly because their handling is, of course, part of translating every noun phrase.

Due to the fact that the processing described in Chapter 5 is intertwined with the general translation machinery, there is no simple way to explicitly measure the time taken just for this processing. However, an examination of the time taken in various sub-routines during translation shows that the processing of number, countability, reference and articles is a negligible part of the overall translation process.

6.1 Results and Evaluation

The algorithms were evaluated on a collection of newspaper articles from the *Nikkei-Sangyō* newspaper, a Japanese financial newspaper published by *Nihon Keizai Shimbun, Inc.* There were three major evaluations. The first was by myself, the second by an English native speaker not connected with the development of the algorithm, and the third by three professional Japanese-English translators. I shall first describe the test set, and then each of the evaluations in turn.

6.1.1 Evaluation Test Data

The test set consists of newspaper sentences describing company merg-
ers and new products from the telecommunications section of the
Nikkei-Sangyō. In the first two evaluations I tested the same 102 sentences; in the last evaluation I added 398 sentences, giving a total of
500. There are an average of 44 characters (kanji, hiragana, katakana
or roman) in each Japanese sentence, or roughly 22 words. The English
translations change as the system changes. In the final evaluation, there
were an average of 26 words per English sentence. An example of the
machine translation output and human translations of the first five
sentences is given in Section 6.1.1.

The evaluations were carried out per noun phrase, with each noun
phrase evaluated as correct or incorrect. That is, for each noun phrase
in its context, I judged whether the number of the noun head and
the choice of determiner was appropriate. There were around 7 noun
phrases per sentence. If a noun phrase contained an embedded noun
phrase, they were each evaluated separately. For example, the translation of *beikoku-no CATV-kyoku*, *a CATV station in the U.S* counts
as two noun phrases *a CATV station in the U.S* and *the U.S*. This
gives the same number of noun phrases as evaluating all **base noun
phrase**s: the base noun phrases in this case would be just *a CATV
station* and *the U.S*.

Results are also given per sentence, as that gives a better idea of how
good the system is from the point of view of the end user — someone
reading the translated text. For a sentence to be judged as correct all
the noun phrases must be correct.

All testing was done on translation of complete sentences, not just
generation from a correctly parsed Japanese source. This was for two
reasons. Firstly, the algorithm includes information from the source
parse, and extracting it correctly is one element that needs to be tested.
Secondly, in any application, there will be errors in the source language
analysis, and the transfer and generation subsystems must be able to
deal with them robustly.

Testing within the machine translation system involved two main
problems. The first was that there is no gold standard to compare the
results against, as they keep changing. As well as changes in the algorithm, other parts of the machine translation system change, which
may completely change the output. Even the number of noun phrases
generated changes along with the system. For example, *a CATV station in the U.S* (two base noun phrases) could also be translated as
a U.S. CATV station, which is only one base noun phrase. A gold

standard could have either of these; they are both good translations. It is acceptable for the machine translation system to produce either of these. However, if the gold standard has *a U.S. CATV station* and the system produces *a CATV station in the U.S*, then there is no way to judge the correctness of the base noun phrase *in the U.S.*. Further, two correct translations could differ in number and countability. In the two translations in (116), *fuku* is translated as either *clothes* or *clothing*. Both these translations are good, with nothing to choose between them: there are multiple gold standards. In this case, choosing either one as the gold standard would mean that the other translation, although perfectly correct, would be unfairly penalized. One solution to this is to provide multiple reference translations. However, producing them is expensive, and judging exactly what range of translations is acceptable is an open-ended problem.

(116) 私 は   服 の   デザイン に 興味 が   ある

watashi-wa fuku-no   dezain-ni kyōmi-ga   aru

I-TOP   clothes-ADN design-DAT interest-NOM have

I am interested in designing clothes

I am interested in designing clothing

The second major problem was that if the overall translation of the sentence was too poor, then it was sometimes not possible to judge a noun phrase as either correct or incorrect. For this reason, I chose a test set that was also used as a test set by other members of the NTT Machine Translation Research Group, and so gave reasonable translations overall.

Sample Text

In this section I give an example of the newspaper text used in the evaluations, its transliteration, **ALT-J/E**'s machine-translated output, and two human translations. The text is first five sentences of the *Nikkei-Sangyō* test data. The machine translation was done on 1998-01-20. There is considerable variation in the quality of the human translations. The first was done by a professional translator who was a native speaker of Japanese, the second by a professional translator who was a native speaker of English and had access to the first translation.

Japanese Input 住友商事は米国のＣＡＴＶ局を買収するため、四月をメドに投資グループを結成する。同社と提携関係にあるＣＡＴＶ局向け大手番組供給会社、ビアコム・インターナショナルおよび投資銀行と三社で結成する。早ければ今夏中にも米国のＣＡＴＶ局を買収する。米国では投資対象としてＣＡＴＶ局の買収が活発だが、住商はＣＡＴＶ運営のノウハウの取得などもねらう。日本企業が米国のＣＡＴＶ局を買収する第一号になりそうだ。

Japanese Input (transliteration) *Sumitomo Shōji-wa beikoku-no CATV kyoku-o baishū-suru-tame, shi-gatsu-o medo-ni tōshi gurūpu-o kessē-suru. dōsha-to tēkē kankē-ni-aru CATV kyoku-muke ōte bangumi tēkyō kaisha, Biakomu Intānashonaru oyobi tōshigingkō-to sansha-de kessē-suru. hayakereba kon-natsu-chū-ni-mo bēkoku-no CATV kyoku-o baishū-suru. bēkoku-dewa tōshi taishō-toshite CATV kyoku-no baishū-ga kappatsu-daga, sumishō-wa CATV unē-no nōhaū-no shutoku-nado-mo nerau. nihon kigyō-ga bēkoku-no CATV kyoku-o baishū-suru dai-ichigō-ni nari-sōda.*

Machine Translation Output Sumitomo Corp. will organize the investment group to acquire a CATV station in the U.S. by April. It will organize the investment group in this company, the company of the service of a major program aimed at CATV stations in a cooperative relation, Beercom International Corp., an investment bank and 3 companies. The investment group acquires a CATV station in the U.S. during this summer at the earliest time. Although the purchase of CATV stations is active as an investment in the U.S., Sumitomo Corporation also aims at the acquisition of the know-how of CATV management and so on. It is likely to total first that a Japanese enterprise acquires a CATV station in the U.S.

Human Translated Output (1) The Sumitomo Corporation will organize an investment group by April for acquiring a CATV station in the United States. The group will consist of three companies, the Sumitomo Corp., their affiliate, the Beerman International Corp., a major supplier of programs to CATV stations, and an investment bank. A CATV station in the United States may be acquired by this summer providing things progress smoothly. Activity in the purchase of CATV stations as investments is brisk in the United States, but the Sumitomo Corp. is also aiming to acquire mainly the know-how of CATV management. It is likely to become the first case of a Japanese enterprise acquiring a CATV station in the United States.

Human Translated Output (2) Sumitomo Corporation will organize an investment group by April to acquire a CATV station in the United States. The group will consist of three companies; Sumitomo, their affiliate Beerman International Corp., a major supplier of programs to CATV stations, and an investment bank. It may acquire an American CATV station by as early as this summer. Activity in the purchase of CATV stations as investments is brisk in the United States, but Sumitomo is also aiming to acquire CATV management know-how. It is likely to be the first time that a Japanese enterprise acquires an American CATV station.

6.1.2 First Evaluation

The first evaluation was on the set of test sentences constructed from linguistic examples (training data), and on a collection of newspaper articles (test data). The results are summarized in Table 23. These results were reported at COLING-94 (Bond et al., 1994). The evaluation was carried out by the developer (the author).

TABLE 23 Correct Generation of Determiners and Number (First Evaluation).

Algorithm	Test Sentences		Newspaper Articles	
	NPs (240)	Sentences (120)	NPs (717)	Sentences (102)
Version-1	94%	90%	73%	12%
Original	70%	46%	65%	5%

In the newspaper articles tested, there was an average of 7.0 noun phrases in each sentence. The introduction of the proposed method improved the percentage of correct sentences from 5% to 12%.

The **original** processing used heuristics similar to those outlined by Kikui and McClure (1991)(§ 3.1). The **version-1** processing was the initial implementation of the algorithms described here. This version lacked most of the clause and case element level rules. Even so, it was an improvement over the general heuristics. In particular, a modest improvement in the percentage of correct noun phrases made a large difference in the percentage of correct sentences. This was because most mistakes are in long complicated sentences with more than the average number of noun phrases. Shorter sentences with fewer noun phrases are easier to handle at all stages of the translation process.

6.1.3 Second Evaluation

In the second evaluation, only the newspaper articles were used as test data. New rules had been added using the results of the first evaluation, so the test data is no longer unseen data. The major change was the addition of the clause and case element level rules along with rules to generate possessive pronouns. The results are summarized in Table 24.

The articles were translated by **ALT-J/E** and the raw output examined by an English native speaker, who could compare it with a human translation made by a professional translator. The evaluator was familiar with the machine translation system, but was not involved with the design of the algorithms.

TABLE 24 Correct Generation of Determiners and Number (Second Evaluation).

Algorithm	Newspaper Articles	
	NPs (717)	Sentences (102)
Version-2	85%	36%
Version-1	73%	12%
Original	65%	5%

Each noun phrase was given one of the following values:

Best The most appropriate article and number.

Analysis Problem with the parse.[21]

NP structure Problem with noun phrase structure or choice of translation.

Dictionary Problem with the dictionary.

Reference Problem with referential property.

Number Inappropriate number or countability.

Article Inappropriate article.

Possessive Inappropriate use of possessive determiner.

The success rates were 85% for the system with the revised method and 65% for the original system. The introduction of the revised algorithm increased the percentage of correct sentences from 5% to 36%.

For the purpose of evaluating the algorithm itself, I also calculated the success rate ignoring errors caused by other parts of the system: those noun phrases that had a problem with only **parse/NP structure/dictionary**. This gave a success rate of 90% for the revised method.

Knight and Chander (1994), in a small pilot study, showed that humans could replace definite and indefinite articles in an English text in which the articles had been replaced by blanks with an accuracy of only around 95%. This would then be an upper limit on the accuracy of the evaluation. Raw machine translation output is less coherent than normal English text and so deciding which article is appropriate is an even harder task. Even using a third party evaluator did not give a perfectly reproducible, absolute level of success. This is because the goal is to produce a translation, which is new text, therefore, there can be no fixed objective target to compare the results with. Be that as it

---

[21]This includes any major problems not connected with articles or number, such as outputting Japanese characters or ungrammatical output.

may, the evaluation does successfully show the overall level of improvement/degradation, and helps to identify the remaining problems. In the final evaluation (§ 6.1.4), I explored whether it is possible to produce a perfectly reproducible, absolute level of success.

Analysis of Errors

After the second evaluation, I looked at the differences between the proposed algorithm and the original algorithm, as well as a full analysis of the errors. Identifying the cause of the errors was done jointly by the evaluator and the developer (the author).

An example of successfully identifying a generic noun phrase is given in (117). Here the sentence is characterizing, and so the (English) subject is marked as generic. Rules such as this one, which are based on the sentence as a whole, need to be defeasible, as they are often overridden elsewhere:

(117) 会員 は 　　　三万 七千 円、 　　　　非会員 は
　　　 kai'in-wa 　　 *sanman-nanasen-en,* *hikai'in-wa*
　　　 member-TOP 37,000 yen, 　　　　 non-member-TOP

　　　 4万 七千 円の 　　　 参加費 が 　　　　 必要.
　　　 yonman-nanasen-en-no sankahi-ga 　　　　 *hitsuyō.*
　　　 47,000 yen-ADN 　　　 registration fee-NOM necessary

　　　 <u>Members</u> need 37,000 yen as the registration fee and <u>non members</u> need 47,000 yen. 　　　　　　　　 (Version-2)

　　　 <u>A member</u> needs 37,000 yen as the registration fee and <u>a non member</u> needs 47,000 yen. 　　　　　　 (Version-1)

There was some problem for 108 of the 717 noun phrases in the machine translation of the newspaper articles. A brief analysis of the errors is given in Table 25.

One large source of errors was problems with the source language analysis and dictionaries (14% in all). These are not problems with the proposed algorithm but with the machine translation system as a whole. As errors were identified, they were passed on to the researchers responsible for the areas they occurred in. This is part of the feedback that improves the overall system.

Another major source of errors is the translation of complex noun phrases (18%). For example, in (118), instead of the noun phrase *denwagaisha-no madoguchi* "telephone company outlets" being correctly made plural, only *denwagaisha* "telephone company" becomes plural. The rules for number give the correct result, but are applied to the wrong noun phrase, in this case due to an error in the analysis of the Japanese noun phrase structure (the modifier *zenkoku-no*

TABLE 25 Errors in the Generation of Articles and Number.

Problem	Freq.	Description of error [108 errors in 717 noun phrases]
Analysis	7%	The Japanese noun phrase was parsed incorrectly so the rules did not trigger.
Noun Phrase	18%	Complex noun phrases were translated badly: for example, *384 Kbits of networks per second* should be *a 384 Kbit/s network*
Dictionary	7%	The dictionary entry was incorrect.
Reference	13%	Miscellaneous errors in determining noun phrase reference.
Number	25%	In many instances rules using common sense and inference are needed to determine the number correctly: for example, *office* should be plural in *there is an office on the fourth floor and above*
Article	26%	The rules for deciding whether a noun has been restrictively described by an embedded sentence are too coarse.
		There needs to be a rule for indirect anaphora. *Two models should be definite in NTT introduced video-tel 111 and video-tel 222 in June. *(The) two models are the first to have video receivers.*
		There needs to be a rule to make a noun phrase definite if its pre-head dependent restricts it sufficiently: for example *NTT will enter the/*a video rental business*
Possessive	5%	The antecedent of the possessive pronoun was sometimes misidentified.

"throughout the whole country" is given narrow scope, instead of wide scope: *[A-no-B]-no-C* instead of *A-no-[B-no-C]*):

(118) 全国 の   電話会社 の   窓口
       zenkoku-no   <u>*denwagaisha-no*</u>   <u>*madoguchi*</u>
       whole country-ADN phone company-ADN windows

       <u>telephone company outlets</u> throughout the country   (Human)

       * <u>the window of telephone companies</u> throughout the country
       (MT)

In the generation of articles and numbers for referential noun phrases some of the errors can still be reduced by the addition of new rules: for example, adding rules which use the meanings of noun-noun combinations, or rules using pre-head dependents to determine definiteness. The problems of common sense deduction and indirect anaphora, however, require a large-scale knowledge base and inference rules. While both are being researched at the moment, they are unlikely to be implemented soon.

A simplified example of an unrecognized noun anaphor giving trouble is given in (119). The noun phrase *shingaisha* "new company" should be definite the second time it appears in the same news article:

(119)   *a.* ＮＴＴ は   新会社
          NTT-wa   *shingaisha*
          NTT-TOP new company
          ＮＴＴ テレコム エンジニアリング 東京 を
          NTT-terekomu-enjiniaringu-tōkyō-o
          NTT Telecom Engineering Tokyo-ACC
          8 日 付けで   設立 する
          hachi-nichi-dzuke-de setsuritsu-suru
          8-day-on   establish

          NTT will establish <u>a new company</u>, NTT Telecom Engineering Tokyo, on the 8th

   b. 新会社 の   資本金 は   8千万円
          shingaisha-no   *shihonkin-wa hassenman-en*
          new company-ADN capital-TOP   80,000,000 yen

          The capital of *a/<u>the new company</u> is 80,000,000 yen

Anaphora turned out to be less of a problem than expected. One reason was that in many cases reference to known entities was already marked by a focus marker (*-wa* or *-mo*), so they were correctly marked as definite even without any explicit discourse tracking. Because of this, it was decided that adding full noun anaphor resolution to **ALT-J/E** did not offer enough improvement to warrant the effort. Murata (1996) added direct and indirect noun anaphor resolution to his system, but it occurred after the determination of reference and definiteness. No results were given as to how much, if at all, the anaphor resolution improved the determination of reference and definiteness.

After examining this test set in detail, I came up with only one major addition to the algorithm for determining noun phrase reference: the check for arguments of derived nominals and verbal nouns (§ 5.2.2).

6.1.4 Final Evaluation

In the final evaluation, done with data taken in 1998, I looked especially at the problem of reproducibility of the evaluation.

Three native speakers of English who can also read Japanese were presented with English paragraphs of translated text **with the determiners deleted**, separated into numbered sentences. The Japanese originals were also available. 500 sentences were provided, the 102 sentences used in the first two evaluations and an additional 398 sentences from the same genre. The last 398 sentences were not translated as accurately by **ALT-J/E**, as they had not been the subject of extensive testing. The output was raw machine translation output, so the English was often incorrect. In many cases, words or phrases were output in the original Japanese. Two sentences failed to translate at all, and have been excluded from the analysis of results.

The testers determined appropriate determiners for each noun phrase. Noun phrases were identified and numbered (sentence-number/phrase-number), roughly as shown below (deleted determiners are shown struck out, in the actual task they were not shown at all; noun phrases have been underlined):

(1) オーストラリア の 人 が 右手 で 鼻 を かく

ōsutoraria-no hito-ga migi-te-de hana-o kaku

All Australian people scratch ~~their~~ nose in ~~their~~ right hand.

(1/1) All Australian people
(1/2) nose
(1/3) right hand

(2) 二本 で 会った 人 が 全員 左手 を 使う

nihon-de atta hito-ga zen'in hidarite-o tsukau

All ~~the~~ people I've ever met in Japan use ~~their~~ left.

(2/5) All people I've ever met in Japan
(2/6) I
(2/7) Japan
(2/8) left

The testers had the following task:

- Give each noun phrase one or more appropriate determiners from the following list: *every, either, neither, each, another, a(an), both, dozen, score, several, we, us, you, many, few, fewer, a few, much, many, little, less, a little, overmuch, too many, more, most, this, these, that, those, which, what, the, some, any, no, my, your, its, her, his, our, their, such, enough*, any cardinal numeral (1, 2, 3, ...) or numeral equivalent (*dozen, score* etc). If you think no determiner is needed, please mark as: **N** (for null). If you cannot tell (for example, if the translation is so bad that it is meaningless), then mark it with a question mark: **?**.

  In some cases, there may be more than one possible determiner. In that case, please list all the ones you think are acceptable: e.g. (*a/the*).

The testers varied considerably, particularly in their decision as to whether a noun phrase was unevaluable (marked with **?**). There was some confusion by the testers on the marking of non-article determiners. To reduce the effects of this, all non-article determiners except the most common three (*this, its* and *their*) are treated as none (**N**). As there were so few possessive pronouns, I also treat *its* and *their* as one class. Finally, to simplify the calculations, only the first answer was counted for multiple answers (e.g. only *a* for *a/***N**). The raw totals of the simplified scores are given in Table 26.

To test the reproducibility of the results, I calculated inter-annotator agreement and κ coefficients for the testers' selection of articles. The κ coefficient corrects for the expected chance agreement between testers, and is defined as follows (Carletta, 1996):

$$\kappa = \frac{P(A) - P(E)}{1 - P(E)} \tag{6.1}$$

P(A) is the inter-tester agreement (how many times two testers agreed, divided by the number of test instances); P(E) is the proportion of times the testers are expected to agree by chance.

The average pairwise agreement for the first 102 sentences was 0.69 ($\kappa = 0.52$). This was even worse in the last 398 sentences, where the pairwise agreement was down to 0.58 ($\kappa = 0.39$). The major reason for this decrease was the increased number of unevaluable NPs. In the first 102 sentences 13.6% of NPs were marked with **?** and 21.3% were in the next 398. This is because the last 398 sentences had not been used for system testing, and were therefore translated worse overall.

The low inter-tester agreement shows that the testing task is not a

TABLE 26 Distribution of Determiners in Machine Translation Output

First 102 Sentences (725 NPs)

Detr	A	B	C	Total	
no	351	388	363	1,102	50.7%
the	164	163	127	454	21.1%
a(n)	88	81	95	264	12.1%
this	11	9	4	24	01.1%
its	17	14	5	36	01.7%
?	94	70	131	295	13.6%

Last 398 Sentences (3,000 NPs)

Detr	A	B	C	Total	
no	1,165	1,559	1,294	4,018	44.6%
the	582	622	341	1,545	17.2%
a(n)	309	558	445	1,312	14.6%
this	41	38	21	100	01.1%
its	39	42	24	105	01.2%
?	864	181	875	1,920	21.3%

reproducible absolute standard. Even so, the testing shows trends in the system's performance and provides useful data for the analysis of errors. However, both of these things were done equally well, and far more economically, by the developer evaluating the results. Therefore, until the overall machine translation quality improves, it is not worth conducting expensive multi-evaluator tests of how well determiners can be generated. Although I did not test other components in this much detail, I would argue that the same is true for most other subtasks: it is not efficient to conduct multi-evaluator tests until the overall system performance has increased. Instead, the emphasis should be on regression testing to determine whether the system is improving or not, and analyses of the remaining errors. In any case, it is important to keep testing on different text, not always on the same sentences.

There has been a recent emphasis in NLP research toward making sure that all research has reproducible evaluations. While this has increased performance in many areas, particularly in POS tagging and parsing, it has had the unfortunate side effect of concentrating research on a few sometimes slightly artificial problems, such as syntactic parsing (for further discussion of these issues, see Romacker and Hahn (2000)).

The final score for generating articles is given in Table 27. Three numbers are given: the first is the number of noun phrases with the same article generated by the system as given by a majority of the evaluators; the second is the number of unevaluable noun phrases; the third is the number of noun phrases with a different determiner generated than that given by the majority of evaluators.

TABLE 27 Correct Generation of Determiners (Final Evaluation).

	Training (102 sentences)		Test (398 sentences)	
	NPs	(%)	NPs	(%)
Correct	556	76.7%	2015	67.2%
Unevaluable	100	13.8%	701	23.3%
Erroneous	69	9.5%	284	9.5%

From the developer's point of view, it was gratifying to see that the percentage of errors is the same in the test data as the training data. I made an effort to construct only rules and lexical entries that were generally applicable, and it was successful.

There are several figures that could be used to describe the overall system performance. The percentage generated correctly, 67.2%, underestimates the results, as it does not take into account the unevaluable noun phrases. The error rate of 9.5% overstates the accuracy for the same reason. The best figure of accuracy is $\frac{\text{Number correct}}{\text{Number evaluable}}$ which gives a figure of 87.6% for the test data and 89.0% for the training data. The baseline is to always choose no article, which gives an accuracy of 58.6% (1,716 no article out of 2,924 evaluable NPs). Many of the unevaluable noun phrases are proper nouns which take no article. Therefore, the baseline would be higher if the overall translation accuracy improved. Minnen et al. (2000) found that 70.0% of all noun phrases in the Wall Street Journal had neither *a(n)* or *the*, but this figure includes all possessive determiners and demonstratives (and also considered noun phrases in titles) so it starts off higher than the baseline that is evaluated here.

Analysis of Errors

I present confusion matrices for the two test sets in Tables 28 and 29. The correct answer was taken to be the answer given by the majority of testers. If no two testers gave the same answer, then the noun phrase was taken to be unevaluable.

Overall, there was not a lot of difference between the two data sets. The biggest difference, as noted earlier, is that there were far more

TABLE 28 Confusion Matrix for First 102 Sentences

Human Choice	Determiner Generated					
	no	the	a(n)	this	its	?
no	**360**	10	15	0	0	0
the	14	**108**	11	3	0	0
a(n)	3	11	**72**	0	0	0
this	0	0	0	**8**	0	0
its	0	0	2	0	**8**	0
?	41	33	20	4	2	**0**

Training data: 725 NPs

TABLE 29 Confusion Matrix for Last 398 Sentences

Human Choice	Determiner Generated					
	no	the	a(n)	this	its	?
no	**1242**	37	49	0	3	0
the	59	**400**	32	2	0	0
a(n)	32	54	**331**	0	2	0
this	2	1	0	**34**	0	0
its	3	4	4	0	**8**	0
?	333	205	149	8	6	**0**

Test data: 3000 NPs

unevaluable noun phrases in the test data, due to the overall worse quality of the output. This also decreased the inter-tester agreement.

Non-referential noun phrases were quite common. There were 86 generic noun phrases (2.31%) and 175 ascriptive noun phrases (4.7%), making 7.01% non-referential in all. Because articles and number are generated very differently for generic noun phrases, they would all have been translated incorrectly without the referentiality processing.

There were 70 noun phrases headed by inherently possessed nouns (1.9%), but possessive pronouns were only generated for 20 of them (0.5%). In general, there were not enough possessive pronouns generated in the translations of the test set. Some of these were due to deficiencies in the dictionary: (1) not all the inherently possessed nouns have been identified; and (2) there were some idiomatic constructions that had not had the required possessive pronouns marked. An example of the latter is *N1-ga za-o mamoru* "N1 maintains N1's position (lit. N1-NOM seat-ACC protect)", for which the incorrect dictionary entry was *N1 maintains the position*. These are simple to enter into the lexicon once they have been identified. It is difficult to identify inherently possessed nouns and constructions fully automatically due to the possibility of external possession. However, it is possible to find candidates from parallel corpora for manual checking (Nakaiwa, 1997). There were also some more problematic examples, where product names and classes should be modified by possessives, as in (120):

(120)   N 社 は   ファクシミリ の 輸出 価格 を   引き上げる
       N-sha-wa   *fakushimiri-no yushutsu kakaku-o hikiageru*
       Company N-TOP facsimile-ADN   export price-ACC   raise

       Company N will raise the export price of its facsimiles (Human)

       * Company N raises the export price of a facsimile   (MT)

The word *fakushimiri* "facsimile" appears many times in the texts, but should be possessively modified only when it is being referred to as a product, so making it inherently possessed in the lexicon is not an option. It is only treated as a product once, so statistical methods will not help. There is no way to generate this without a deeper analysis than is currently feasible. This deeper analysis would have to identify the facsimiles as products in this particular context, and then make them inherently possessed, again just for this context.

6.2   Discussion

Using heuristics based on the referentiality of the noun phrases was useful. In total, finding the referentiality of the noun phrases made a difference for 7% of the noun phrases.

The generation of possessive pronouns also proved to be important, although less so. Possessive pronouns were generated for 20 noun phrases (4%). However, over 70 noun phrases were headed by inherently possessed nouns. The additional constraints used to determine when to generate a pronoun were extremely important (as outlined in Section 5.4.4). It is not enough to generate possessive pronouns based only on the type of the head noun itself.

It is hard to say what an acceptable error rate is. The error rate of 9.5% is already lower than the percentage of unevaluable nouns. Thus, from the developers point of view, it seems good enough under the circumstances. From the point of view of a translator, however, having to correct one noun phrase in ten is a considerable burden. For casual use, such as web browsing, users are more tolerant of errors and online Japanese-English systems typically have a higher error rate than this.

Finally, although reproducible evaluation is essential for competitive evaluations, it is not always either necessary or possible. The inter-tester agreement was so low on the raw machine translation output that the results can not be considered reproducible. They were, however, extremely useful, both in showing trends in performance (improvement/degradation), and in identifying the remaining problems. For competitive evaluation, having all the systems tested on the same input, by the same evaluator, should give good enough results to compare systems.

With an error rate of 9.5% there is still room for improvement. However, the process of translation needs to be thought of as a whole. There is a limit to how much one area can be improved on its own. Some of the more detailed rules here could be implemented only after redoing entire sections of the transfer process, in particular, the translation of adnominal noun phrases and numeral classifiers.

Looking specifically at the system on which this algorithm was tested, it became unrewarding to work on solving the remaining problems in English generation without increasing the overall accuracy and quality of the Japanese analysis. Further, as this algorithm has reduced the number of errors in the determination of number and generation of determiners, other problems, such as prepositional choice and the translation of tense and aspect, have become more noticeable. After these, and other problems, have been improved, the analysis stage should give more accurate and more detailed information. This information can then be used to refine further rules for determiners and number. Progress needs to be approached as an ever-increasing spiral, where a full circuit should be done before returning to tackle the same area again.

6.2.1 Comparison with Other Systems

In Murata (1996), success rates of 85.5% for referential property and 89% for number were given for training data and 68.9% and 85.6% for test data. This shows that their approach is effective, although it is only just above the baseline for their test corpus. It is impossible to directly compare my results to Murata's for two reasons. First, the granularity of the results is different. Murata gives only three values for definiteness, compared to the nine possible in my system (three values of reference times three values of definiteness). In addition, the actual values are not comparable: for example, proper nouns are `definite` for Murata, but mainly `null` in my system, as they have no overt article. Second, Murata's testing was all carried out in Japanese by the developers, so the problems of generating the English and getting an impartial evaluation were not addressed.

Heine (1997), using rules quite similar to those presented here, achieves an accuracy of 88.8% for determining the definiteness of Japanese noun phrases to be translated into German. These excellent results are the result of comprehensive coverage of a very narrow domain: meeting scheduling. However, some of the rules will not work in a larger domain: for example, the rule that any noun phrase marked with an adnominal marker is definite. Because the rules are not defeasible, this means that they must be changed as different domains are considered; they cannot be overwritten by later rules (although they may be preempted by earlier ones).

Knight and Chander (1994), obtain a success rate of 78% for learning to replace articles when they have been removed from English texts. At present, however, the prototype cannot be used to post-edit output from a typical machine translation system. This is because it assumes the knowledge that an article should be used in a given position, which is not normally available. In addition, it has not been shown that the post-editing rules will be successfully triggered by raw machine translation output. Further, Knight and Chander use only information from within the NP or for two words before or after it. This means that information from further away, such as that used in my clause level or even case element level rules, is not generally available.

Chander (1998) does takes into account the possibility of generating no article. He cites accuracy results of around 96%, but this figure is applicable only to the postediting task as he considers whether to generate an article at every interword position. As it is trivial to predict that articles are inapplicable in most interword positions in a sentence, his results appear high.

When Chander (1998) tested his system on raw MT output the accuracy was 88%, lower than the MT system's built-in rules, which gave 95% accuracy (using the per word metric). It could only outperform the MT system's rules if it used the system's knowledge of where an article could be inserted, which raised the accuracy to 95.5%.

Converting my error rate of 9.5%/NP to an error rate/word gives an error rate of 2.7%/word (7.45 NPs per 26 word sentence). The per word accuracy of 97.3% for both articles and number is slightly above Chander's results of 95.5–6% for articles alone. However, the evaluation was done over different text translated from different languages on different systems, so too much cannot be read into it.

7

Construction of the Lexicon

The semantic representation described in Chapter 4 and the processing described in Chapter 5 both rely on detailed syntactic and semantic information in the lexicons. In this chapter, I give some more details of the lexical representation, and some tests for determining the lexical features. The first section describes the relevant lexical information stored for nouns (§ 7.1). This is followed by a description of the relevant lexical information for other parts of speech (§ 7.2). In the next chapter, I present methods for automatic and semi-automatic acquisition of some of the lexical information.

In the implementation discussed in Chapter 5, English lexical information is mainly stored in the Japanese-English transfer dictionaries. This is done because that is where word senses are distinguished: each Japanese-English pair is a different sense. Using translations to delineate senses has the advantage that the sense distinctions are clear — a word will have as many senses as it has translations. There is, however, a major disadvantage: information about the same word in English is stored separately for each pair. For example, *-mai* "slice" and *-kire* "slice" both need to record the lexical information for the English word *slice* that they are countable, portion classifiers, singular by default, and are not inherently possessed. Because the information stored is complex, it is easy for the lexicographers to overlook inconsistencies.

One way to avoid this is for the information to be kept separately for each language. The transfer dictionary would then contain just that information needed during transfer, plus links to the monolingual dictionaries. In practice, this is difficult for two reasons. The first is that the entry granularity is often different: there are far more multiword expressions in the transfer lexicon. The second is that the transfer entry is neither the union nor intersection of the monolingual entries, so it itself must contain information. This adds another rich layer, which also complicates maintenance.

7.1 Lexical Information for Nouns

In the lexicon, each word has the basic information needed to drive the transfer process — the Japanese equivalent, part of speech, semantic classes, selectional restrictions and so on. For example, *hana* "nose" is translated as *nose* by default, but if it is an elephant's nose then it will be translated as *trunk*. In addition, each noun has associated with it the following information: countability preference; default number; default definiteness; whether it is inherently possessed; and whether it is a classifier. If necessary, it also has an idiomatic class; a classifier type (if it is a classifier) or a default classifier and its type (if it is uncountable or plural only). A simplified example of the entry for *hana* "nose" is given in Figure 21. [22] A full list of the attributes and the values they can take are shown in Figure 22. The idiomatic classes are listed in Table 32.

$$
\begin{bmatrix}
\text{INDEX} & \text{鼻 } hana \\
& \text{SENSE}_1 \begin{bmatrix}
\text{ENGLISH TRANSLATION} & nose \\
\text{PART OF SPEECH} & \text{noun} \\
\text{SEMANTIC CLASSES} & \langle\text{nose}\rangle \\
\text{COUNTABILITY PREF.} & \text{fully countable} \\
\text{DEFAULT NUMBER} & \text{singular} \\
\text{INHERENTLY POSSESSED} & \text{t}
\end{bmatrix} \\
& \text{SENSE}_2 \begin{bmatrix}
\text{ENGLISH TRANSLATION} & trunk \\
\text{SEMANTIC CLASSES} & \langle\text{nose}\rangle \\
\text{SELECTIONAL RESTR.} & \begin{bmatrix}\text{MOD-BY} & z\bar{o} \text{ "elephant"}\end{bmatrix} \\
\text{PART OF SPEECH} & \text{noun} \\
\text{COUNTABILITY PREF.} & \text{fully countable} \\
\text{DEFAULT NUMBER} & \text{singular} \\
\text{INHERENTLY POSSESSED} & \text{t}
\end{bmatrix}
\end{bmatrix}
$$

FIGURE 21 Japanese-English Noun Lexical Entries (*hana* ⇔ *nose/trunk*)

---

[22] ALT-J/E's transfer lexicon has 6 translations for *hana* with the Chinese character meaning nose: *nose, trunk, muzzle, snout, nostril* and the proper name *Hana*.

INDEX	Japanese Word	
	ENGLISH TRANSLATION	English Word
	PART OF SPEECH	noun
	SEMANTIC CLASSES	⟨from Goi-Taikei⟩
	SELECTION RESTR.	(Choose this sense if . . .)
	COUNTABILITY PREF.	{fully countable, strongly countable, weakly countable, uncountable, plural only, collective, semi-countable}
SENSE	DEFAULT NUMBER	{singular, plural}
	DEFAULT DEFINITENESS	{indefinite, definite, null, depends}
	IDIOMATIC CLASS	(See Table 32)
	INHERENTLY POSSESSED	{t, nil}
	WORD IS CLASSIFIER	{t, nil}
	CLASSIFIER TYPE	{sortal, portion, measure, container group, taxonomic}
	DEFAULT CLASSIFIER	English Word (e.g. *piece*)

FIGURE 22 Lexical Information in the Japanese-English Transfer Lexicon

Over half of the English translation equivalents are multiword expressions: for example, *takuan* "pickled radish". In this case, information on countability and number applies to the whole noun phrase but is normally expressed only on the head word. The default article is for the entire noun phrase, any embedded noun phrases will have their article included explicitly. Some expressions include an explicit quantifier: for example, *Nihon-sankei* "three noted views of Japan", which is marked as `fully countable, plural, definite`, and so will be generated as *the three noted views of Japan*. Some even have an explicit determiner, such as *hon-an* "this proposal", which is marked as `fully countable, singular, null`. The `null` value blocks the generation of a new article so it will be generated as *this proposal*.

Because the information is stored for Japanese-English pairs, the nouns are largely disambiguated: *paper* "a material made of cellulose pulp" and *paper* "a scholarly article" are different entries (the first linked to *kami* "paper", and the second to *ronbun* "paper").

7.1.1 Countability Preferences

A noun's countability preference determines how it will behave in different environments, as described in Section 4.4.1.

To determine a noun's countability preference, the lexicographers use two sets of tests. First, there are three tests to determine the noun's base countability, then supplementary tests to determine the minor types. Combining the test results for the tests gives the noun countability preferences as shown in Table 30.

Test 1 Does it have a plural form?
Animals are dangerous.

Test 2 Can it take the indefinite article *a(n)* directly?
Words that fail this test may require a default classifier when used with a/an: *a piece of equipment*.

Test 3 Can it be modified by *much*?
much activity can be dangerous.

Weakly and strongly countable nouns can not be distinguished using grammaticality judgments. The difference between them is which usage (countable or uncountable) should be considered the default. In order to choose this default, the lexicographers considered the behavior of the noun with the modifier *takusan* "much/many", which can appear with either individual or substantive referents:

- If *many Ns* sounds better then `strongly countable`
- If *much N* sounds better then `weakly countable`

TABLE 30 Noun Countability Preference Test Results

Countability Preference	Test 1 ? Pl	Test 2 a(n)	Test 3 much	Other
Fully Countable	+	+	-	
Collective	+	+	-	Si/Pl V agreement
Strongly Countable	+	+	+	Default countable
Weakly Countable	+	+	+	Default uncountable
Uncountable	-	-	+	* Add Classifier
Semi-countable	-	+	+	Can take *a*
Plural Only	+	-	-	* Add Classifier

Section 8.3 discusses methods of determining a noun's countability preference from corpora in detail.

If the noun is uncountable, the default classifier also needs to be determined (§ 7.1.7). If there seems to be no suitable candidate, but instead a countable form is used, then the countability preference should be weakly countable.

Collective nouns are distinguished because the singular noun heading a subject allows either singular or plural verb agreement, as shown in (121):

(121)   *The committee*   *has met and it has*   *rejected the proposal*
        have met and they have

The default value for noun countability preference is `fully countable`. This value is also used for unknown words.

7.1.2 Default Number

The default value for number is `singular`. Nouns that are commonly used as plural with no modification, such as *noodles*, are marked as `plural`. This is purely a default value, used to determine the number in the absence of other information.

`plural only` nouns, and nouns made explicitly plural due to modification in the entry itself, are also marked as `plural`: *hasami* "scissors", *morote* "both hands".

Distribution of Noun Countability Preferences and Default Number

The distribution of noun countability preferences and default number for common nouns and technical terms at the time of the final evaluation (§ 6.1.4) is given in Table 31. Singular, fully countable nouns are the most common entry, followed by uncountable nouns.

TABLE 31 Distribution of Noun Countability Preferences and Default
Number

| Noun Count. Preference | Common Nouns | | Technical Terms | | Total |
	Singular	Plural	Singular	Plural	
Fully Countable	46,895	941	62,018	15	109,869
— Collective	3	0	0	0	3
Strongly	3,091	19	6	1	3,117
Weakly	3,371	6	142	0	3,519
Uncountable	15,443	6	142	0	15,591
Plural Only	1	2,110	9	4	2,124

134,223 common nouns in **ALT-J/E**'s Japanese-English dictionary.

There were some practical issues that have affected the distribution.
The first is that in the system used, there was no mechanism for selecting between the singular and plural agreement during generation,
so there was no motivation to mark collective nouns. Therefore, there
are almost no collective nouns entered into the dictionary.

There are some theoretically impossible combinations (such as uncountable nouns with plural number and plural only nouns with singular number). Some of these are errors. One of the problems in maintain-
ing a large dictionary is that new entries are often created by copying
and changing an existing entry. When this is done, it is easy to change
one feature and neglect to change a related one. Two things could be
done to guard against this. One is to add cross-field consistency checking in the lexicon, so that uncountable nouns can only be singular, and
plural only nouns can only be plural. The second solution would be
to offer a menu of combined countability preferences and number, and
only let the lexicographers select the permissible combinations.

Some of the entries that appear to be inconsistent, are however, for
entries that can not be cleanly described using the features we defined.
For example, *touzai-ryō-doitsu* "East and West Germany" has a morphologically singular head but plural agreement: *East and West Germany have agreed*. It was marked as **uncountable** and **plural**, which
works for the system. The only way to handle examples like this correctly would be to store the entry as a set of lexical items, syntactic
rules and known relations. This extra layer of complexity would take
us beyond the current approach. Another approach is to add more and
more sub-types (similarly to Ozawa et al. (1990): Section 3.1), but this
complicates the interpretation rules. Entries like this make it impossi-

ble to add cross-field consistency checking as a hard constraint. Instead, a lexicographic tool should alert lexicographers when an inconsistent entry is being created or maintained. This should greatly reduce the number of errors.

7.1.3 Default Definiteness

The default value for definiteness is `indefinite`. The value `definite` is used mainly for nouns that have (generally accepted) unique reference: *[the] earth*, *[the] sun*, . . . , or for multiword expressions that include a restrictive modifier: *gedan* "[the] lowest tier". Many human bilingual dictionaries list entries such as *tsuki* "the moon" as multiword expressions. However, this leads to incorrect predictions when the word is used as a modifier: *yumi-hari tsuki* "crescent moon" is indefinite by default, and the whole noun phrase is neither *crescent [the moon]* or *the [crescent] moon*. Therefore, it is essential that the definite article is treated as a feature.

The value `depends` is used to mark words that have idiomatic article use depending on the context; these nouns will also belong to an idiomatic class, as described below.

7.1.4 Nouns with Idiomatic Article Usage

This feature is used to mark noun classes with various idiomatic uses, primarily for articles, but also for selection of prepositions. The classes are listed in Table 32. These are mainly semi-productive classes of nouns that head defective noun phrases, as discussed in Section 5.4.5. Nonproductive idioms can be listed as full expressions, and fully productive expressions need to be handled by rules.

Classes 1–12 are used for the generation of temporal expressions as discussed in Section 5.4.5.

Classes 13–15 trigger special processing when used in prepositional phrases denoting means-of-transport. All of them have no determiner (`null`) when following *by* or *via*. Classes 13 and 14 take a definite article (`definite`) when used in a locative prepositional phrase following *on*: *on the train*. Class 15 takes the preposition *on* in means-of-transport prepositional phrases: *I went on foot*.

Classes 16 and 17 are institutions. Class 16 typically takes no article if the noun is unmodified after *to* as locative goal: *I am going to school* vs *I am going to a good school*; or in stative locative prepositional phrases: *at school*. Which nouns act as institutions differs considerably between American and Australian English. Class 17, which consists of the single word *home*, does not need a preposition to become a locative goal: *I am going home*.

TABLE 32 Nouns with Idiomatic Article Use

No.	Examples	Comment
Temporal		
1	dark	
2	morning, afternoon, evening	periods of time
3	noon, daybreak, nightfall, midnight, dusk, sunrise, sunset, dawn	moments of time
4	night	night
5	Monday ... Friday	days of the week
6	January ... December	months
7	today, yesterday, tomorrow	deictic-days
8	spring, summer, autumn, winter	seasons
9	Christmas, New Year, Easter ...	holidays
10	Golden Week, ...	named-weeks
11	Ramadan	named-months
12	Lent, *O-bon*, Easter	Other set periods
PP: Means of Transport		
13	bike, train, ship, ...	means of transport
14	road, sea, air, phone, email, ...	+ information transport
15	horseback, foot	*on*
PP: Locative		
16	school, university, town, ...	institutions
17	home	
Role Nouns		
18	guide, interpreter, president, secretary, leader, ...	
Meals		
19	breakfast, lunch, supper, dinner, tea, morning tea, afternoon tea, brunch, ...	Meal times
Name Elements		
20	river, canal, hall ...	proper names
21	series, islands ...	proper names
Other Idiosyncratic Nouns		
22	average, ground, normal, par, price, sea-level	above & below
23	beginning, end, left, right	end points
24	field, area, market	areas of endeavour
25	weather	the weather

Class 18 are role nouns, which are discussed in Section 5.4.5.

Class 19 (meals) are often used to represent times or locations, in which case they take no article: *I will meet you at breakfast*.

Classes 20 and 21 are used to construct names. Ideally, all names are identified during the source language analysis. Even so, the form that the name takes is language dependent. Noun phrases headed by members of class 20 form a name if they are modified by a proper noun. The resulting noun phrase takes a definite article, and is typically written with initial capitalization: *the Sumida River, the Aoi Hall*. The same holds for class 21, but in this case the noun phrase is plural: *the Ryukyu Islands*. There are some exceptions, for example, *the River Thames*, where *river* proceeds the proper noun. These have to be listed in the lexicon.

Finally, there are a set of small classes which required further processing. Members of class 22 take no article if they are modified by *above* or *below*: *This analysis is below par*. Members of class 23 take the definite article after the preposition *in*: *in the beginning*. Class 24 consists of words that are typically definite if premodified by any modifier: *the semi-conductor field, the local market*. Finally, Class 25 consists of the single word *weather*, which is normally determined by a definite article when unmodified: *What do you think of the weather?*. When modified, it takes no article: *This is filthy weather*.

Some of these special classes would not be necessary if the system was capable of perfectly determining when something is being used countably or uncountably, when habitually, when specifically and so on. Many of the words are on the borderline between common nouns and proper nouns, such as week-days or *the Aoi Hall*. However, in most cases, the idiosyncrasy is language specific — other languages behave slightly differently — and accordingly the idiosyncrasy must be encoded in the lexicon (Himmelmann, 1998, Baldwin et al., 2003). These collections of idiomatic rules are extremely important for the overall quality of a machine translation system.

7.1.5 Inherently Possessed Nouns

Some nouns have an argument structure and are inherently possessed. These nouns trigger special processing to generate possessive pronouns, as discussed in Section 5.4.4. The default value for inherently possessed is `nil`. The semantic hierarchy of 2,710 categories (§ 5.1.1) used in the implementation is not finely grained enough to identify these words by their denotation alone. It is also not easy to identify such nouns using only monolingual data, because any noun can be modified by a possessor, and inherently possessed nouns are not always possessed (due to different senses or the influence of verbs). Therefore, these nouns are identified by examining bilingual corpora. All nouns where the Japanese has no possessive marking but the English does are flagged in the first stage. They are then hand checked and, if necessary, marked as inherently possessed in the lexicon. This was then extended by considering nouns from the same semantic classes.

One coarse monolingual test is given in (122). If DETVE is conventionally *my* rather than *a* or *the*, then the noun is inherently possessed:

(122)   *I lost* DETVE NOUN.

Some examples of inherently possessed nouns, sorted by semantic class are given below:

kin, partners *father, sister, family, brother, daughter, son, parent, sibling aunt, uncle, relative, cousin, nephew, mother, grandfather, husband, wife, family, sweetheart, ...*

body-parts *arm, body, brain, mind, ear, hand, heart, leg, nose, finger, throat, stomach, belly, gut, eye, shoulder, wrist, hair, ...*

work *duties, answer, examination paper, examination, homework, home-task, income, job, class work, review, school life, school work, test, thought, thinking, train of thought, way of thinking, work, ...*

roles *assailant, class, group, doctor, friend, leader, maid, neighbor, partner, subordinate, superior, teacher, ...*

meals *box lunch, breakfast, meal, supper, ...*

attributes *height, depth, character, rate of climbing, grades, speed, strength, fault, age, name, ...*

others *annexation, appearance, appointment, appreciation, thanks, hope, base, bath, cell, conclusion, headquarters, ...*

As with other features, the lexical marking for all the features, including this one, is at the sense level: *cell* "a room where a prisoner is kept" is inherently possessed, but *cell* "a fundamental biological unit" is not. This feature can also be extracted from parsing the definitions in human oriented dictionaries (Barnbrook, 2002, 228–231). For example, words in Collins Cobuild Student's Dictionary (Sinclair, 1990) whose definition is of the form *a person's* **headword** *is a* **superordinate term**, tend to be inherently possessed. For example, the sense of *girlfriend* defined as *a woman's* **girlfriend** *is a female friend* is inherently possessed.

7.1.6 Classifier Type

Because nouns that require classifiers cannot themselves be classifiers, two fields are collapsed into one. The classifier type field applies to the English head word itself if the `word is classifier` flag is true, otherwise it refers to the type of the default classifier. For example, *mob* is flagged as `word is classifier`, so the classifier type `group` refers to it, whereas *asparagus* has a default classifier *spear* to which its classifier type (`sortal`) refers.

The classifier types are discussed in detail in the section on classifiers (§ 4.2.3). For English, the classifier type describes the behavior and restrictions placed by and on a noun in the partitive construction: CLASSIFIER *of* NP.

Test fragment *an* N_1 *of* N[ominal]$_2$.
If a noun N_1 can be used meaningfully in this construction it is probably a classifier.

Sortal nouns combine with an uncountable or singular countable N_2 to make a countable noun phrase: *a piece of paper*.

Portion nouns combine with an uncountable or singular countable N_2 to make a countable noun phrase, and also serve to delimit a set amount: *a slice of cake, a piece of a loaf*.

Group nouns combine with plural noun phrases to make a countable noun phrase: *a flock of birds, a pair of scissors*.

Species nouns are partitives of quality and can occur with countable or uncountable noun phrases, the embedded noun phrase will agree in number with the partitive noun if possible (i.e. for fully and strongly countable nouns): *a kind of car, two kinds of cars, a kind of equipment*.

Measure nouns can occur with any noun phrases, the new noun phrase formed can have singular verb agreement: *2 meters of rope is not enough; a row of figures*. Only units are marked in the lexicon as they principally occur in measure noun phrases, although any noun can be used in a measure noun phrase (Flickinger and Bond, 2003).

Container nouns can occur with any noun phrases, the new noun phrase formed will have normal verb agreement: *2 boxes of rope are not enough*. These nouns can refer to an amount, or an actual container. Many containers can be made into measure nouns by appending *-ful*: *spoon* ⇒ *spoonful*.

7.1.7 Classifier

Uncountable and plural only nouns can have default classifiers listed with them. For example, the default classifier for *asparagus* is *spear*. The classifier is given in its index form with no article or following preposition: *piece, pair*. If there is no classifier listed, uncountable nouns will be generated with *piece*. Plural only nouns do not have a classifier generated if one is not listed. This is to allow for words such as *clothes*.

7.2 Information for Modifiers

Words that modify nouns or take noun phrases as arguments can have preferences for the referential use, countability, number, definiteness and use of a possessive pronoun of their heads or arguments respectively. These are not selectional restrictions, as they are defeasible (see Chapter 5 for further discussion).

Referential use can be marked with a preference for `referential`, `generic` or `ascriptive` (§ 4.3).

Preferences for number and countability are marked using the IN-TERPRETATION feature (§ 4.4.2). It can have the values `individuated-singular`, `individuated-plural`, `non-bounded-1`, `non-bounded-2` and `substance` or `depends` (§ 4.4.2).

The most common value is unmarked. For the marked entries, the most common values are `non-bounded-1` and `non-bounded-2`. Around 400 predicates were identified that should be thus marked in our lexicon (3% of the total of the semantic valency dictionary (Ikehara et al., 1997)).

Identifying Relevant Arguments

The most common values marked on arguments are either `generic` or `non-bounded-2`. This section describes a method for lexicographers to identify the relevant arguments of verb patterns (Japanese/English pairs).

1. Construct an example so that every English argument slot is filled with singular indefinite noun phrases headed by non-collective countable nouns. If it is acceptable, then there is no need to enter any preferences.
   gakusei-ga ringo-wo taberu → A student eats an apple
   kawa-wa ari-ni afureru → ? A river overflows with an ant
   kodomo-wa ari-ga kirai da → ? A child dislikes an ant

2. If it is unacceptable, try it with plural noun phrases replacing the unacceptable ones:
   kawa-wa ari-ni afureru → A river overflows with ants

kodomo-wa ari-ga kirai da → *A child dislikes ants*

3. If making the noun phrase in question plural increased its acceptability, then it is one of the patterns in question.[23] Now try it with *all* modifying the noun phrase.

   kawa-wa ari-ni afureru → *? A river overflows with all ants*
   kodomo-wa ari-ga kirai da → *A child dislikes all ants*

   If it sounds all right with *all* then it should be `generic`, if not then it should be `non-bounded-2`.

4. If even those tests fail to convince then try translating it with the Japanese noun phrase in question modified by *kono* "this/these".

   kawa-wa kono-ari-ni afureru
   → *A river overflows with these ants/? this ant*
   kodomo-wa kono-ari-ga kirai da
   → *A child dislikes this ant/these ants*

   If the translation sounds better with *these* then the slot should be marked `non-bounded-2`. If it could be either *this* or *these* then the slot should be marked `generic`.

Sometimes a pattern should be marked `non-bounded-2`, even though it does not have non-specific reference. For example, in *N1-wa N2-o N3-kara erabu* → *N1 chooses N2 from N3*, N3 should be plural because you need to have more than one item to make a choice. However, the noun phrase will normally be definite: *watashi-wa sore-o sono-empitsu-kara eranda* → *I chose it from those pencils*.

Identifying Relevant Modifiers

An adjective (or other dependent) modifying a noun, or a word selecting for it, can restrict the choice of articles in the noun phrase. For example, *next, first, last* all imply that there is a definite object in mind and so the noun phrase must be definite. These are marked with a preference for `definiteness`, which can be `definite`, `indefinite`, `null` or unmarked (§ 4.5).

In addition, a modifier can indicate that the noun phrase should be marked as inherently possessed, for example, *dokuji* "[one's] own". This can be marked with a flag.

---

[23] If it still sounds strange then you may have chosen inappropriate noun phrases or there's something strange with the entry.

8

Automatic Acquisition of Lexical Information

This chapter discusses the automatic acquisition of lexical information. The first section discusses the acquisition of semantic classes (§ 8.1) from existing lexicons. The second discusses determining countability from semantic classes (§ 8.2), and finally acquiring countability from corpora (§ 8.3).

Dictionaries could be extended more easily if it were possible to learn the lexical information, such as the default definiteness use and noun countability preferences, from corpora. While there is some work on learning rules from corpora for selecting articles (Knight and Chander, 1994, Chander, 1998, Minnen et al., 2000), these approaches learn rules based on the orthographic form of the head of the noun phrase. However, lexical information can vary for different senses. Therefore, a method is needed to learn rules for noun senses rather than just for words.

8.1 Acquisition of Semantic Classes

Some of the processing for determining the correct interpretation requires the use of semantic classes: for example, deciding whether a sentence is defining (§ 5.2.1) or a noun phrase is locative (§ 5.2.2). In addition, semantic classes are crucially important in the general translation task, for parse selection, transfer and generation. In this section, I present a method of determining lexical information for unknown words (including the part of speech, semantic class and noun countability preference).[24] The method has only been applied to nouns, as that is where the semantic hierarchy was most useful.

---

[24]This was first presented in Ikehara et al. (1994b), and is described in more detail in Ikehara et al. (1995).

8.1.1 Acquiring Classes for New Words

The approach leverages existing entries in the lexicon. It is based on two observations: (1) most new entries are multiword entries, and (2) most multiword entries are **endocentric** in that they have the same the part-of-speech (common or proper noun), semantic classes and countability as their heads.

The approach works as follows: for each Japanese-English pair (J_U, E_U), find the closest equivalent in each language (J_S, E_S) in the system dictionaries. The new entry then takes the attributes of the equivalent entry. The method is outlined in Figure 23. Although this method can, in theory, work for all part of speech classes, we only discuss its use for nouns. A similar approach for verbs is outlined in Fujita and Bond (2004).

If an exact match cannot be found, then the word is simplified until a match can be found, or it cannot be simplified any further. As Japanese is largely head-final and nouns do not inflect, the process of simplification is straightforward: delete the initial character. Deleting a single character often results in a non-word, but this candidate will be eliminated when the system dictionary is accessed. The meaning often changes considerably going from a two character word to just the right-most character, so the algorithm stops when there are two characters left.

Simplifying English is more complicated. Because of number inflection, the entry is searched for first with the number it has, and then with singular inflection. If there is no match, then any post-head modifiers are deleted (everything after the last preposition or complementizer — *which*, *that*, ...) and the system dictionary is searched again with both inflections. If there is still no match, then pre-head modifiers are eliminated, starting with the leftmost.

Some examples of unknown word pairs being matched are shown in Table 33. Parts that matched in the system dictionaries are underlined.

The semantic classes acquired are compared to those added by lexicographers in Table 34. There are two test sets with a total of 238 nouns. Semantic classes were acquired for 211 of the 238 nouns. The reference data was made by checking the semantic classes along with the output of the machine translation system and adding and subtracting classes as necessary to get the best translation (Ikehara et al., 1995). In many cases, both for the manual and automatic assignment, the assigned semantic classes were close but either one level too high or too low. The results counting these as a match is given in the row marked (± 1).

1. For each unknown pair (J_U, E_U)
2. Look up the Japanese in the J-E system dictionary
   - If no match, simplify and look up again
     (a)delete leftmost character (until length ≤ 2)
3. Look up the English in the J-E system dictionary
   - If no match, simplify and look up again
     (a)if plural head, look up singular
     (b)delete post head modifiers (PP and relative clause)
     (c)delete leftmost word (until only one remains)
4. If match is **proper noun**, then entry is **proper noun**
5. Assign the semantic classes of the match to the unknown pair

FIGURE 23 Automatic Deduction of Semantic Classes

TABLE 33 Examples of Automatic Deduction of Semantic Classes

Japanese	**User Dictionary** English	Semantic Class
chiryō	*treatment*	⟨treatment⟩
teate	*cure*	⟨treatment⟩
suushi-seigyou-robotto	*numerically controlled robot*	⟨machine⟩

Japanese	**System Dictionary** English	Acquired Sem. Class
chiryō	*cure*	⟨treatment⟩
seigyou-robotto	*controlled robot*	⟨machine⟩

TABLE 34 Results of Automatically deducing Semantic Classes

Method	Newspapers		Manuals	
	Precision	Recall	Precision	Recall
Automatic	38.1%	58.3%	19.6%	35.1%
(±1)	49.0%	74.8%	25.5%	45.5%
Manual	84.5 %	73.2%	56.9 %	38.7%
(±1)	100.0%	86.6%	70.0%	47.6%

Manual lexicon construction gave better results than the automatic construction, but was still not perfect. Although the dictionary has been extensively used in a machine translation system, errors still exist. There were errors in 11–21% of the entries. A particularly common source of errors was words being placed one level too high or low in the hierarchy. Automatically assigning semantic classes is less accurate and words are, in general, assigned to too many semantic classes. However, even this level of accuracy is useful in practice.

A further test shows that using the automatically assigned classes improved the machine translation system translation quality (Table 35), measured by the percentage of sentences judged useful translations from a test set of 207 sentences (Ikehara et al., 1995). Although automatic acquisition is not as good as manual construction, it is still definitely useful (an increase of 10.5–16.7%). Further, manual construction, even by expert lexicographers, is better than automatic acquisition (by 4.7–5.1%) but seldom perfect. Corpus based reviews of manual entries improves accuracy yet again (3.9–8.6%), but at an increased cost. This is generally the case. Automatic acquisition is not as good as manual construction, but is far better than nothing; manual construction is good, but rarely perfect, and can almost always be improved by further testing. Accordingly, trade-offs can be made depending on the relative importance of coverage and accuracy.

TABLE 35 Improvement in Translation using deduced Semantic Classes

Method	Newspapers		Manuals	
	Accuracy	Gain	Accuracy	Gain
No Classes	56.7%	0.0%	65.7%	0.0%
Automatic	69.6%	+16.7%	71.4%	+10.5%
Manual	71.5%	+21.6%	71.4%	+15.2%
Reference	72.5%	+25.5%	73.3%	+23.8%

The two great advantages of this method is that it places words in classes in the hierarchy used by the system and is very simple to implement, requiring only the existing system dictionary.

8.2 Acquisition of Countability from Semantic Classes

It is generally agreed that there is some link between countability and meaning (§ 2.3). However, it is not a simple one, and as a result the feature `countability` is not directly connected to the semantic classes.

Using the transfer lexicons, it is possible to measure how well the semantic classes predict the countability preferences.[25]

The experiments are run under different conditions to test the effect of combinations of semantic classes and single word or multiword entries. In all cases the baseline is to give the most frequently occurring noun countability preference (`fully countable`).

TABLE 36 Results of Deducing Countability from Semantic Classes

Conditions	Entries	%	Range	Baseline
Training=Test	all	77.9	76.8–78.6	65.8
Tenfold Cross Validation	all	71.2	69.8–72.1	65.8
Tenfold Cross Validation	single word	66.6	65.6–67.7	58.6
Tenfold Cross Validation	multiword	74.8	73.9–75.8	71.1

In the experiments, I use five noun countability preferences (`fully`, `strongly`, `weakly countable`, `uncountable` and `plural only`). The two minor classes and default number are ignored.

For each combination of semantic classes in the lexicon the most common noun countability preference is calculated. If two preferences tied for the most common, then the tie is resolved as follows: `fully countable` beats `strongly countable` beats `weakly countable` beats `uncountable` beats `plural only`. For example, consider the semantic class `910:tableware` with four members: *shokki* ⇔ *tableware* (UC), *yōshokki* ⇔ *dinner set* (CO), *yōshokki* ⇔ *Western-style tableware* (UC) and *tōkirui* ⇔ *crockery* (UC). The most common noun countability preference is UC, so the noun countability preference associated with this class is `uncountable`.

How well the semantic classes predict noun countability is measured by the percentage of entries whose noun countability preference was the same as the most common one. For example, the noun countability preference associated with the semantic class `910:tableware` is `uncountable`. This is correct for three out of the four words in this semantic class. This is equivalent to testing on the training data, and gives a measure of how well semantic classes predict noun countability in **ALT-J/E**'s lexicon: 77.9% of the time. This is better than the baseline of all `fully countable` which would give 65.8%. The results are presented in Table 36.

---

[25]This work was done jointly with Caitlin Vatikiotis-Bateson (Bond and Vatikiotis-Bateson, 2002)

In order to test how useful semantic classes are in predicting the countability of unknown words, the experiment was repeated using stratified 10-fold cross validation. In order to ensure an even distribution, the data was stratified by sorting according to semantic class with every 10th item included in the same set. If the combination of semantic classes was not found in the test set, the countability is set to the overall most common noun countability preference: `fully countable`. This default was used 11.6% of the time. Using only nine tenths of the data, the accuracy went down to 71.2%, 5.4% above the baseline. In this case, the training set for `910:tableware` will always contain a majority of `uncountable` nouns, so it will be associated with `UC`. This will be correct for all the words in the class except *yōshokki* ⇔ *dinner set* (`CO`).

Finally, I divided the dictionary into single and multiple word entries (looked at from the English side) and re-tested. It was much harder to predict countability for single words (66.6%) than it was for multiword expressions (74.8%).

8.2.1 Discussion of Semantic-based Acquisition

The upper bound of 78% is quite low. There are several reasons for this. One is that there were some problems with the granularity of the hierarchy. In English, the class names of heterogeneous collections of objects tend to be uncountable, while the names of the actual objects are countable. For example, the following terms are all hyponyms of *tableware* in Wordnet (Fellbaum, 1998): *cutlery, chopsticks, crockery, dishware, dinnerware, glassware, glasswork, gold plate, service, tea set,* ...: see (123). Most of the entries are either uncountable, or multiword expressions headed by group classifiers, such as *service* and *set*. The words below these classes are almost all countable, with a sprinkling of plural only nouns (like *tongs*). Thus in the three levels of the hierarchy, two are mainly uncountable, and below that mainly countable. However, **ALT-J/E**'s ontology only has two levels here: `910:tableware` has four daughters, all leaf nodes in the semantic hierarchy: `911:crockery`, `912:cookware`, `913:cutlery` and `914:tableware (other)`: (124). The majority noun countability preferences for all four of these classes are `fully countable`. The question arises as to whether words such as *cutlery* should be in the upper or lower level. Using countability as an additional criterion for deciding which class to add a word to makes the task more constrained, and therefore more consistent. In this case, *cutlery* should be assigned to the parent node `910:tableware` on the basis of its countability (or a new layer added to the ontology). Using this additional criterion helps to solve the problem noted in Section 8.1

of words being assigned a semantic class one level too high or too low.

(123) `WordNet`

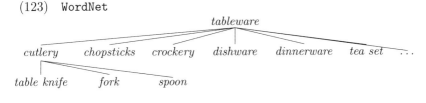

(124) **ALT-J/E**

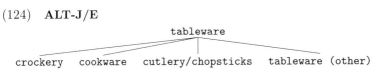

Because the major differentiator for bipartite nouns is physical shape (a bipartite structure), they are not distinguished by the semantic hierarchy and their countability cannot be learned by this method. Therefore, almost all of them are wrongly predicted, slightly less than 3% of the total. Although there are some functional similarities, such as a large percentage of 820:`clothes for the lower body`, it was more common to get one or two in an otherwise large group, such as *tongs* in the 913:`cutlery` class, which is overwhelmingly `fully countable`. In order to link the syntactic class to the meaning, the ontology would have to include information about physical shape so that it is accessible for linguistic processing.

The correspondence between semantics and syntax could be made closer by exploiting the relation between under-specified semantics and countability. Words such as *usagi* ⇔ *rabbit* are marked with the semantic classes for `animal` and `meat`, and the single noun countability preference `strongly countable`. If countability is associated with the animal sense, and uncountability with the meat sense, it is possible to learn noun countability preferences for each semantic class individually (ignoring `plural only`). Countability could then be assigned dynamically during sense disambiguation. Learning noun countability preferences for each class individually would also make it possible to predict noun countability preferences for entries with unseen combinations of semantic classes. In the ten fold cross validation tests 11.6% of the semantic combinations were unseen, and they were all simply assigned `uncountable`.

Multiword entries were easier to predict then single word entries because single word entries tended to have more semantic classes per word (1.38 vs 1.34) and more varied combinations of semantic classes. This meant that there were 5.1 entries per combination to train on for the multiword entries, but only 3.7 for the single word entries. Therefore, it was harder to train for the single word entries.

As can be seen in the case of *tableware* given above, there were classes where the single word and multiword expressions in the same semantic class had different countabilities. Therefore, even though there were fewer training examples, learning the noun countability preferences differently for single and multiword expressions and then combing the results gave an improved score: 72.0%.

Finally, there were also substantial numbers of genuine errors, such as *sofuto karā* which has two translations *soft color* and *soft collar*. Their semantic classes should have been `hue` and `clothing` respectively, but the semantic labels were reversed. In this case, the countability preferences were correct, but the semantic classes incorrect.

An initial analysis of the erroneous predictions suggested that the upper bound with all genuine errors in the lexicon removed would be closer to 85% than 78%. I speculate that this would be true for languages other than English: our ontology is not specifically tuned to English, it was developed for Japanese analysis.

van der Beek and Baldwin (2004) look at both Dutch and English. Dutch also distinguishes between countable, uncountable and plural only, although plural only is a small closed class. They used **EuroWordNet** as the ontology and considered the countability of the superordinate and subordinate classes in predicting the countability of each class (or synset). Dividing nouns into countable and uncountable, they could predict countability with an accuracy of 82.9% for English and 78.3% for Dutch. Interestingly, training on Dutch nouns and transferring the countability values over to English did slightly better (83.4%), as did training on English and testing on Dutch (80.2%). This confirms that not only is countability predictable from meaning, but that these predictions hold across languages (or at least across two typologically very similar languages). The very best results were obtained by training on data from both languages. This doubled the size of the training data and allowed the classifiers to predict the countability 87.4% of the time for English and 81.6% of the time for Dutch.

O'Hara et al. (2003) determine countability in English on the basis of semantic descriptions using the much richer CYC ontology (Lenat and Guha, 1990). They use an approach where the 256 most-frequent semantic classes (atomic terms) are used to give a feature vector. Each noun in the CYC ontology can thus be represented as a vector of 1's for each term which subsumes it and 0 for all other terms. A decision tree learner is used to learn the countability (uncountable (mass) or not) from these vectors. The baseline is slightly higher than for **ALT-J/E** (68.2% countable). Using these vectors, O'Hara et al. (2003) can predict whether a noun sense is mass or not with an accuracy of 89.5% using the Cyc ontology. These results show convincingly that countability is largely predictable from semantics.

From a psycho-linguistic point of view, it would be interesting to test whether unpredictable countabilities (that is, those words whose countability is not motivated by their semantic class) are harder for non-native speakers to use, and more likely to be translated incorrectly by humans. In this case, words with unpredictable countabilities should be given special emphasis in language teaching.

8.2.2 Applications

In general, many errors in countability that had been overlooked by the lexicographers in the original compilation of the lexicon and its subsequent revisions became obvious when looking at the words grouped by semantic class and noun countability preference. Most entries in the system tested (**ALT-J/E**) were made by Japanese native speakers, who do not make countability distinctions. They were checked by a native speaker of English, who in turn did not always understand the Japanese source word, and was, accordingly, unable to identify the correct sense. This state of affairs is all too common in system development, where speakers fluent in both languages are often hard to find.

Adding a checker to the dictionary tools, which warns if the semantic class does not predict the assigned countability, would help to avoid such errors. Such a tool could also be used for fine tuning the position of words in the semantic hierarchy, and spotting flat-out errors.

Another application of these results is in automatically predicting the countability of unknown words. Semantic classes for new noun entries can be automatically assigned (§ 8.1.1). These semantic classes can then be used to predict the countability at a level substantially above the baseline.

8.3 Acquisition of Countability from Corpora

As on-line text becomes more common, more and more research is focusing on knowledge-rich lexical acquisition from unannotated corpora. It is possible to take unstructured text and extract out linguistically-precise categorizations of word and expression types. In this section, I show how to learn the countability preferences of English nouns from unannotated corpora.[26] Similar research has shown success in classify-

---

[26]This work was done jointly with Timothy Baldwin (Baldwin and Bond, 2003a,b).

ing the semantics of derivational affixes (Light, 1996) and in learning verb aspect (Siegel and McKeown, 2000). The basic method is to annotate the text automatically and then train classifiers using a set of gold standard data. These are then run over the corpus to classify unknown words.

In the preliminary step, features that are relevant to countability are identified, such as the number of the head, or the presence of certain dependents. In the first learning step, the classifier looks at each feature as it appears with examples of the training data in the corpus. It then learns whether these features positively or negatively predict each class. For example: if a noun appears only with singular number it is a good predictor that the noun is uncountable, and not plural only. Appearing as both singular and plural is a good indicator that something is countable, and so on. When the classifier is applied, it looks at which features appear with the noun, and classifies accordingly. For example, *gaslight* appears 21 times in the British National Corpus (Burnard, 2000). It is always singular, appears multiple times in constructions like *brilliance/flare/shaft of gaslight* and *by/with gaslight*, but only once as *a gaslight*. It is, therefore, classified as `uncountable`.

There are several problems in attempting to learn countability from raw corpora. The first is that words are frequently converted to different countabilities, sometimes in such a way that other native speakers will dispute the validity of the new usage. A system does not necessarily wish to learn such rare examples, and may not need to learn more common conversions either, as they can be handled by regular lexical rules (Copestake and Briscoe, 1995). The second problem is with idiomatic article use. For example, role nouns (§ 5.4.5), which are typically countable, can appear without an article in some constructions (e.g. *We elected him treasurer*). Similarly words that normally require an article can appear without them in some prepositional phrases (e.g. *on foot, to school, in line*) or in lists, titles and headers (§ 5.4.5, 7.1.4). The third is that different senses of a word may have different countabilities: *interest* "a sense of concern with and curiosity" is normally countable, whereas *interest* "fixed charge for borrowing money" is uncountable. More commonly, senses with related meanings have different countability: *gaslight* "a light that burns illuminating gas, a gas lamp" is countable, while the light it produces ("light yielded by burning gas") is uncountable.

8.3.1 Resources

Information about noun countability was obtained from two sources. One was **COMLEX** 3.0 (Grishman et al., 1998), which has around

22,000 noun entries. Of these, 12,922 are marked as being `countable` (`COUNTABLE`) and 4,976 as being `uncountable` (`NCOLLECTIVE` or `:PLU-RAL *NONE*`). The remainder are unmarked for countability.

The other was the common noun part of **ALT-J/E**'s Japanese-to-English semantic transfer dictionary (described in Section 7.1). It contains 71,833 linked Japanese-English pairs. Considering only unique English entries with different countability and ignoring all other information gave 56,245 entries.

In order to combine the two resources, words are classified into only four possible noun countability classes (§ 4.4.1), with some words belonging to multiple classes. The first class is `countable`: **COMLEX**'s `COUNTABLE` and **ALT-J/E**'s `fully`, `strongly` and `weakly countable`. The second class is `uncountable`: **COMLEX**'s `NCOLLECTIVE` or `:PLU-RAL *NONE*` and **ALT-J/E**'s `strongly` and `weakly countable` and `uncountable`.

The third class is `bipartite` nouns. Nouns in **ALT-J/E** marked `plural only` with a default classifier of *pair* are classified as `bipartite`. **COMLEX** does not have a feature to mark bipartite nouns. The last class is `plural only` nouns: those that only have a plural form, such as *goods*. Nouns marked `:SINGULAR *NONE*` in **COMLEX** and nouns in **ALT-J/E** marked `plural only` without the default classifier *pair* are classified as `plural only`. There was some noise in the data, so this class was hand-checked, giving a total of 104 entries; 84 of these were attested in the training data.

The classification of countability uses only the three basic classes of `countable`, `uncountable` and `plural only`, (and `bipartite` as a separate class, not a subclass). As the countability classifications are derived from corpus evidence, it is possible to reconstruct countability preferences (i.e. `fully`, `strongly`, or `weakly countable`) from the relative token occurrence of the different countabilities for that noun.

In order to get an idea of the intrinsic difficulty of the countability learning task, I tested the **agreement** between the two resources in the form of classification accuracy. That is, the average proportion of (both positive and negative) countability classifications over which the two methods agree. For example, **COMLEX** lists *tomato* as being only `countable` where **ALT-J/E** lists it as being both `countable` and `uncountable`. Agreement for this one noun, therefore, is $\frac{3}{4}$ (75%), as there is agreement for the classes of `countable`, `plural only` and `bipartite` (with implicit agreement as to negative membership for the latter two classes), but not for `uncountable`. Averaging over the total set of nouns countability-classified in both lexicons, the mean was 93.8%. Almost half of the disagreements came from words with two countabilities in **ALT-J/E** but only one in **COMLEX**. Many of the disagreements can be attributed to the annotation of different senses. For example, *gaslight* is marked as countable in **ALT-J/E** (it is the translation of the Japanese *gasutō* "a light that burns illuminating gas, a gas lamp"), and uncountable in **COMLEX**, where it probably means "light yielded by burning gas", and is an example of a mismatch. There were no matches in the bipartite class, as **ALT-J/E** stores the head of plural only nouns as plural by default (*trousers*), and **COMLEX** stores them as singular (*trouser*).

8.3.2 Learning Countability from Corpora

The classifiers use **linguistic indicators**: lexical and/or constructional features associated with the countability classes. These are identified by hand. Next, I determine the relative corpus occurrence of these features for each noun. These are then fed into a classifier which makes a judgment on the membership of the given noun in each countability class.

In order to extract the feature values from corpus data, some basic phrase structure, and particularly noun phrase structure is needed. I use three different sources for this phrase structure: part-of-speech tagged data, chunked data and fully-parsed data, as detailed below. The corpus of choice throughout this section is the written component of the British National Corpus (BNC version 2, Burnard (2000)), totaling around 90 million word units (POS-tagged items).

Below, I outline the linguistic indicators used in this research and methods of describing feature interaction, and the classifier architecture. The full range of different classifier architectures tested as part of this research, and the experiments to choose between them are described in Baldwin and Bond (2003b).

Feature space

For each target noun, I compute a fixed-length feature vector based on a variety of features intended to capture linguistic constraints and/or preferences associated with particular countability classes. The feature space is partitioned up into **feature clusters**, each of which is conditioned on the occurrence of the target noun in a given construction. Feature clusters take into account not just the relative corpus frequency, but also the frequency relative to the target word frequency, and the frequency relative to other features in the same feature cluster.

How the linguistic indicators are encoded as feature clusters is described next, along with a representative example. A summary of the number of base features and prediction of positive feature correlations

Feature cluster (base feature no.)	Countable	Uncountable	Bipartite	Plural only
Head number (2)	sg,pl	sg	pl	pl
Modifier number (2)	sg,pl	sg	sg	pl
Subj–V agreement (2×2)	[sg,sg],[pl,pl]	[sg,sg]	[pl,pl]	[pl,pl]
Coordinate number (2×2)	[sg,sg],[pl,sg],[pl,pl]	[sg,sg],[sg,pl]	[pl,sg],[pl,pl]	[pl,sg],[pl,pl]
N of N (11×2)	[100s,pl],…	[lack,sg],…	[pair,pl],…	[rate,pl],…
PPs (52×2)	[per,–DET],…	[in,–DET],…	—	—
Pronoun (12×2)	[it,sg],[they,pl],…	[it,sg],…	[they,pl],…	[they,pl],…
Singular determiners (10)	a,each,…	much,…	—	—
Plural determiners (12)	many,few,…	—	—	many,…
Neutral determiners (11×2)	[less,pl],…	[BARE,sg],…	[enough,pl],…	[all,pl],…

(sg=singular, pl=plural)

TABLE 37 Predicted feature-correlations for each feature cluster

with countability classes is also given in Table 37.

Head noun number: the number of the target noun when it heads an NP (e.g. *a shaggy dog* = $\underline{\text{sg}}$)

Modifier noun number: the number of the target noun when it is a modifier in an NP (e.g. *dog food* = $\underline{\text{sg}}$)

Subject–verb agreement: the number of the target noun in subject position vs. number agreement on the governing verb (e.g. *the dog barks* = $\langle \text{sg}, \underline{\text{sg}} \rangle$)

Coordinate noun number: the number of the target noun vs. the number of the head nouns of conjuncts (e.g. *dogs and mud* = $\langle \text{pl}, \underline{\text{sg}} \rangle$)

N *of* N constructions: the number of the target noun (N_2) vs. the type of the N_1 in an N_1 *of* N_2 construction (e.g. *the type of dog* = $\langle \text{TYPE}, \underline{\text{sg}} \rangle$). There are a total of 11 N_1 types for use in this feature cluster, mainly kinds of classifiers.

- **Mensural Unit**: *acre, billionth, horsepower, ...*
- **Time Unit**: *minute, hour, morning, ...*
- **Individuated Singular**: *measure, piece, portion, ...*
- **Individuated Plural**: *couple, layer, line, ...*
- **Taxanomic Classifier**: *kind, sort, type*
- **Group Classifier**: *caravan, herd, party, ...*
- **LACK**: *lack, shortage*
- **PAIR**: *pair*
- **DEGREE**: *amount, degree, percentage, ...*
- **SET**: *set*
- **OTHER**: any other nouns

Occurrence in PPs: the presence or absence of a determiner ($\pm$DET) when the target noun occurs in **singular** form in a PP (e.g. *per dog* = $\langle per, \underline{\text{−DET}} \rangle$). This feature cluster exploits the fact that countable nouns occur determinerless in singular form with only very particular prepositions (e.g. *by bus, *on bus, *with bus*) whereas with uncountable nouns, there are fewer restrictions on what prepositions a target noun can occur with (e.g. *on furniture, with furniture, ?by furniture*).

Pronoun co-occurrence: what personal and possessive pronouns occur in the same sentence as singular and plural instances of the target noun (e.g. *The dog ate its dinner* = $\langle \underline{its}, \text{sg} \rangle$). This is a proxy for pronoun binding effects, and is determined over a total of 12 third-person pronoun forms (normalized for case, e.g. *he, their, itself*).

Singular determiners: what singular-selecting determiners occur in NPs headed by the target noun in singular form (e.g. $\underline{a}$ $dog = \underline{a}$). All singular-selecting determiners considered are compatible with only countable (e.g. *another, each*) or uncountable nouns (e.g. *much, little*). Determiners compatible with either are excluded from the feature cluster (cf. *this dog, this information*). Note that the term "determiner" is used loosely here and below to denote an amalgam of simplex determiners (e.g. *a*), no determiner, complex determiners (e.g. *all the*), numeric expressions (e.g. *one*), and adjectives (e.g. *numerous*), as relevant to the particular feature cluster.

Plural determiners: what plural-selecting determiners occur in NPs headed by the target noun in plural form (e.g. $\underline{few}$ $dogs = \underline{few}$). As with singular determiners, the focus is on those plural-selecting determiners which are compatible with a proper subset of count, plural only and bipartite nouns.

Non-bounded determiners: what non-bounded determiners occur in NPs headed by the target noun, and what is the number of the target noun for each (e.g. $\underline{more}$ $\underline{dogs} = \langle \underline{more}, \mathtt{pl} \rangle$). Here again, the focus is on non-bounded determiners that select for singular-form uncountable nouns (e.g. *sufficient furniture*) and plural-form countable, plural only and bipartite nouns (e.g. *sufficient dogs*).

The above feature clusters produce a combined total of 1,284 individual feature values.

These determiner features are mainly denumerators and classifiers, as described in Section 4.4.2. Candidates were initially generated by considering the dictionary entries for modifiers marked with the `inter-pretation` feature. The linguistic classes used in deep processing are also useful for automatic acquisition. Singular determiners are marked as `individuated-singular`, `substance` or `depends`; plural determiners with `individuated-plural` and `depends`; and non-bounded determiners with `non-bounded-1` and `non-bounded-2`. `interpretation` is also a feature on some predicate arguments, but it was not used in acquisition due to the lack of precision in automatically identifying verbs and their arguments.

Feature extraction

In order to extract the features described above some parsing of the text must be done. I adopt three approaches. First, to use part-of-speech (POS) tagged data and POS-based templates to extract out the necessary information. Second, to use chunk data to determine NP and PP boundaries, and medium-recall chunk adjacency templates to recover inter-phrasal dependency. Third, to fully parse the data and simply read off all necessary data from the dependency output.

As the full parser, I used RASP (Briscoe and Carroll, 2002), a robust tag sequence grammar-based parser. RASP's grammatical relation output function provides the phrase structure in the form of lemmatized dependency tuples, from which it is possible to read off the feature information. RASP has the advantage that recall is high, although precision is potentially lower than chunking or tagging as the parser is forced into resolving phrase attachment ambiguities and committing to a single phrase structure analysis.

Although all three systems map onto an identical feature space, the feature vectors generated for a given target noun diverge in content due to the different feature extraction methodologies. In addition, I only consider nouns that occur at least 10 times as head of an NP, causing slight disparities in the target noun type space for the three systems. There were sufficient instances found by all three systems for 20,530 common nouns.

Classifier architecture

Four parallel supervised classifiers are used, one for each countability class. This makes it possible to classify a single noun into multiple countability classes, e.g. *demand* is both countable and uncountable. Baldwin and Bond (2003b) experimented with a wide range of classifier architectures and found this design to be optimal for the task. The supervised classifiers were built using TiMBL version 4.2 (Daelemans et al., 2002), a memory-based classification system based on the k-nearest neighbor algorithm.

8.3.3 Results and Evaluation

The evaluation of the corpus-based evaluation is broken down into two components. First, the optimal classifier configuration for each countability class is determined by way of stratified cross-validation over the gold-standard data. I then run each classifier in optimized configuration over the remaining target nouns for which there are feature vectors.

Cross-validated Results

The cross-validated results for each classifier are presented in Table 38, broken down into the different feature extraction methods. For each countability class I give the classification accuracy, baseline and F-score. The classifiers are run over the concatenated feature vectors for the three basic feature extraction methods, producing a 3,852-value feature space ("Combined"). In each case, the score is given for 10-fold stratified cross-validation. The final classification accuracy and F-score

TABLE 38 Cross-validation Results for Acquiring Countability from Corpora

Class	Accuracy	Baseline	F-score
Countable	.939	.746	.960
Uncountable	.952	.783	.892
Bipartite	.996	.994	.722
Plural only	.990	.985	.582

$(\frac{2 \cdot precision \cdot recall}{precision + recall})$ are averaged over the 10 iterations. The system does better than the baseline for all countabilities.

Results for New Nouns

The next task evaluated is classifying all unseen common nouns. In each case, the classifier is run over the best-500 features rather than the full feature set, in order to reduce processing time. The baseline method is to classify every noun as being uniquely countable.

There were 11,499 feature-mapped common nouns not contained in the union of the gold-standard datasets. Of these, the classifiers were able to classify 10,355 (90.0%). 7,974 (77.0%) were classified as countable (e.g. *alchemist*), 2,588 (25.0%) as uncountable (e.g. *ingenuity*), 9 (0.1%) as bipartite (e.g. *headphones*), and 80 (0.8%) as plural only (e.g. *damages*). Only 139 nouns were assigned to multiple countability classes.

The classifier outputs are evaluated in two ways. In the first, I compared the classifier output to the union of the **COMLEX** and **ALT-J/E** lexicons: a lexicon with countability information for 63,581 nouns. The classifiers found a match for 4,982 of the nouns. The predicted countability was judged correct 94.6% of the time. This is marginally above the level of match between **ALT-J/E** and **COMLEX** (93.8%) and substantially above the baseline of all-countable at 89.7% (error reduction of 47.6%).

To evaluate how useful the results are for describing the use of words appearing in the corpus, Baldwin and Bond (2003a) used BNC corpus evidence to blind-annotate 100 randomly-selected nouns from the test data, and tested the correlation with the system output. This is intended to test the ability of the system to capture corpus-attested usages of nouns, rather than independent lexicographic intuitions as are described in the **COMLEX** and **ALT-J/E** lexicons. Of the 100 words, 28 were classified by the annotators into two or more groups (mainly countable and uncountable). On this set, the baseline of all-countable was 87.8%, and the classifiers gave an agreement of 92.4% (37.7% error reduction), agreement with the dictionaries was also 92.4%. Again, the main source of errors was that the classifier only returned a single countability for each noun. Based on this limited evaluation, therefore, the automated method is able to capture corpus-attested countabilities with equivalent precision to the manually compiled lexicon.

8.3.4 Discussion of Corpus-based Acquisition

The above results demonstrate the utility of the proposed method in learning noun countability from corpus data. In the final system configuration, the system accuracy was 94.6%, even higher than deducing the countability from semantic classes.

The classifiers were trained to determine whether or not a noun could be a member of a certain countability class. The next step is to store the distribution of countability for each target noun and build a representation of each noun's countability preferences. This can be done by isolating token instances strongly supporting a given countability class analysis for that target noun. With this evidence, it is possible to estimate the overall frequency of the different countabilities. This would represent a continuous equivalent of the discrete 4-way scale (fully, strong, weak, and un- countable) given in Section 4.4.1, tunable to different corpora/domains.

For practical purposes, however, it is preferable to learn the countability per sense, not word, as machine translation deals with senses. There are two possible ways to do this. The most straightforward way is to sense tag the corpus in the feature extraction phase, and then learn the features per sense rather than per word. Robust open class word sense disambiguation is becoming available (Stevenson, 2003), although it is still far below the accuracy of tagging, chunking or parsing. The number of examples for each sense will be fewer than for the word itself, especially for rare senses, but this is becoming less of a problem as corpora increase in size. If the words are sense tagged with multiple senses (or classes), then a second possible approach is to exploit the regularity in relations between the senses, as suggested in Section 8.2.1. For example, there are several words that can be used both to mean a source of light and the light itself (e.g., *light*, *gaslight*, *limelight*) but some words can only mean one (*flashlight*) or the other (*torchlight*). By looking at non-polysemous words, it is possible to learn that the source sense is countable and the light sense uncountable, and this can then be applied to split words such as *gaslight* into countable and uncountable senses.

8.4   Progress in Lexical Acquisition

One of the major perceived problems with knowledge rich approaches
to natural language processing is the knowledge acquisition bottleneck:
it is hard to acquire detailed syntactic and semantic information. However, with advances in machine learning techniques, it is now possible
to take a small core of hand annotated data, and then use it to train
classifiers on unannotated text. In this chapter, I showed that countability can be learnt with a precision rivalling manual annotation. There
is no reason to suppose that other features cannot also be acquired
in similar ways. Further, the links between syntax and semantics, and
between phenomena in different languages, make it possible to further
cross check and improve the quality of this acquired knowledge.

In addition, following the free software movement, more and more
lexical resources are being freely released. For example, taggers, chun-
kers and even parsers can be downloaded for many languages. Further, high quality dictionaries are now being developed and made freely
available (for example, in the Papillon Multi-lingual Lexical Database
Project: `http://www.papillon-dictionary.org/`). This combination
of improved learning and sharing of existing resources is beginning to
put an end to the knowledge acquisition bottleneck, at least for some
languages.

9

Conclusion

The algorithms outlined in this book provide a robust method to generate determiners and to determine number and countability when translating from Japanese to English. The method is linguistically motivated, and has been tested by implementation in a large-scale machine translation system.

As well as using syntactic and semantic information, the algorithm uses the information available in the source language text to determine the referential use of a noun phrase: **generic**, **referential**, **ascriptive** or **idiomatic** reference. It also distinguishes universal features of boundedness, and combines them with English-specific information on countability. Finally, the system generates determiners, in particular, articles and possessives, with an accuracy of over 85%.

9.1 Further Refinements

The accuracy of the solution presented here is so high compared to the overall translation accuracy that, as noted in Section 6.2, there are more pressing problems that should be addressed before attempting to further improve the generation of determiners and determination of number. Considering machine translation as a whole, the basic problems of source language analysis and target language lexical selection still need to be improved, and other sub-areas such as prepositional choice and the translation of tense and aspect remain problematic. However, considering only the problem of generating articles, this research could be extended in the following ways.

1. Extending the translation process to translate texts as coherent passages, not just as single sentences. This would allow the algorithm to use information on anaphoric relations within the text, which would permit better generation of both *the* and *this*. This would also bring the system even closer to the artificial intelli-

gence goal of text understanding.

2. Looking at the less frequent determinatives *some*, *any* and the demonstratives. However, because they are so infrequent, there is no point in doing this until the overall translation accuracy improves.

3. Combining with word sense disambiguation.

4. Making more use of explicit statistical models to decide values.

9.2 Other Applications

The semantic features and rules used to generate number and determiners can be used in several other applications. I will outline four applications here: generating from underspecified input other than machine translation; generating other languages; translation from English to Japanese; and teaching English as a second language.

9.2.1 Generating from Under-specified Input

The first application is other natural language processing tasks where the input is underspecified. One common task is report generation or summarization where several texts are combined. Another important application is in the field of augmentative and alternative communication. In particular, people who have lost the ability to speak sometimes use a text-to-speech generator as a prosthetic device. But most disabilities which affect speech, such as strokes or amyotrophic lateral sclerosis (ALS or Lou Gehrig's disease), also cause some more general motor impairment, which means that prosthesis users cannot achieve a text input rate comparable to normal typing speeds even if they are able to use a keyboard. Many have to rely on a slower physical interface (head-stick, head-pointer, eye-tracker etc). Article choice is particularly important for this application: many disabled users drop articles and resort to a sort of telegraphese, but this causes degradation in comprehension of synthetic speech and contributes to its perception as unnatural and robot-like (Copestake, 1997, Minnen et al., 2000). Producing default articles from underspecified input allows the user to only enter content words and non-default articles, which significantly reduces the number of words that have to be input.

9.2.2 Application to Different Language-Pairs

The second application is to use the semantic features and rules in generating number and determiners for different languages. The rules are straightforwardly useful for other languages with determiners and number (such as French, German, Spanish and so on), although the final decision as to which article to generate under what conditions is, of course, language specific. However, as the processing was designed with target-source independence in mind, it is easy to adapt to new language pairs. The rules have already been shown useful in generating Malay, which does not have obligatory articles, but must use possessive modifiers for a small class of inherently possessed nouns heading referential noun phrases. Ogura et al. (1999) show that the processing outlined in Section 5.4.4 for generating English possessive pronouns can be directly used to generate appropriate Malay possessives. Determination of the noun phrases reference is crucial: the possessive modifiers are not used for generic or ascriptive reference.

9.2.3 Generating from Over-specified Input

The third application is for the reverse task of translating a language with overt articles and number to one without them, such as English-to-Japanese machine translation. Here the problem is to decide when a noun phrase is overspecified and should therefore have information deleted. For example, for possessive pronouns it is necessary to delete default and idiomatic possessives, leaving only explicit ones. Idiomatic possessives should be stored within transfer rules and can be simply deleted by them. To remove excess possessive pronouns, a reverse process to generation can be used: if a noun phrase with a possessive pronoun is headed by an inherently possessed noun, and the possessive is co-referential with the subject, then delete it. The process is simpler than Japanese-to-English translation: the difference is between trying to determine a value for an under-specified feature (Japanese to English) and mapping a specific feature to a less specific one (English to Japanese).

Current commercial systems do not delete excess possessive pronouns. This makes their output understandable but very unnatural Japanese. For example, *I scratched my nose* is translated as *watashi-wa watashi-no hana-o kizutsuketa* "I I-ADN nose-ACC scratched" by an on-line translation service.[27] The second use of *watashi* "I" is both unnecessary and unnatural. Incorporating the processing described here would lead to a distinct improvement in quality.

9.2.4 Computer Aided Language Learning

The final application discussed here is language education. Problems with articles and number are the most frequent types of errors for Japanese speakers of English (Izumi et al., 2003). In an analysis of audio-recorded data from Japanese learners of English undergoing interview tests (the Standard Speaking Test), they found errors in article

---

[27]Translated at http://babelfish.altavista.com/tr on 2004-11-10.

use in 9% to 18% of noun phrases (18% for beginners, 16% for intermediate learners and 9% for advanced learners). Han et al. (2004) found errors in 6% of noun phrases in TOEFL exams by native speakers of Japanese, Chinese and Russian. These problems surface for learners in many other language pairs.

The research shown here can help language education in two ways. The first is in identifying specific words whose countability (and thus number) are likely to be hard for learners, because the syntax is not predictable from the semantics. The second is in providing learners with a fundamental explanation of how and why languages such as Japanese and English differ.

9.3 Summary

Ultimately, the problem of determining number can be solved only with world knowledge. For example, in (125), the Japanese sentence does not say whether there is one office or more than one, and this information was not contained anywhere in the surrounding text. However, the structure of English forces a choice, as a noun phrase headed by a countable noun must be either singular or plural. In this case the only thing for a translator to do, whether machine or human, is to provide a reasonable default choice.

(125)　A 社 は　　　7 回 に　　オフィスが　あります
　　　　A-sha-wa　　nana-kai-ni ofisu-ga　arimasu
　　　　A-company-TOP 7-floor-LOC office-NOM have

Company A has an office/offices on the seventh floor

Gawrońska (1993, 11) starts off a detailed and perceptive analysis of the problem of generating articles in machine translation with the pessimistic disclaimer:

> "No matter how powerful your computer is or how sophisticated your programs, it will not be possible to bring about a perfect automatic translation. Postedition will always be necessary. The demands for implementing a procedure for article choice in English and Swedish and aspect choice in Russian and Polish are so enormous that you had better leave this task to a well educated native speaker."

In this book, I have shown that this task can in fact be attempted by a reasonably sophisticated program, even though errors still remain and there will always be some cases that are undecidable. For a perfect translation, revision will always be necessary, just as it is for a human translation. However, this task can be made significantly less burdensome by reducing the number of errors in the output: in this case from 35% of noun phrases to 9.5%.

References

Allan, Keith. 1980. Nouns and countability. *Language* 56(3):541–67.

Allan, Keith. 1998. The semantics of English quantifiers. In P. Collins and D. Lee, eds., *The clause in English: In honour of Rodney Huddleston*, pages 1–31. John Benjamins.

Arakawa, Naoya. 1998. The recognition of noun usage and pronominal anaphora in Japanese. Tech. Rep. TR-IT-0280, ATR, Kyoto.

Backhouse, A. E. 1993. *The Japanese Language: An Introduction*. Oxford: Oxford University Press.

Baldwin, Timothy, John Beavers, Leonoor van der Beek, Francis Bond, Dan Flickinger, and Ivan A. Sag. 2003. In search of a systematic treatment of determinerless PPs. In *Proceedings of the ACL-SIGSEM Workshop on the Linguistic Dimensions of Prepositions and their Use in Computational Linguistics Formalisms and Applications*, pages 145–56. Toulouse, France.

Baldwin, Timothy and Francis Bond. 2003a. Learning the countability of English nouns from corpus data. In *41st Annual Meeting of the Association for Computational Linguistics: ACL-2003*, pages 463–470. Sapporo, Japan.

Baldwin, Timothy and Francis Bond. 2003b. A plethora of methods for learning English countability. In *2003 Conference on Empirical Methods in Natural Language Processing: EMNLP 2003*. Sapporo, Japan. 73–80.

Barker, Chris. 1995. *Possessive Descriptions*. Dissertations in Linguistics. Stanford: CSLI Publications.

Barnbrook, Geoff. 2002. *Defining Language — A local grammar of definition sentences*. Studies in Corpus Linguistics. John Benjamins.

Bender, Emily and Dan Flickinger. 1999. Peripheral constructions and core phenomena. In G. Webelhuth, J.-P. Koenig, and A. Kathol, eds., *Lexical and Constructional Aspects of Linguistic Explanation*, pages 199–214. Stanford: CSLI.

Bies, Ann, Mark Ferguson, Karen Katz, and Robert MacIntyre. 1995. *Bracketing Guidelines for Treebank II Style*. Penn Treebank Project, University of Pennsylvania.

Bond, Francis, Daniela Kurz, and Satoshi Shirai. 1998. Anchoring floating quantifiers in Japanese-to-English machine translation. In *36th Annual Meeting of the Association for Computational Linguistics and 17th International Conference on Computational Linguistics: COLING/ACL-98*, pages 152–159. Montreal, Canada.

Bond, Francis, Kentaro Ogura, and Satoru Ikehara. 1994. Countability and number in Japanese-to-English machine translation. In *15th International Conference on Computational Linguistics: COLING-94*, pages 32–38. Kyoto. (http://xxx.lanl.gov/abs/cmp-lg/9511001).

Bond, Francis, Kentaro Ogura, and Satoru Ikehara. 1995. Possessive pronouns as determiners in Japanese-to-English machine translation. In *2nd Pacific Association for Computational Linguistics Conference: PACLING-95*, pages 32–38. Brisbane. (http://xxx.lanl.gov/abs/cmp-lg/9601006).

Bond, Francis, Kentaro Ogura, and Hajime Uchino. 1997. Temporal expressions in Japanese-to-English machine translation. In *Seventh International Conference on Theoretical and Methodological Issues in Machine Translation: TMI-97*, pages 55–62. Santa-Fe.

Bond, Francis and Kyonghee Paik. 2000. Re-using an ontology to generate numeral classifiers. In *18th International Conference on Computational Linguistics: COLING-2000*, pages 90–96. Saarbrücken.

Bond, Francis and Caitlin Vatikiotis-Bateson. 2002. Using an ontology to determine English countability. In *19th International Conference on Computational Linguistics: COLING-2002*, vol. 1, pages 99–105. Taipei.

Briscoe, Ted and John Carroll. 2002. Robust accurate statistical annotation of general text. In *Proc. of the 3rd International Conference on Language Resources and Evaluation (LREC 2002)*, pages 1499–1504. Las Palmas, Canary Islands.

Briscoe, Ted and Ann Copestake. 1999. Lexical rules in constraint-based grammars. *Computational Linguistics* 25(4):487–526.

Burnard, Lou. 2000. *The British National Corpus Users Reference Guide*. Oxford University Computing Services.

Carletta, Jean. 1996. Assessing agreement on classification tasks: the kappa statistic. *Computational Linguistics* 22(2):249–254.

Carlson, Gregory N. and Francis Jeffry Pelletier. 1996. *The Generic Book*. Chicago, London: University of Chicago Press.

Chander, Ishwar. 1998. *Automated Postediting of Documents*. Ph.D. thesis, University of Southern California, Marina del Rey, CA.

Chase, Lesley. 1983. *Classification of the Determiners in English*. Master's thesis, University of Queensland, Brisbane.

Chesterman, Andrew. 1991. *On definiteness: A study with special reference to English and Finnish*. No. 56 in Cambridge studies in linguistics. Cambridge: Cambridge University Press.

Clancy, Patricia M. and Pamela Downing. 1987. The use of *wa* as a cohesion marker in Japanese oral narratives. In Hinds et al. (1987), pages 3–56.

Copestake, Ann. 1997. Augmented and alternative NLP techniques for augmentative and alternative communication. In *Proceedings of the ACL workshop on Natural Language Processing for Communication Aids*, pages 37–42. Madrid.

Copestake, Ann and Ted Briscoe. 1995. Acquision of lexical translation relations from MRDs. *Machine Translation* 9(3–4):183–219.

Cornish, Tim, Kimikazu Fujita, and Ryochi Sugimura. 1994. Towards machine translation using contextual information. In *15th International Conference on Computational Linguistics: COLING-94*, pages 51–56. Kyoto.

Daelemans, Walter, Jakub Zavrel, Ko van der Sloot, and Antal van den Bosch. 2002. TiMBL: Tilburg memory based learner, version 4.2, reference guide. ILK technical report 02-01. Available from `http://ilk.kub.nl/downloads/pub/papers/ilk.0201.ps.gz`.

Dale, Robert. 1992. *Generating Referring Expressions*. Cambridge, MA: MIT Press.

Declerk, Renaat. 1988. *Studies on Copular Sentences, Clefts and Pseudoclefts*. Leuven, Belgium: Leuven University Press.

Downing, Pamela. 1995. The anaphoric use of classifiers in Japanese. In Downing and Noonan (1995), pages 345–375.

Downing, Pamela. 1996. *Numeral Classifier Systems, the case of Japanese*. Amsterdam: John Benjamins.

Downing, Pamela and Michael Noonan, eds. 1995. *Word Order in Discourse*, vol. 30 of *Typological Studies in Language*. Amsterdam: John Benjamins.

Ehara, Terumasa and Hozumi Tanaka. 1993. kikaihonyaku-ni-okeru shizengengo shori [natural language processing in machine translation]. *Journal of Information Processing Society of Japan* 34(10):1266–1273. (in Japanese).

Fellbaum, Christine, ed. 1998. *WordNet: An Electronic Lexical Database*. MIT Press.

Flickinger, Dan. 1996. English time expressions in an HPSG grammar. In Gunji (1996), pages 1–8.

Flickinger, Dan and Francis Bond. 2003. A two-rule analysis of measure noun phrases. In *The 10th International Conference on Head-Driven Phrase Structure Grammar*, pages 111–121. Michigan.

Fujita, Sanae and Francis Bond. 2004. An automatic method of creating new valency entries using plain bilingual dictionaries. In *10th International Conference on Theoretical and Methodological Issues in Machine Translation (TMI-2004)*. Baltimore. 55-64.

Fukui, Naoki. 1995. *Theory of Projection in Syntax*. Tokyo & Stanford: Kuroshio & CSLI.

Ganeshsundaram, P. C. 1980. Technical translation as information transfer across language boundaries. *Journal of Information Science* 2:91–100.

Gawron, Jean Mark. 1999. Abduction and mismatch in machine translation. `http://www.ai.sri.com/~gawron/mt_paper.ps`.

Gawrońska, Barbara. 1990. "Translation Great Problem" on the problem of inserting articles when translating from Russian into Swedish. In *13th International Conference on Computational Linguistics: COLING-90*. Helsinki.

Gawrońska, Barbara. 1993. *An MT Oriented Model of Aspect and Article Semantics*. Sweden: Lund University Press.

Grishman, Ralph, Catherine Macleod, and Adam Myers. 1998. *COMLEX Syntax Reference Manual*. Proteus Project, NYU. (http://nlp.cs.nyu.edu/comlex/refman.ps).

Gunji, Takao. 1987. *Japanese Phrase Structure Grammar: A Unification-Based Approach*. Dordrecht: D. Reidel (Kluwer).

Gunji, Takao. 1996. Studies on the universality of constraint-based phrase structure grammars. Tech. Rep. 06044133, International Scientific Research Program, Osaka University, Japan.

Han, Na-Rae, Martin Chodorow, and Claudia Leacock. 2004. Detecting errors in English article usage with a maximum entropy classifier trained on a large, diverse corpus. In *4th International Conference on Language Resources and Evaluation (LREC 2004)*, vol. V, pages 1625–1628. Lisbon.

Hawkins, John A. 1978. *Definiteness and indefiniteness. A study in reference and grammaticality prediction.*. London: Croom Helm.

Hawkins, John A. 1991. On (in)definite articles: implicatures and (un)grammaticality prediction. *Journal of Linguistics* 27:405–442.

Heine, Julia. 1997. Ein Algorithmus zur Bestimmung der Definitheitswerte japanischer Nominalphrasen [An algorithm for determining the definiteness of Japanese noun phrases]. Diplomarbeit, Universität des Saarlandes, Saabrücken. (in German).

Heine, Julia. 1998. Definiteness predictions for Japanese noun phrases. In *36th Annual Meeting of the Association for Computational Linguistics and 17th International Conference on Computational Linguistics: COLING/ACL-98*, pages 519–525. Montreal, Canada.

Himmelmann, Nikolaus P. 1998. Regularity in irregularity: Article use in adpositional phrases. *Linguistic Typology* 2:315–353.

Hinds, John. 1987. Thematization, assumed familiarity, staging, and syntactic binding in Japanese. In Hinds et al. (1987), pages 83–106.

Hinds, John, Senko K. Maynard, and Shoichi Iwasaki, eds. 1987. *Perspectives on Topicalization: The Case of Japanese wa*, vol. 14 of *Typological Studies in Language*. Amsterdam: John Benjamins.

Hockey, Beth Ann and Dania Egedi. 1994. Determining determiner sequencing: A syntactic analysis for English. In *3e Colloque International sur les grammaires d'Arbres Adjoints (TAG+3)*. Université Paris 7.

Huddleston, Rodney. 1984. *Introduction to the Grammar of English*. Cambridge textbooks in linguistics. Cambridge: Cambridge University Press.

Huddleston, Rodney. 1988. *English grammar: an outline*. Cambridge: Cambridge University Press.

Huddleston, Rodney and Geoffrey K. Pullum. 2002. *The Cambridge Grammar of English*. Cambridge: Cambridge University Press. (principal authors).

Ikehara, Satoru, Masahiro Miyazaki, Satoshi Shirai, Akio Yokoo, Hiromi Nakaiwa, Kentaro Ogura, Yoshifumi Ooyama, and Yoshihiko Hayashi. 1997. *Goi-Taikei — A Japanese Lexicon*. Tokyo: Iwanami Shoten. 5 volumes/CDROM.

Ikehara, Satoru, Masahiro Miyazaki, and Akio Yokoo. 1993. nichiē kikaihonyaku-no-tame-no imikaisekiyō-no gengo chisiki-to sono bunkainō [classification of language knowledge for meaning analysis in machine translation]. *Transactions of the Information Processing Society of Japan* 34(8):1692–1704. (in Japanese).

Ikehara, Satoru, Satoshi Shirai, and Kentaro Ogura. 1994a. gengo hyōgen taikē-no chigai-ni chakumokushita nichiē kikaihonyaku shiken kōmoku-no kōsē [criteria for evaluating the linguistic quality of Japanese to English machine translations]. *Journal of Japanese Society for Artificial Intelligence* 9(4):569–579. (in Japanese).

Ikehara, Satoru, Satoshi Shirai, Akio Yokoo, Francis Bond, and Yoshie Omi. 1994b. Automatic determination of semantic attributes for user defined words in Japanese-to-English machine translation. In *Fourth Conference on Applied Natural Language Processing: ANLP-94*, pages 184–185. Association for Computational Linguistics, Stuttgart.

Ikehara, Satoru, Satoshi Shirai, Akio Yokoo, Francis Bond, and Yoshie Omi. 1995. Automatic determination of semantic attributes for user defined words in Japanese-to-English machine translation. *Journal of Natural Language Processing* 2(1):3–17. (in Japanese).

Ikehara, Satoru, Satoshi Shirai, Akio Yokoo, and Hiromi Nakaiwa. 1991. Toward an MT system without pre-editing – effects of new methods in **ALT-J/E–**. In *Third Machine Translation Summit: MT Summit III*, pages 101–106. Washington DC. (http://xxx.lanl.gov/abs/cmp-lg/9510008).

Imai, Mutsumi and Dedre Gentner. 1997. A crosslinguistic study of early word meaning: Universal ontology and linguistic influence. *Cognition* 62:169–200.

Iwasaki, Shoichi. 1987. Thematization, assumed familiarity, staging, and syntactic binding in Japanese. In Hinds et al. (1987), pages 107–141.

Izumi, Emi, Saiga Toyomi, Thepchai Supnithi, Uchimoto Kiyotaka, and Isahara Hitoshi. 2003. Error tag tuki nihonjingakushuusha hatuwa corpus o mochiita gakushuusha no kanshishutokukeikou no bunseki [analysis on article acquisition for learners based on an error-tagged sst corpus]. In *9th Annual Meeting of The Association for Natural Language Processing*, pages 19–22. Yokohama. (in Japanese).

Jackendoff, Ray. 1991. Parts and boundaries. In B. Levin and S. Pinker, eds., *Lexical and Conceptual Semantics*, pages 1–45. Cambridge, MA & Oxford, UK: Blackwell Publishers.

Jackendoff, Ray. 1992. *Languages of the Mind*. Cambridge, MA: MIT Press.

Jackendoff, Ray. 1996. The proper treatment of measuring out, telicity and perhaps even quantification in English. *Natural Language and Linguistic Theory* 14:305–354.

Jackendoff, Ray. 1997. *X-bar Syntax: A study of Phrase Structure*. Cambridge, MA: MIT Press.

Jackendoff, Ray. 1998. Why a conceptualist view of reference? A reply to Abbott. *Linguistics and Philosophy* 21(2):211–219.

Jakobson, Roman. 1966. On linguistic aspects of translation. In R. A. Brower, ed., *On translation*, pages 232–239. New York: Galaxy Books.

Kikui, Gen-ichiro and William McClure. 1991. nichiē kikaihonyaku-ni-okeru kanshi-no kettē-ni-tsuite [determination of articles in Japanese-to-English machine translation]. (handout presented at the Kyoto Linguistics Colloquium, in Japanese).

Kim, Alan Hyun-Oak. 1995. Word order at the noun phrase level in Japanese: quantifier constructions and discourse functions. In Downing and Noonan (1995), pages 199–246.

Knight, Kevin and Ishwar Chander. 1994. Automated postediting of documents. In *Proceedings of the 12th National Conference on Artificial Intelligence: AAAI-94*, pages 779–784. Seattle. (http://xxx.lanl.gov/abs/cmp-lg/9407028).

Koiso, H. 1994. *On classifiers*. Master's thesis, Department of Literature, Chiba University.

Krifka, Manfred, Francis Jeffry Pelletier, Gregory N. Carlson, Alice ter Meulen, Godehard Link, and Gennaro Chierchia. 1996. Genericity: An introduction. In Carlson and Pelletier (1996), pages 1–124.

Kuno, Susumu. 1973. *The Structure of the Japanese Language*. Cambridge, MA: MIT Press.

Kurafuji, Takeo. 1998. Definiteness of *koto* in Japanese and its nullification. In *RuLing 1: Rutgers Working Papers in Linguisitics*, pages 169–174. New Jersey: Rutgers University. http://equinox.rutgers.edu/resources/rsrc_arch.html.

Lakoff, Robin. 1969. Some reasons why there can't be any *some-any* rule. *Language* 45:608–15.

Langkilde, Irene and Kevin Knight. 1998. Generation that exploits corpus-based statistical knowledge. In *36th Annual Meeting of the Association for Computational Linguistics and 17th International Conference on Computational Linguistics: COLING/ACL-98*, pages 704–710. Montreal, Canada.

Lenat, Douglas B. and Ramanathan V. Guha. 1990. *Building Large Knowledge-Based Systems: Representation and Inference in the CYC Project*. Addison-Wesley.

Levin, Beth. 1993. *English Verb Classes and Alternations*. Chicago, London: University of Chicago Press.

Light, Marc. 1996. Morphological cues for lexical semantics. In *34th Annual Meeting of the Association for Computational Linguistics: ACL-96*, pages 25–31. Santa Cruz.

Link, Godehard. 1997. *Algebraic Semnatics in Language and Philosophy*. Stanford: CSLI.

Lunde, Ken. 1999. *CJKV Information Processing*. Sebastopol, CA: O'Reilly.

Mahesh, Kavi, Sergei Nirenburg, Stephen Beale, Evelyne Viegas, Victor Raskin, and Boyan Onyshkevych. 1997. Word sense disambiguation: Why statistics when you have these numbers? In *Seventh International Conference on Theoretical and Methodological Issues in Machine Translation: TMI-97*, pages 151–159. Santa Fe.

Manning, Christopher D. and Hinrich Schütze. 1999. *Foundations of Statistical Natural Language Processing*. MIT Press.

Martin, Samuel E. 1988. *A Reference Grammar of Japanese*. Tokyo: Tuttle, first tuttle edition edn.

Matsui, Tomoko. 1995. *Bridging and Relevance*. Ph.D. thesis, University College London, London.

Matsumoto, Yō. 1996. *Complex Predicates in Japanese*. Tokyo & Stanford: Kuroshio Shuppan & CSLI.

Minnen, Guido, Francis Bond, and Ann Copestake. 2000. Memory-based learning for article generation. In *Proceedings of the Fourth Conference on Computational Natural Language Learning and of the Second Learning Language in Logic Workshop (CoNLL-2000 and LLL-2000)*, pages 43–48. Lisbon. (http://lingo.stanford.edu/pubs/det-ml.pdf).

Mish, Frederick C., ed. 1993. *Merriam Webster's Collegiate Dictionary*. Springfield, MA: Merriam Webster, 10th edn.

Miura, Tsutomu. 1967. *ninshiki-to gengo-no riron [Theory of Recognition and Languages]*. Tokyo: Keiso Shobou. (in Japanese).

Miyazaki, Masahiro, Satoshi Shirai, and Satoru Ikehara. 1995. gengo katēsetsu-ni motozuku nihongo hinshi-no taikēka-to sono kōyō [a Japanese syntactic category system based on the constructive process theory and its use]. *Journal of Natural Language Processing* 2(3):3–25. (in Japanese).

Mufwene, Salikoko S. 1981. Count/mass distinction and the English lexicon. In *Papers from the Regional Meeting of the Chicago Linguistic Society*, vol. 17, pages 221–38. University of Chicago.

Murata, Masaki. 1996. *Anaphor Resolution in Japanese Sentences using Surface Expressions and Examples*. Ph.D. thesis, Kyoto University.

Murata, Masaki, Sadao Kurohashi, and Makoto Nagao. 1996. hyōsōhyōgen-o tegakari-toshita nihongo mēshiku-no shijisē-to sū-no kakutē [an estimate of referential property and number of Japanese noun phrases from surface expressions]. *Journal of Natural Language Processing* 3(4):31–48. (in Japanese).

Murata, Masaki and Makoto Nagao. 1993. Determination of referential property and number of nouns in Japanese sentences for machine translation into English. In *Fifth International Conference on Theoretical and Methodological Issues in Machine Translation: TMI-93*, pages 218–25. Kyoto. (http://xxx.lanl.gov/abs/cmp-lg/9405019).

Murata, Masaki and Makoto Nagao. 1996. mēshi-no shijisē-o riyō-shita nihongo bunshō-ni-okeru mēshi-no shijidaishō-no kakutē [an estimate of referent of nouns in Japanese with referential property of nouns]. *Journal of Natural Language Processing* 3(1):67–81. (in Japanese).

Nagao, Makoto, ed. 1989. *Machine Translation: How far can it go?*. Oxford: Oxford University Press.

Nakaiwa, Hiromi. 1997. Automatic extraction of rules for anaphora resolution of Japanese zero pronouns from aligned sentence pairs. In *Proceedings of ACL-97/EACL-97 Workshop on Operational Factors in Practical, Robust, Anaphora Resolution for Unrestricted Texts*, pages 22–29. Madrid.

Nakaiwa, Hiromi and Satoru Ikehara. 1995. Intrasentential resolution of Japanese zero pronouns in a machine translation system using semantic and pragmatic constraints. In *Sixth International Conference on Theoretical and Methodological Issues in Machine Translation: TMI-95*, pages 96–105. Leuven.

Nariyama, Shigeko. 2003. *Ellipsis and Reference Tracking in Japanese*. John Benjamins.

Nida, Eugene A. 1964. *Toward a Science of Translating*. Leiden, Netherlands: E. J. Brill.

Nishiyama, Yūji. 1990. kopyurabun-ni-okeru mēshiku-no kaishaku-o megutte [Concerning the interpretation of noun phrases in copula sentences]. In *bunpō-to imi-no aida [Between Syntax and Semantics]*, pages 133–148. Tokyo: Kuroshio Shuppan.

Nogaito, Izuru and Hitoshi Iida. 1990. ēgo tēmēshiku sēsē-no-tameno nihongo mēshiku-no rikai (Japanese NP understanding for English definite NP generation). In *Transactions of the 1990 IEICE Spring Conference*, no. 6, page 83. IEICE. (in Japanese).

Ogawa, Yoshiki. 1996. The definiteness of tense and specifier head agreement in Japanese. In M. Koizumi, M. Oishi, and U. Sauerland, eds., *Formal Approaches to Japanese Linguistics 2*, vol. 29 of *MIT Working Papers in Linguistics*, pages 173–192. Cambridge, MA: MIT.

Ogura, Kentaro, Francis Bond, and Yoshifumi Ooyama. 1999. **ALT-J/M**: A prototype Japanese-to-Malay translation system. In *Machine Translation Summit VII*, pages 444–448. Singapore.

O'Hara, Tom, Nancy Salay, Michael Witbrock, Dave Schneider, Bjoern Aldag, Stefano Bertolo, Kathy Panton, Fritz Lehmann, Matt Smith, David Baxter, Jon Curtis, and Peter Wagner. 2003. Inducing criteria for mass noun lexical mappings using the Cyc KB and its extension to WordNet. In *Proc. Fifth International Workshop on Computational Semantics (IWCS-5)*. (to appear).

Ono, Kiyoharu. 1996. Syntactic behaviour of case and adverbial particles in Japanese. *Australian Journal of Linguistics* 16(1):81–129.

Ozawa, Kuniaki, Hiroshi Kinukawa, Kazuaki Maeda, and Hiroyuki Kannari. 1990. Article check in computer aided English text generation system (a method of noun classification). In *40th Annual Convention of the IPSJ*, no. 5F-8, pages 482–483. (in Japanese).

Paik, Kyonghee and Francis Bond. 2002. Spatial representation and shape classifiers in Japanese and Korean. In D. Beaver, S. Kaufmann, B. Clark, and L. Casillas, eds., *The Construction of Meaning*, pages 163–180. Stanford: CSLI Publications.

Pelletier, Francis Jeffry, ed. 1979. *Mass Terms: Some Philosophical Problems*. Dordrecht: Reidel.

Poesio, Massimo, Rahul Mehta, Axel Maroudas, and Janet Hitzeman. 2004. Learning to resolve bridging references. In *42nd Annual Meeting of the Association for Computational Linguistics: ACL-2004*, pages 144–151. Barcelona.

Poesio, Massimo and Renata Vieira. 1998. A corpus-based investigation of definite description use. *Computational Linguistics* 24(2):183–216.

Prince, Ellen. 1981. Toward a taxonomy of given-new information. In P. Cole, ed., *Radical Pragmatics*, pages 223–255. New York: Academic Press.

Quinlan, John Ross. 1993. *C4.5: Programs for Machine Learning*. San Mateo, CA: Morgan Kaufmann.

Raskin, Victor and Sergei Nirenburg. 1998. An applied ontological semantic microtheory of adjective meaning for natural language processing. *Machine Translation* 13(2–3):135–227.

Romacker, Martin and Udo Hahn. 2000. An empirical assessment of semantic interpretation. In *The 1st Meeting of the North American Chapter of the ACL: ANLP-NAACL-2000*, pages 327–334. Seattle.

Ross, John Robert. 1995. Defective noun phrases. In *Papers from the Regional Meeting of the Chicago Linguistic Society*, vol. 31, pages 398–440. University of Chicago.

Sakahara, Shigeru. 1996. ēgo-to nihongo-no mēsiku gentē hyōgen-no taiō kankē [correspondence of determiners in English and Japanese]. *Cognitive Studies: Bulletin of the Japanese Cognitive Science Society* 3(3):38–58. (in Japanese).

Shibatani, Masayoshi. 1990. *The languages of Japan*. Cambridge Language Surveys. Cambridge University Press.

Siegel, Eric V. and Kathleen McKeown. 2000. Learning methods to combine linguistic indicators: Improving aspectual classification and revealing linguistic insights. *Computational Linguistics* 26(4):595–628.

Siegel, Melanie. 1996a. Definiteness and number in Japanese to German machine translation. In D. Gibbon, ed., *Natural Language Processing and Speech Technology*, pages 137–142. Berlin: Mouton de Gruyter.

Siegel, Melanie. 1996b. Preferences and defaults for definiteness and number in Japanese to German machine translation. In B.-S. Park and J.-B. Kim, eds., *Selected Papers from the 11th Pacific Asia Conference on Language, Information and Computation*, pages 43–52. Language Education and Research Institute, Kyung Hee University, Seoul.

Siegel, Melanie. 1998. Japanese particles in an HPSG grammar. Tech. Rep. 220, Verbmobil, Universität des Saarlandes.

Siegel, Melanie. 1999. The syntactic processing of particles in Japanese spoken language. In J.-F. Wang and C.-H. Wu, eds., *Proceedings of the 13th Pacific Asia Conference on Language, Information and Computation (PACLIC-99)*, pages 43–52. Taipei, Taiwan.

Siegel, Muffy E. A. 1994. Such: Binding and the pro-adjective. *Linguistics and Philosophy* 17(5):481–497.

Sinclair, J.M., ed. 1990. *Collins Cobuild Student's Dictionary*. London & Glasgow: Collins.

Sornlertlamvanich, Virach, Wantanee Pantachat, and Surapant Meknavin. 1994. Classifier assignment by corpus-based approach. In *15th International Conference on Computational Linguistics: COLING-94*, pages 556–561. Kyoto. (http://xxx.lanl.gov/abs/cmp-lg/9411027).

Stevenson, Mark. 2003. *Word Sense Disambiguation*. CSLI Publications.

Takano, Hisako. 1995. Japanese common nouns and their unquantificational nature. In N. Akatsuka, ed., *Japanese/Korean Linguistics*, vol. 4, pages 379–395. Stanford: CSLI.

Taylor, Ann, Mitchel Marcus, and Beatrice Santorini. 2003. The Penn treebank: an overview. In A. Abeillé, ed., *Treebanks: Building and Using Parsed Corpora*, chap. 1, pages 5–22. Kluwer Academic Publishers.

Tokieda, Motonaga. 1941. *kokugogaku genron [The Principle of Japanese Linguistics]*. Tokyo: Iwanami Shoten. (in Japanese).

Trujillo, Arturo. 1995. Towards a cross-linguistically valid classification of spatial prepositions. *Machine Translation* 10:93–141.

Tsujimura, Natsuko. 1996. *An Introduction to Japanese Linguistics*. Cambridge, MA: Blackwell. ISBN 0-631-19856-3.

Uszkoreit, Hans. 2002. New chances for deep linguistic processing. In *19th International Conference on Computational Linguistics: COLING-2002*, pages XIV–XXVII. Taipei.

van der Beek, Leonoor and Timothy Baldwin. 2004. Crosslingual countability classification with EuroWordNet. In *Proceedings of the 14th Meeting of Computational Linguistics in the Netherlands (CLIN 2003)*, Antwerp Papers in Linguistics. Antwerp.

Vieira, Renata and Massimo Poesio. 2000. An empirically based system for processing definite descriptions. *Computational Linguistics* 26(4):539–594.

Wierzbicka, Anna. 1988. *The Semantics of Grammar*. Amsterdam: John Benjamins.

WordNet. 1997. *WordNet - a Lexical Database for English*. Cognitive Science Laboratory, Princeton University, 221 Nassau St., Princeton, NJ 08542. Version 1.6, (http://www.cogsci.princeton.edu/~wn/).

Yoshimoto, Kei. 1998. *Tense and Aspect in Japanese and English*. Frankfurt am Main: Peter Lang.

Zelinsky-Wibbelt, Cornelia. 1992. Exploiting linguistic iconism for article selection in machine translation. In *Fifteenth International Conference on Computational Linguistics: COLING-92*, pages 792–798. Nantes.

Index